Rulers and Ruled:

An Introduction to Classical Political Theory from Plato to the Federalists

This book illuminates several timeless principles of political philosophy that have come down to us through the ages in the writings of Plato, Aristotle, Machiavelli, Hobbes, Locke, Montesquieu, Rousseau, and the authors of the Federalist Papers, Madison, Hamilton, and Jay. Among these principles are the following: that a good society is based on law; that a good constitution balances social classes against each other; that a mixed constitution is best for this purpose; that popular sovereignty is the best foundation for a just and stable constitution; and that representative government is best for a large, complex society.

In this valuable and accessibly written guide to the fundamentals of political thought, Irving Zeitlin shows that certain thinkers have given us insights that rise above historical context – 'trans-historical principles' that can provide the political scientist with an element of foresight, an ability not to predict events but to anticipate a certain range of possibilities. While the historian studies unique and unrepeatable circumstances such as those, for example, that gave rise to Julius Caesar, the political theorist, using these trans-historical principles, recognizes the conditions that can lead to Caesarism.

Zeitlin draws on an unusual depth of knowledge, offering a lucid, interesting, and memorable summation of his chosen classic texts, in a work that will appeal strongly to his intended audience at the undergraduate level and no less strongly to the general reader interested in the subject.

IRVING M. ZEITLIN is Professor Emeritus in the Department of Sociology at the University of Toronto.

RULERS AND RULED

*An Introduction to
Classical Political Theory
from Plato to the Federalists*

IRVING M. ZEITLIN

UNIVERSITY OF TORONTO PRESS
Toronto Buffalo London

© University of Toronto Press Incorporated 1997
Toronto Buffalo London
Printed in Canada

ISBN 0-8020-0894-1 (cloth)
ISBN 0-8020-7877-X (paper)

Printed on acid-free paper

Canadian Cataloguing in Publication Data

Zeitlin, Irving M.
    Rulers and ruled : an introduction to classical political
    theory from Plato to the Federalists

    Includes bibliographical references and index.
    ISBN 0-8020-0894-1 (bound)   ISBN 0-8020-7877-X (pbk.)

    1. Political science – History.   2. Political science –
    Philosophy.   I. Title.

    JA81.Z44 1997   320′.01   C96-931539-2

University of Toronto Press acknowledges the financial assistance to its
publishing program of the Canada Council and the Ontario Arts Council.

For Esther

Contents

Introduction

There is a tradition in political theory that has come to be called 'classical' because the ideas constituting that tradition have stood the test of time – not in the sense that the proposed ideas have always proved to be valid, but rather in the sense that the authors of those ideas have raised the key issues and have provided fruitful conceptual tools with which to grapple with those issues. However, the thinkers considered in this book have often provided more than analytical tools by proposing that the constitution of a good, just, and stable society requires the guidance of certain fundamental political principles. By principles I mean valid trans-historical insights. The insights those thinkers proposed after a careful reflection on historical experience can provide us with foresight. History does not literally repeat itself, but there are enough similarities between the human experiences of the past and those of the dynamic present to give us a sense of *déjà vu* – a sense that humanity has been there before.

It is such similarities that enable us not to predict events, but at least to anticipate the range of possibilities. The historian studies unique and unrepeatable circumstances such as those that gave rise to Julius Caesar; the political theorist, thanks to his or her grasp of certain trans-historical principles, recognizes the circumstances that can lead to Caesarism. In this book, then, I give primary attention to the search for principles and comparatively little attention to the task of situating thinkers in their historical and social contexts. The social context of an idea and its validity are two distinct questions. And it is an error to suppose that the social origin of an idea has necessary implications for its validity.

As one reads the classical texts with the aim of searching for principles, one soon learns that from the time of Plato political theorists have reflected on this central question: What is a good society and how is it achieved? This question, in turn, implied another: What roles should the rulers and the people play in constituting a good society? Plato, in the *Republic*, placed all authority in the hands of a small ruling élite, assigning no political role at all to the vast majority of the subjects of his ideal state. The *Laws*, Plato's last thoughts on politics, written when he was almost eighty years of age, suggests that his disappointing experiences with the tyrants of Syracuse prompted him to modify his position. Evincing a somewhat more favourable attitude towards democracy, Plato now allowed the people a more significant role, albeit a rather passive and shadowy one. At the end of the *Laws*, however, Plato comes full circle, returning to the sovereignty of the philosopher-rulers of the *Republic*, but in the guise of theocrats. The tension between the rulers and the people was thus resolved in favour of the former.

Aristotle, in his *Politics*, followed Plato in assessing the relative merits of the rule of the one, the few, and the many. Although he was quite critical of both the *Republic* and the *Laws*, he was sufficiently impressed with the latter work to propose that a good society must be founded on the rule of law. Aristotle also showed a more favourable attitude to the multitude, recognizing from his reflections on history that the people were capable, in the right circumstances, of being wiser and better than the one or the few. Addressing the question of how civil peace may be established and maintained, Aristotle underscored the importance of a large middle class in stabilizing a political society. The greatest number of citizens should possess moderate property – a material stake in the system – and extreme inequalities should be eliminated. There are, of course, other valid insights in Aristotle's *Politics*, which will be taken up later in this book.

The view still prevails that Machiavelli espoused an amoral, beyond-good-and-evil pragmatic doctrine in which the pursuit of a political end justified the employment of any and all means of attaining it. This view could not be further from the truth. As we shall see, Machiavelli was morally and politically committed to a republican form of government. Along with other substantial contributions to our understanding of politics, Machiavelli proposed that ultimately, in his words, 'the populace is the prince.'

Thomas Hobbes may be regarded as the giant of seventeenth-century political thought. His *Leviathan* remains unsurpassed for its intellectual rigour and logical consistency. Living through and reflecting on the tumultuous events of the English civil war, he concluded that civil peace can be secured only when the sovereignty of the ruler remains absolute and undivided. Too often, however, the *Leviathan* is read as if Hobbes were merely defending royal absolutism. Such a reading overlooks the fact that Hobbes expressly applies his doctrine of sovereignty not only to monarchy, but to aristocracy and democracy as well. Moreover, he allows, in an earlier work, for an original democracy of the multitude in the state of nature, a democracy that the multitude may preserve by delegating authority to a common power *conditionally*.

Hobbes's contemporaries and critics failed, however, to discern the important qualifications of his central thesis, and they concluded that the *Leviathan* was nothing more than an apologia for the rule of an absolute monarch. This impression was strengthened by Hobbes's statement in that work that 'tyranny' is simply monarchy disliked; just as 'oligarchy' and 'anarchy' are, respectively, aristocracy and democracy disliked. This statement, suggesting that tyranny is no reality but merely an unsavoury epithet, provoked the extraordinarily fruitful contributions of Locke and Montesquieu. Recognizing tyranny as a fearful reality, both thinkers maintained that unchecked power is bound to become tyrannical. Montesquieu's contributions, as will be seen, go beyond the structure of government, enriching our understanding of several dimensions of political society.

Although Rousseau, like Locke and Montesquieu, also quarrels with Hobbes over his conception of the 'state of nature,' he agrees with Hobbes that sovereignty must be absolute and undivided. However, whereas Hobbes's social contract required that subjects surrender their liberty, Rousseau's contract was founded on popular sovereignty, a doctrine in which the people retain their liberty. Viewing government as necessary but also dangerous, in that it can undermine the people's sovereignty, Rousseau confined his democracy to societies that were small, both demographically and geographically. Only by means of frequent assemblies could the people hope to retain their sovereignty.

The framers of the American Constitution and the Federalists, who most clearly grasped the need for such a Constitution, had carefully read and reflected on the classical tradition of political thinking from Plato to Rousseau. It is no exaggeration to say that the authors of *The Federalist Papers* – Madison, Hamilton, and Jay – had successfully integrated in their intellectual consciousness many of the valid insights of the classical tradition, applying them to the challenge of practical politics with extraordinary acuity and wisdom. The Federalist synthesis of classical principles thus constitutes an original contribution in its own right.

The aim, then, of this review of political theory is to clarify the roles of ruler and ruled in forming a good society.

RULERS AND RULED:

AN INTRODUCTION TO CLASSICAL POLITICAL
THEORY FROM PLATO TO THE FEDERALISTS

Chapter One

Plato

The dialogue that has come to be called the *Republic* bears the original Greek title *Politeia* ('the state'), which not too long afterwards was rendered in Latin as *res publica*. The dialogue's additional Greek title was *e peri dikaiou* ('or concerning justice'). The central question Plato set himself in the *Republic* was this: What is a good individual, and how is such an individual formed? To Plato, it was obvious that an individual could be made good only through membership in a good society. Hence, the first question presupposed a second: What is a good society? – or, on the foundations of what principles is a good society formed?

In one of its important aspects the *Republic* is a polemic directed against the sophists who argued from nature that 'might is right.' Laws of morality, from their standpoint, were not more than arbitrary conventions, which had to be destroyed to make way for the rule of nature where the strong and superior rule the weak and inferior. In opposition to this view Plato wants to argue that the laws of morality are in fact rooted in the nature of the universe and in the nature of the human soul. In an earlier dialogue called the *Gorgias*, we hear a sophist named Callicles insisting that no truly strong and superior individual would enter politics and assume the responsibilities of a ruler if he could not gain materially and otherwise from his position of power in the state. In the *Republic*, another sophist named Thrasymachus espouses an even more extreme view. Plato therefore takes upon himself the task of proving rationally that a state should no longer be the field for the self-satisfaction of the ruler. A state, Plato avers, should rather be the organism of which the ruler is a part and in which he fulfils a vital function. The good society should demand from its rulers that they sacrifice their personal ends to the interests of the general welfare.

In the Greek city-states of Plato's time the conflict between two opposing socio-political systems continued to rage. Indeed, the Peloponnesian War was at one and the same time a struggle for territory and
spheres of influence and an ideological conflict between oligarchy and
democracy. This is a fact that Thucydides repeatedly stresses: 'Practi-
cally the whole of the Hellenic world was convulsed with rival parties in
every state – democratic leaders trying to bring in the Athenians, and
oligarchs trying to bring in the Spartans' (Thucydides, III, 82).[1]

For Plato, both systems were defective. Athenian democracy was fundamentally flawed in that it allowed ignorance to reign in politics.
Statesmanship, like any art or craft, required knowledge and expertise.
Yet in Athens any man, whatever his background and experience, might
be elected to office by the chance of the lot. This was not only a mis-
guided and false equality, it was also unjust. For justice, in Plato's view,
meant that every individual should do the work for which he is suited
by his capacities. Everything has its proper function. One could use an
axe or a knife or any other sharp tool to trim vine branches, but nothing
would do the job as well as a pruning hook fashioned for that purpose
(*Rep.*, 353A).[2] Hence, anyone who attempts to govern others when at
best he is fit only to be an artisan is doubly unjust; for he not only fails to
do his own work, but he also prevents the properly qualified individual
from doing his.

But oligarchy also had its distinctive flaw – a rampant egoism that
prompted individuals to seek offices of state in order to wield power for
their own selfish purposes. Every oligarchical city was divided into two
hostile camps of rich and poor, oppressors and oppressed. Not only that,
but the ruling body itself was torn by dissension, and the root of the evil
was, of course, greed. The rich, striving to become still richer, captured
political office for the sake of the material advantages that its corrupt
use might bring them. This remained so characteristic of oligarchies that
Aristotle later remarked, 'Nowadays owing to the benefits to be derived
from public sources and from holding office men seek to be in office continuously' (*Politics*, III, iv, 6). Thus government, instead of mediating
between the classes and moderating their conflicts, furthered the interests of the rich and privileged.

For Plato, however, political selfishness was not unique to oligarchies.
From the time of Pericles the citizens of Athenian democracy not only
paid themselves from the public coffers for their political services, they
used their authority, on the slightest pretext, to confiscate the estates of
the rich and to plunder their wealth by imposing upon them heavy

financial obligations ('liturgies'). In oligarchies and democracies alike, then, intense and often violent social strife (*stasis*) was the rule. Plato's mission, therefore, was to propose a theory of the state that would avoid the evil of both political systems – the evil in which rulers are like watchdogs who, far from guarding the flocks, themselves attack the sheep and behave like wolves instead of dogs (*Rep.*, 416A).

Oligarchies and democracies alike failed to recognize that statesmanship was a calling, requiring specialized knowledge and moral responsibility. Since both political regimes are blind to this, Plato begins the construction of his ideal state by enunciating the principle of *specialization* as justice. He divides the state into three classes: the rulers, the warriors, and the farmer-producers – the men of gold, silver, and iron-and-brass, respectively. Each of the three classes is assigned its specialized function, and each is to concentrate exclusively on the discharge of that function. Throughout the *Republic* Plato concerns himself with the governing and warrior classes, saying virtually nothing about the third class.

Plato denies private property to both the rulers and the warriors, seeking thereby to free them from any temptation to pursue material interests. He imagined that if a distinct class were designated for the work of government, that would eliminate the struggle for power so characteristic of other political systems. Moreover, if each class remained within its own boundaries, concentrating on its exclusive function, there would be no reason for one class to come into conflict with another. Selfishness (*pleonexia*), for Plato, meant trespassing on another's sphere; so a properly trained governing class would never commit such trespass. To instil the virtue of selflessness in this class, Plato subjects its candidates to a demanding and rigorous series of trials and tests; and only those who have distinguished themselves by their dedication to the common weal of the state are admitted. Besides the spiritual education for unselfishness, Plato introduces the material guarantee of communism: the rulers are to have no family, nor any home or private property of their own. With communism, Plato assumed, the rulers would have no temptation to selfishness, no material interest in holding their positions of authority. With the rulers having nothing in private possessions but their bodies, and everything else in common, one could count on their being free from the dissensions that arise among individuals from the possession of family and property (*Rep.*, 464D–E). That is the way Plato proposes that each should do his own specialized work in contentment. The fundamental principle of social life is 'justice' – which for Plato means neither more nor less than an individual's fulfilment of the role assigned to him in the interest of society as a whole.

The Challenge of Thrasymachus (*Rep.*, 336A–54C)

Thrasymachus represents the view of the radical sophists of the late fifth century. He defines justice as 'the interest of the stronger' – that is, 'might is right.' An individual is entitled to whatever he can get. The state, he argues, simply lays down as the law whatever it deems to be in its own interest, equating 'justice' with whatever it can claim as its right by virtue of its superior power. If this standard of conduct is good enough for the ruler, why should it not also be good for every individual in the community? If one looks at things realistically, says Thrasymachus, all individuals act in their own interest, and the strongest always get what they want; and since the rulers are the strongest in any society, they strive to get whatever they want for themselves and, most often, succeed. Why, asks Thrasymachus, is it just for the ruler to realize his will against the resistance of others, and yet unjust for others to do the same? What is true for the one must be true for the rest. The real standard of action is plain for everyone to see: every individual strives to satisfy himself.

If, therefore, the meaning of justice is unselfishness, it is injustice, for Thrasymachus, that constitutes the truly wise standard for all rational individuals. Injustice is better than justice; and the unjust individual is wiser than the just. The truly wise individual will satisfy his ruler's selfish definition of justice if he must; but he will be unjust if he can and pursue his own interests. Thrasymachus thus espouses an ethical nihilism that is, perhaps, more thoroughgoing than the master-morality expounded by Callicles in the *Gorgias*.

How does Plato strive to counter this extreme form of individualism? The essence of Plato's rebuttal is the argument that the individual is no isolated unit, but rather a part of an organic order with definite functional obligations in that order. This is the argument that Plato unfolds in the course of the *Republic* as a whole. First, however, he tries to meet Thrasymachus on his own sophistic ground by countering with the attempt at a formal logical refutation. Thrasymachus had stated two propositions: (1) rulers rule in their own interest, and (2) injustice (i.e., selfishness) is better than justice. To the first proposition Plato opposes the Socratic conception of government as an art. All arts, he contends, come into being in order to eliminate the defects in the materials with which they deal. The physician attempts to eliminate the afflictions of the body, the teacher those of the mind. The aim of every art is to ensure the well-being of its material. It followed, for Plato, that a ruler who acts in accordance with the demands of his art is thoroughly unselfish, his one and only aim being the welfare of the citizens committed to his care.

In response to Thrasymachus's second proposition Plato argues that the just man is not only wiser and stronger, but also happier than the unjust. He is wiser because he follows the teaching of the Delphic Oracle and recognizes the need of a limit – nothing in excess. With his aim being excellence in discharging his specialized function, the just man competes with others only incidentally – not because he loves competition for its own sake, but because he loves excellence. The just man is also stronger because he acknowledges his interdependence with his fellows. He recognizes that on the principle of reciprocity he gains greater strength by acting justly towards his fellows. The just individual is stronger than the unjust by virtue of the principle that binds him to his fellow human beings. Hence, he is also the happier individual.

The argument by which Plato wishes to prove that the just individual is also happier is so formal in character that it is not entirely convincing. Everything, he argues, has its specialized function (*ergon*), which cannot be fulfilled equally well by any other thing. The virtue of any given thing consists in the fulfilment of its function. The special function of the soul is life (*to Zen*), and its virtue is a good life (*to eu Zen*). The soul fulfils its appointed function only if it possesses the virtue of good living. And since specialization in one's function is called 'justice' by Plato, he concludes that if the soul possesses the virtue of good living, it also possesses happiness (*eudaimonia*), and the just individual is happier than the unjust. This is Plato playing with the sophists at their game of words, and we are left with strong doubts that he has in fact beat them at their own game. Thus far he has not persuaded us, by means of this type of rational discourse, that the unegoistic individual is necessarily the happier one.

The Challenge of Glaucon (*Rep.*, 357–67E)

Without adopting Thrasymachus's position that justice is the will of the strongest directed towards his own interests, Glaucon nevertheless contends that justice is an *artificial* thing, an unnatural social convention. Anticipating the modern social-contract theorists, Glaucon argues that in a state of nature individuals do injure and suffer injury (read injustice), and nothing restrains the perpetrators of injury. Finding this state of affairs insufferable, the weak, who suffer more injustice than they can inflict, take the initiative and make a contract with others neither to do nor to suffer injustice. In accordance with this contract they create laws and conventions that thereafter become the code of justice. In this way humans turn against their natural instincts, which strive for self-satisfaction, and consent to the authority of the unnatural law.

Thus justice, for Glaucon, is the offspring of fear: it is a compromise between the best, which is to injure others with impunity, and the worst, which is to suffer wrong or injury and be powerless to do anything about it. Justice is accepted and approved not because it is a real good, but because one is too weak to wrong others and get away with it. For it is obvious, Glaucon claims, that anyone who was a real man and who, in fact, possessed the power to get away with injuring others would never agree to such a contract. Thus while Thrasymachus has defined justice as the interest of the stronger, Glaucon defines it as an invention to which the weaker resort out of fear. Though he is in fundamental agreement with Thrasymachus on the artificiality of justice, Glaucon posits the fears of the weak rather than the interests of the strong as the origin of the social contract. Plato intends the rest of what he has to say in the *Republic* as a rebuttal of the claims made by Thrasymachus and Glaucon.

The Human Soul-Mind and the Construction of the Ideal State

Under the influence of the Pythagorean doctrines, Plato proposed that the human soul consists of three components: the appetitive, the rational, and the spiritive. The appetitive or non-rational element (*epithymia*) is the desire for pleasure; it is the source of erotic love, hunger, thirst, and other appetites (*Rep.*, 439D). The second component is reason (*logos*), the faculty by which human beings gain knowledge. The third element is spirit (*thymos*), which refers to the condition in which both humans and animals may be either high or low spirited. For Plato, this element accounts in humans for the sense of honour, inspiring men for battle. It is the source of ambition and competition, but at the same time an ally of reason, prompting individuals to resist and fight injustice. In the internal struggle of these soul-elements, when, say, an individual's desires impel him in a direction contrary to his reason and well-being, the spiritive element becomes an ally of reason, turning him back in the proper direction (*Rep.*, 440B). Each of these soul-elements becomes, respectively, the basis of the classes in Plato's ideal state.

As noted, Plato's central doctrine in the *Republic* is that each individual should 'do his own' (*to autou prattein*) – each should fulfil a single, specific function. Hence, in shaping the division of labour Plato begins with the appetitive or economic function as the foundation of the state. The fundamental human need for food and shelter requires cooperation in the form of a division of labour; and it is the division of labour that demonstrates the inevitability of human *interdependence*: each participant in it provides something for the others that they, in turn, provide for him or her. The specialization of functions inevitably brings with it reciprocal exchange and interdependence. No individual is self-sufficient; every individual needs others. Plato applies this logic to the political sphere. If, say, the cobbler produces better work by sticking to his task, why should it be less true that the statesman will produce better results if he too sticks to his vocation? And if the economic organization for the satisfaction of basic human needs is based on specialization and reciprocity, why should not the entire organization of the society and state be based on the same principles? In this way Plato reasoned that reciprocity and the mutual exchange of services between ruler and ruled could displace the self-seeking in which one strives to get everything for oneself. Plato's aim, then, was to design a state in which all citizens must be set to the specific tasks for which their natures have fitted them, so that the whole society becomes not a multiplicity of interest groups and factions, but rather an organic unity (*Rep.*, 423D).

If the economic organization of the state is a manifestation of the appetitive element in the soul, then the military factor is an expression of the soul's spiritive component. Human beings are not content with mere vital necessities. They crave the higher things in life – art, music, and other needs of a refined taste. An extension of the division of labour and, hence, a larger population and territory are therefore required to satisfy such needs. War thus enters as an essential function of the state (*Rep.*, 373D), whose responsibility it is to gain and defend a territory sufficient for the society's general needs. 'Spirit,' the soul-element that inspires men to battle, finds expression in the organization of the state by constituting the military stratum of guardians (*Rep.*, 347D). There must be a caste of warriors whose sole business it is to plan the defence and security of the state, and Plato gives considerable attention to the education and training of the professional warrior (*Rep.*, II, 376E–III, 412A).

The warrior is a guardian (*phylanx*) of the state. Here Plato characteristically employs an analogy: the guardian, like a watchdog, must be gentle to those he guards, but ferocious to every stranger. The watchdog possesses the cognitive capacity to distinguish between friend and foe (*Rep.*, 376A–B). Likewise, the guardian of the state must develop his faculty of reason so as to recognize an enemy deserving of attack. In the warrior, reason is mixed with the soul-element of spirit, by which reason is aided. But reason in its purest form expresses itself not in the guardian, but in the 'perfect guardian,' or ruler. The class of guardians is now split by Plato into two: the military guardians whose chief characteristic is 'spirit' and who are now termed 'helpers' (*epikouroi*), and the philosophic guardians whose chief strength lies in their superior capacity for reasoning. These are the guardians *par excellence* of the Platonic state.

Watchdogs show affection for those whom they know and protect. Similarly, the 'perfect guardians' will not only recognize but love the general interest of the state. They will zealously dedicate themselves to the common weal. If this soul-element, reason-love, becomes manifest in government, it will be unselfish; and in place of the self-seeking that Thrasymachus espoused, government will be realized as an art practised for the good of its subjects. Appetite draws individuals together in an interdependent division of labour; reason mixed with spirit binds the military guardians to those they protect; and the pure reason of the philosophic guardians bears the primary responsibility of holding the society together as an organic whole. They are *the* ruling class. There being no exception to Plato's principle of specialization, they will give themselves to ruling, and to ruling alone.

The real ruler, Plato insists, must be a philosopher; but the philosophic faculty is present in only a few, rare souls. Philosophy, or the love of wisdom, says Plato, is impossible for the multitude (*Rep.*, 494A). Candidates for rulership will be carefully selected and subjected to an elaborate system of intellectual and moral tests. If they are to become members of the philosopher-guardian class, they must come to know the essence of Goodness, Justice, Beauty, and Temperance as standards or forms in whose likeness they will shape the characters of those whom they rule. The state is capable of perfection if it is guided by a superlative, philosophic reason. This, in fact, is the underlying premise of the *Republic*: the state is the product of the human mind, and each component of the state is the product of an element of the soul-mind. The state is, unavoidably, an economic, military, and rational organization, for these are, respectively, expressions of the appetitive, spiritive, and rational aspects of the mind. Hence, the 'philosopher-king' is a logical outcome of Plato's method in which the constitution of the state is guided by his conception of the human soul.

The Third Class of the Platonic State

To the philosophers and guardians Plato now adds a third class – the class of producers who fulfil the fundamental economic function. Like the philosopher-rulers and the warriors, the members of the third class – by far the vast majority of the populace – will also confine themselves to a single function. So the Platonic state as a whole is a society consisting of a division of labour between three specialized classes: the rulers or 'perfect guardians'; the warriors (who were at first called 'guardians,' but later called 'helpers'); and the producing classes, whom Plato calls the 'farmers.'

Plato's scheme implies that each of the component elements of the soul-mind (appetite, spirit, and reason) is prominent in particular individuals or groups of individuals. There is one very small group in which reason is prominent; a second, larger group in which the spiritive element prevails; and a third category, comprising the vast majority of the people, in which appetite is paramount. Criticisms of this scheme are therefore warranted. On the one hand, Plato proposes a pan-human conception of the soul in which the soul-mind of every human being consists of the three elements of reason, spirit, and appetite. On the other hand, he proposes that the social structure of the state should be divided into classes, which correspond strictly to the respective elements of the mind. The result is that each member of a particular class is limited by Plato to the use of only one component element of the mind, the other elements remaining unused and atrophying for all practical purposes. The ruler lives by reason and is forced by Plato to abandon appetite. He is subjected to a highly ascetic, communistic regime that represses the role of appetite and deadens an essential element of human nature. The farmer-producer, in contrast, lives solely for the satisfaction of appetite. His activity in the economic sphere, to which he is restricted, is guided not by his own internal reason, but by the reason of the perfect guardians. How, therefore, can the farmer-producers not suffer an atrophy of their rational faculties?

For Plato, not only is the soul made up of three distinct elements, but each element is responsible for a certain kind of activity. We learn with one part, feel anger with the second, and desire with the third. The mind is not a homogeneous entity, but rather the home of elements that often conflict with one another. Appetite and reason, for example, are often engaged in a struggle resembling the conflict of factions in a state (*Rep.*, 440B). The distinct and often contradictory elements of the soul can only be brought into harmony if and when the rational part, the source of wisdom and forethought, rules with the 'spiritive' part as its subject and ally (*Rep.*, 441E). It is this doctrine of the tripartite soul that led Plato to the creation of the three-class system of his ideal state, which may be criticized on the following grounds: it rests on a hierarchy of classes possessing the features of an order of castes; it posits a great gulf between the producing and the ruling classes; and it seeks to unify the rulers with one another and the rest of society by depriving them of family and property, which are so essential to a full, human personality. Furthermore, Plato's polity seeks to unify the society by subjecting it to the absolute sovereignty of a class. He thus transposes from the mind to the state an autocratic view of reason. If, however, we start with Plato's own pan-human conception of the mind, in which the soul-mind of every human being possesses the faculty of reason, and if we then transfer this conception to the state, we find reason animating each and every member of the society. This strongly suggests that it is not the chosen few, but the will of the whole community that should rule.

In fairness to Plato we need to observe that he acknowledges the possibility that individuals of one class may possess the faculties required for another. When that occurs, such individuals should be enabled to rise to the class to which their capacities entitle them. Plato's Socrates expresses this principle in the form of a myth. Although it is true, he says, that all members of our ideal society are brothers, yet the gods, in fashioning those who are best fitted to rule, placed gold in their beings, which is why they are the most precious; just as the gods placed silver in the 'helpers,' and iron and brass in the farmers and other producers. And though for the most part gold would breed gold and the others would breed their own kind, it may sometimes happen that a golden father will beget a silver son, and a golden offspring will come from silver parents, and the rest would likewise beget exceptions. The rulers are therefore admonished to observe carefully the mixture of these metals in the souls of their offspring, and if children are born to them with a predominance of brass or iron in their souls, the rulers shall by no means give way to pity, but shall assign them to the class of farmer-producers. And if in this class are born children with a predominance of gold and silver in their souls, they shall be promoted to the statuses they deserve (*Rep.*, 415A–C).

Plato's View of Justice

'Justice' in the *Republic*, as already observed, is neither more nor less than specialization: the duty to discharge one's own function and not interfere with or encroach on that of another. Human beings with different capacities and skills come together under the impulse of their mutual needs; by thus coming together in one society and concentrating on their distinct functions, they create a functionally integrated, harmonious whole. But the price individuals pay for this integration, as we have seen, is that they act with only a fraction of their total soul-minds or personalities. Moreover, Plato's peculiar conception of justice fails to provide a principle by which to deal with the diverse, competing, and conflicting interests of classes. But it is precisely such a principle that we seek in a fruitful conception of justice. And although Plato urges upon all of his state's members the virtue of self-control, this is a moral, not a legal principle. Indeed, in the *Republic* Plato makes no provision at all for law, as the philosopher-kings rule strictly by virtue of their own superior wisdom.

Candidates for the philosopher-king class undergo a long and rigorous physical and mental training. They study mathematics to prepare themselves for the study of dialectic. If mathematics teaches one to see the relation between objects of sense and objects of thought, dialectic enables one to grasp the objects of thought themselves – the perfect and pure forms – and ultimately the supreme form of the good. For fifteen years, from the age of thirty-five to fifty, candidates devote themselves to the service of the state, holding military and other offices and gaining experience of life (*Rep.*, 539E). Throughout this period they are tried and tested, and finally, at the age of fifty all those who have passed every trial and test with distinction are allowed to devote the greater part of their time to the study of philosophy – while continuing, when their turn comes, to toil in the service of the state.

In Plato's educational theory, as in his own life, we may observe a certain tension between the ideal of contemplation and that of action. There are passages in which the goal of life seems to be grasping adequately the form of the good; but there are other passages in which life's purpose is the moral betterment of humanity, requiring one's devotion to a life of social service. Plato resolves this tension in favour of the active life, acknowledging that the abstention from politics is only a 'second-best' option. In a life of contemplation alone, the philosopher will not, after all, have accomplished anything great. However, it is only in a state hospitable to his calling that a philosopher can attain his full stature and help save both his country and himself (*Rep.*, 497A). The ideal of the *Republic* is to constitute such a state so that the philosopher can bind the subjects together to form a commonwealth. In the *Republic*, therefore, the philosopher must not refuse 'to go down again' into the 'cave,' into the world of affairs; he must not take false advantage of the privilege society has granted him by remaining in the upper world of vision and contemplation (*Rep.*, 519D). Having pursued and grasped the good, the philosopher is bound to communicate it as a 'way of life' to his fellow humans.

The Political Structure of the *Republic*

The state of the *Republic* must be guided by philosophers: either philosophers must become kings, or present-day kings must become philosophers, so that political power and philosophical intelligence are joined. For so long as the two remain separate, there will be no end to the troubles plaguing states. The rule of the 'philosopher-kings' may be either a monarchy or an aristocracy (*Rep.*, 445D, 587D). Whether it is one who rules or a few, their power is absolute in the sense that it is uncontrolled by any written law. In this respect Plato abandons in the *Republic* the common Greek conception of the state as an association governed by the sovereignty of the law. However, although Plato makes no provision for a written law-code, he does lay down certain principles: (1) the rulers must guard against the intrusion into the state of the extremes of wealth and poverty (*Rep.*, 421E); (2) the size of the state must be limited so as to be consistent with unity and self-sufficiency (*Rep.*, 423C–D); (3) the rulers must maintain justice in Plato's peculiar sense – that is, they must ensure that every citizen is occupied exclusively with the fulfilment of his specific function (*Rep.*, 423D); (4) the rulers must also guard against innovations in the system of education and in art and music 'For modes of music are never changed without unsettling the most fundamental political and social conventions' (*Rep.*, 424B–C).

The governing class of the *Republic* is compelled to embrace a form of communism in which members are deprived of family and private property. Communism, for Plato, is a material corollary of the rigorous spiritual education of the philosopher-rulers. Two of the *Republic's* three classes – the rulers and the warriors – must live under a communistic regime. They represent, respectively, the soul-elements of reason and spirit; so if they are to fulfil the special duties of those elements, they must have nothing to do with the element of 'appetite,' which is the special duty of the third class of farmers and producers. Plato believed that communism is necessary for the rulers because experience had shown that wherever economic and political power are held in the same hands, corruption of government is inevitable. The third class, however, retains private property, but under the supervision of the rulers who regulate trade and industry – not by means of law, but by means of their own wisdom. True to the central principle of the *Republic* – specialization as justice – each member of the third class practises his own craft and never encroaches on that of another.

It is important to remind ourselves that the two highest classes of the *Republic* are not merely a spiritual or intellectual élite, but a military élite as well, and the third class resembles a class of serfs. The rulers, Plato tells us, are to choose a strategic site in the city for their encampment, 'the best position from which they could put down rebellion from within and repel aggression from without' (*Rep.*, 415E). This passage strongly suggests that notwithstanding Plato's effort to create a harmonious and organic social whole, he realized that the third class might have cause for rebellion, and that the rulers must prepare themselves for such a contingency. The propertyless rulers are to live on an income paid in kind by the farmer-producer class, who in their subordinate status would presumably be willing to make such payments. As we shall see, this scheme is quite problematic.

Plato imagines that the philosopher-rulers will be loved by those they rule because they are their wise helpers, not their masters. The rulers, in turn, will love their subjects to whom they owe their sustenance (*Rep.*, 463A–B). Rulers and subjects will be bound together by mutual need, respect, and gratitude. Several questions thus beg to be addressed: How can one have a society in which one part lives under a communistic regime while the other part is based on the institution of private property? Would not such an arrangement produce the very same dissension and conflict that Plato aims to avoid? If private property is the cause of dissension, why should it be allowed in the third and most populous class? Given the institution of private property in the third class, why should not the existence of, say, larger and smaller farms and the diversity of crafts produce intense conflict, or a 'war of each against all'? In the absence of a legal code, how would the rulers regulate conflict in the third class? Finally, why exactly is it in the interest of the third class to go along with this scheme and yield to the authority of the philosopher-kings?

We return, then, to the contradiction between Plato's pan-human soul and his ideal state. If every human being possesses a mind consisting of three elements, why should not every member of Plato's state be allowed and enabled to employ all three elements? Plato will not hear of any such thing because it implies democracy, and Plato is certainly no democrat. He remains adamant that rational knowledge is a rather esoteric thing; so he posits a great gulf between the few individuals who are capable of attaining such knowledge and the rest of humanity who are not.

Communism of Wives

To protect the rulers of his ideal state from the temptations of material self-interest, Plato deprived them of private property. If he had left the family intact, he would have failed to accomplish that aim, since one's family is an extension of oneself, and one can hardly avoid wanting the best for one's offspring, whether material or spiritual. Hence, the abolition of family life among the rulers was a logical corollary of the abolition of private property.

To understand Plato's discussion of women, one must remember that public life in the Greek city-state was a masculine affair. The man lived in the open as a 'political being' while the woman, except in Sparta, lived a secluded life in the family's private household. Taking his cue from Sparta – as he does frequently in the *Republic* – Plato develops an argument designed to emancipate women from their traditional seclusion (*Rep.*, 451C–56B). The traditional status and role of women, he observes, meant not only that their own development was thwarted, but that society lost the contributions of half of its members. Earlier Plato had compared the guardians to watchdogs; now he places another dog-analogy in the mouth of Socrates to make a new point: we expect the female dogs to guard and to hunt and to join the males in all the tasks we assign to those creatures, and we train the females accordingly. If, then, we are to employ women for the same things as men, we must also teach them the same things. Music, gymnastics, and the military arts are the training we give to the men as members of the philosopher-guardian class, so we must give the same training to the women if we expect them to join that class in their service of the state.

The women-guardians, like the men-guardians, are to live in common and open barracks; and with the family among them having been abolished, a communal system is introduced in which wives and children of the male guardians are to be held in common (*Rep.*, 457C–66D). The analogy of the domesticated animal world suggested that if one desires good stock, the state must join male to female in a careful and selective manner. Sexual intercourse will therefore be strictly regulated in the interest of the state. The children of these unions will be taken at birth from their mothers and transferred to public nurseries, and the mother will no longer have anything at all to do with her child, nor even know her own child. All couples married and becoming parents at the same time will be taught to regard their offspring as their common children; and the children will be taught to regard themselves as brothers and sisters of one another. In this way Plato envisions that the philosopher-guardians will come to feel themselves as one body, sharing a way of life and loving the same persons. There is, then, a strong eugenic element in Plato's scheme. Believing that offspring should be bred from the best stock in its prime, Plato designates the period of reproduction for men between the ages of twenty-five and fifty-five, and for women between twenty and forty. He prescribes the strict rule that if intercourse takes place outside those periods, the offspring is to be put to death. He objects, moreover, to the employment of medical skill to prolong the lives of chronic invalids (*Rep.*, 459E–60E).

Plato's communism raises a fundamental question: Has he not, in effect, impoverished and drastically diminished the individual self by denying to the philosopher-guardians the experience of family and the minimal household property necessary for a healthy family life? In Plato's demand that the individual philosopher-guardian shall identify with the state, he not only abolishes the family and family households, but other vital human associations as well. None of the 'secondary associations' so characteristic of Greece appears in Plato's ideal state. There are no clans, villages, tribes, demes, or religious associations. Plato has thus thought away many conditions that are still with us today; and he has thought into being other conditions, such as common wives and children, that seem no less than preposterous.

Plato on the Actual Greek States

In the eighth and ninth books of the *Republic* Plato analyses the political societies of his time: Sparta, a form of timocracy and oligarchy; Athens, a form of democracy; and Syracuse, a form of tyranny. Plato's ideal state is founded, as we have seen, on the three soul-elements of reason, spirit, and appetite and, presumably, their harmonious union through the dominance of reason. Below the ideal state Plato places oligarchy, democracy, and tyranny, all founded on the supremacy of appetite and, therefore, on a discordant relationship of the soul-elements. In any political system, Plato maintains, it is excess that causes its degeneration. Oligarchy perishes from the excessive pursuit of wealth, just as democracy is ruined by the excessive pursuit of freedom. There is a universal law in which any excess is bound to engender an opposite reaction. The law applies equally to plants, animals, and political systems (*Rep.*, 563E–64A). In an oligarchy, for instance, when the rich relentlessly increase their wealth, poverty grows at the other pole, and the discontented poor soon begin to resist and oppose the regime. The result is class-warfare and even revolution (*Rep.*, 556E).

For Plato, all actual states are corruptions of his ideal state. The first corruption is a timocracy – a form of government in which property is necessary for political office, in which honour (*timé*) is the society's central principle. The dominance of reason has given way to the dominance of spirit, as in the case of the war-state Sparta. The second corruption is oligarchy. Timocracy already contains elements of oligarchy. But whereas the aim of the former is war and glory, the aim of the latter is trade and money. A timocracy turning into an oligarchy is the corruption of a military state into a commercial one. In an oligarchy, Plato states plainly, 'the rich hold office and the poor man is excluded' (*Rep.*, 550C). Oligarchy thus violates the ideal state's principle of justice: the rich hold office though they may have no real ability to govern. The third corruption is democracy – a system, for Plato, in which appetite, uncurbed and unbridled, dominates the social psychology of the people. Appetite in a democracy expresses itself in the demand for absolute freedom and equality, guaranteed and sanctioned by the use of the lot in the appointment of all officials. Democracy is anarchy, Plato insists, because its twin pillars, liberty and equality, far from being true principles are the negation of principles – the negation of social hierarchy that is the *sine qua non* of an organic social order.

Democracy is also a negation of justice in Plato's peculiar sense, for it denies the principle of specialization and allows every man to participate in governing the state. Plato ridicules the extremes that popular liberty has reached in democracy, where the male and female purchased slaves appear to be no less free than the owners who paid for them, and where even horses and asses conduct themselves with an audacious freedom and dignity, making way for no one and bumping into everyone (*Rep.*, 563B–D). It is the extremes of democracy that, for Plato, cause it to degenerate into tyranny. This comes about when a democratic city becomes so intoxicated from the strong wine of liberty that the citizens accuse their leaders of being accursed oligarchs (*Rep.*, 562D–E). In the *Republic*, then, the verdict on democracy is one of condemnation. In its life it is anarchic and in its death it paves the way for tyranny. We need, therefore, to observe that the latter notion – that tyranny emerges out of democracy – is contradicted by what Thucydides had to say on the historical origin of tyranny: 'The old form of government was hereditary monarchy with established rights and limitations; but as Hellas [Greece] became more powerful and as the importance of acquiring money became more and more evident, tyrannies were established in nearly all the cities' (Thucydides, I, 13). It is therefore closer to the historical truth to say that tyrants came to power in ancient Greece by making themselves champions of the lower classes who had become discontented with the oppressiveness of oligarchical regimes. The sequence in Greek history is quite the opposite of that proposed by Plato.

The original question from which the whole argument of the *Republic* took its departure was whether the perfectly just individual is happier than the perfectly unjust. In the ninth book of the *Republic* Plato wants to prove the perfect happiness of the just and the perfect misery of the unjust. The ideal state, Plato asserts, is perfectly just and happy; therefore, the philosopher-ruler who shapes and fulfils the highest virtues of the ideal state is perfectly just and happy. Ignoring the third class altogether, Plato discusses only the rulers and warriors in this context, but fails even in their case to prove that they are as happy as they are 'just' (i.e., devoted exclusively to their specific functions). His argument is based on the dubious assumption that their happiness consists less in their own well-being as individuals than in their contribution to the general happiness. Moreover, at the end of the *Republic* we are still uncertain as to why Plato believes that the third class of farmers and producers – the vast majority of the populace – should find happiness in his ideal state. They are, after all, confined to the exercise of only one element of their soul-mind; and in the governing of the ideal state they are allowed no rational, participatory role whatsoever.

The Statesman (*Politicus*)

It is highly probable that the dialogue *Politicus* was written late in Plato's life and that it should be regarded as a prime example of the changes in Plato's thinking following completion of the *Republic*. Perhaps the best way to convey the nature of this transitional phase between the *Republic* and Plato's final work, the *Laws*, is to begin with the myth related in the *Politicus*, which distinguishes two stages in the development of human society. The first is the era of Cronus, when the gods ruled the world and human beings therefore had no need to shoulder the cares of government (271–72A). In this primordial age the human species was a single family, with men holding wives and children in common. The Earth yielded its bounty without the need for cultivation, and the permanent springtime on Earth made clothing and shelter unnecessary. Then came the present era, when the divine helmsmen withdrew and retired to their respective realms. Human beings, now left to their own devices, fell into a state of such helplessness that they were even at the mercy of the beasts until the gods took pity on them. Prometheus gave them fire, Hephaestus and Athena the arts, and other gods gave them seeds and plants. With these divine gifts humans were furnished with the means of managing their own lives and fending for themselves. As the dialogue unfolds we see how Plato makes the transition from the philosopher-king ideal of the *Republic* to the recognition of the validity of less-than-ideal institutions.

Just as one would distinguish the true weaver from all false claimants to his title and calling, one must distinguish the true statesman from imposters (279A). The true statesman is like the genuine weaver in that he has to join together diverse natures so as to create a smooth texture. Statesmanship, like weaving, is an art requiring knowledge. This is Plato's principle: those who possess the art of ruling and those alone should be regarded as rulers, whatever form their rule may take. It is immaterial whether the subjects are willing or unwilling; whether they rule with or without a code of laws; whether they are poor or wealthy (293B). The only true state is one that possesses such rulers. A state will be no more than factions at war with one another so long as it fails to cohere as a unity through the coordinating power of a statesmanship based on knowledge. Echoing the *Republic*, Plato asserts that such knowledge can be attained only by one individual or at most by a few, but never by the multitude (292E).

Thus far in the dialogue Plato retains the view that neither law nor the consent of the governed is an essential principle of a good and just polity. Statesmanship is an art, and it is the essence of every art that the artist works alone, free from any constricting rules determining how he shall do his creative work. The artist moulds his materials according to his specialized knowledge; and the statesman, as an artist, must be free to rule his subjects according to his own wisdom (293C). Employing two additional analogies, Plato argues that neither a ship-passenger nor a doctor's patient has any right to give or withhold prior consent to the exercise of the ship-pilot's or physician's art. Both the passenger and the patient must place themselves under the guidance of specialized knowledge without any claim to a voice in the methods by which that knowledge is to be applied. What is required from the passenger and the patient is not consent, but acquiescence, for if the pilot and physician are truly knowledgeable, they will necessarily do the passenger and patient good. The same must be true, Plato asserts, of the relationship between the statesman and his subjects. If, therefore, the statesman forces his subjects to do things contrary to their will, it must not be said that they have suffered injustice (296D–E).

It needs to be observed, however, that Plato's analogies fail to prove his point. The ship-pilot may not be directly responsible to the passengers, but he is responsible to the ship-owners and, say, to the governmental agency that ensures standards of safety in navigation. Similarly, in the analogy of the physician it is important to remember that a patient voluntarily entrusts himself to a doctor's care and may, therefore, accept or reject his advice. In Plato's view, however, the so-called knowledgeable statesman's power carries with it no real accountability. Hence, in the *Politicus*, as in the *Republic*, law is unnecessary and even detrimental to the statesman's art. Indeed, law in the *Politicus* is still regarded as an evil on the ground that it imposes checks on the free play of the ruler's expert knowledge. Law by its very nature is general, Plato reasons, and cannot prescribe with precision what is good for each individual member of the society. The differences of human personality and the variety of human experiences make it impossible to issue unqualified rules that hold good on all questions and at all times (294B).

Plato, however, overlooks what later political theorists will see rather clearly. Law is essential for at least two reasons: (1) if it is true that power can only be checked by power, then a law-code must stipulate the means by which a ruler's abuse of power may be checked; and (2) if social life is to be peaceful and calculable, members of society must know in advance the rules by which they are to act, and by which they may expect others to act.

In the *Politicus*, in accordance with the teachings of the Delphic Oracle ('nothing in excess') – a well-established principle of Greek wisdom – the statesman-weaver is to be guided by a mean or limit. In the art of music, for instance, the mean is a blending of opposites that produces harmony. Like the weaver, then, who joins in harmony the warp and the woof, the statesman must unite harmoniously the diverse elements of human nature. There are individuals, for example, whose excess of courage (read rashness or recklessness) leads to militaristic adventurism; and there are, in contrast, other individuals whose pacific natures prompt them to indulge their passions for peace at the wrong times, thus making themselves and their community vulnerable to an aggressor (307E–8A). Social life possesses no inherent unity of virtue; it exhibits a variety of virtues that are often even hostile to one another: one type of individual opposed to another type, one class inimical to another (306B–C). The statesman-weaver must therefore enter and fulfil his function by discovering a mean and mixing different natures and classes so as to produce a harmony. The 'classes' of the *Politicus*, however, unlike those of the *Republic*, represent social types, not social occupations.

Towards the end of the dialogue, however, Plato shifts rather abruptly to a new theme. He provides us with two detailed classification schemes of government. The first represents the theory current in his day. Its criterion is number, which yields the three forms of rule – of the one, the few, and the many. With the added criteria of force or consent and the legal or non-legal nature of government, the first two forms are further subdivided into two types (291). There are, therefore, in this first scheme five forms of government: monarchy, tyranny, aristocracy, oligarchy, and democracy. The second scheme is Plato's own (*Politicus*, 302C–3A), in which seven forms of government are distinguished. Adding a new form of monarchy – that of the ideal statesman who governs by perfect knowledge – Plato differentiates three forms of the rule of the *one*: ideal monarchy, legal monarchy, and tyranny. Democracy, of which there was only one type in the first scheme, is now subdivided by Plato into the two forms of legal democracy and extreme (arbitrary) democracy. What this seems to imply, then, is that Plato has arrived at a transitional phase in his theoretical reflections on politics, which will lead him to the new position he takes in the *Laws*. In the *Politicus* there are states based on law and there are states based on arbitrary rule. Those based on law are 'second best' in that they come closest to the state founded on the perfect knowledge of the true statesman. Those states that are devoid of law fall doubly short of the ideal state. This suggests a more realistic and practical conception of politics on Plato's part and a new awareness of the virtue of the 'second-best' system.

At first in the *Politicus* the doctrine of the 'second best' seems not to apply to democracy, which is always the same whether the multitude controls the wealthy by force or by consent, and whether or not the democracy abides strictly by the laws (292A). Later in the dialogue, however, Plato sees some good in democracy. The rule of the many, he asserts, is the weakest in all respects. It is incapable of any real good or any serious evil as compared with the rule of the one and the rule of the few. Plato's reason is that sovereignty in a democracy is dispersed in small portions and vested in a large number of rulers. If, therefore, all three governments are based on law, democracy is the worst of the three; but if all three are 'lawless,' democracy is the best. It is best to live in a democracy if and when all governments are unprincipled. But when they are principled and lawful, democracy is least desirable and monarchy is by far the best. But even here Plato urges us to remember that the real and true best is not just any monarchy, but the ideal, philosophic-monarchy of the *Republic*, which, like a god among mortals, stands higher than all other governmental structures (*Politicus*, 303A–B). In the *Laws*, however, we shall find Plato advocating a law-based government just a notch below the ideal state itself.

The *Laws*

Plato's final thoughts on politics were most likely composed during the last ten years of his life, when he was a man of over seventy years of age. In contrast to Plato's earlier dialogues, Socrates makes no appearance in the *Laws*, which is really something of a monologue by an Athenian stranger (presumably Plato himself) in the company of a Cretan and a Spartan who listen to him rather patiently and politely. The change that Plato's views had undergone between the *Republic* and the *Laws* is clearly indicated in the very title of the latter work. In the *Republic* the philosopher-kings were to rule unencumbered by laws. Plato himself had in fact intended to translate the *Republic*'s theory into practice in 361 BC, when he was involved with Dionysius the Younger, the tyrant of Syracuse. During Plato's stay there he had tried but failed to turn the young tyrant into a philosopher-ruler by means of a philosophical education. Plato's failure and his reflection upon it appears to have given rise to a modification in his theory of government: if he could not train a philosophic ruler to rule without and instead of the law, he would create a philosophic law-code that all states should follow. In that way a law-state would at least be indirectly governed by philosophy, and it would be a 'second-best' state, second only to the ideal state of the *Republic*, which, Plato never totally abandoned.

The ruler in the *Laws* possesses both a family and private property. The communism of the *Republic* is discarded, and the ruled are now given a voice and a vote in the election of the rulers. The chief virtue of the *Laws* is no longer the specialization-as-justice of the *Republic*, but rather temperance or self-control. Hence, the virtue of, say, courage, if it is untempered by self-control and the doctrine of the mean, turns a state into a war-state, which is a perverted state. This is a point that the Athenian, speaking to a Spartan and a Cretan, wishes to make concerning their respective military states. Plato may have been led to press this view by the course of Greek history: Sparta had been defeated by Thebes at the battle of Martinea in 362 BC. The war-state was thus discredited, and an era of criticism of Sparta began, criticism that finds its echo not only in Plato's *Laws*, but also in Aristotle's *Politics*. If the war-states will now listen to the Athenian (Plato) they will renounce expansion, conquest, and annihilation and, by learning the philosophy of peace, turn their policies inward to bring about a social harmony that only self-control can yield. But Plato is no pacifist. He is opposed to offensive warfare, not warfare necessary for a state's defence (760–61A).

As a state renounces offensive warfare and turns inward, it recognizes that law is the expression of reason; and if reason is to be sovereign in a state's domestic policy, law must be sovereign. Law is also the means by which the virtue of self-control is realized, since self-control is nothing other than a harmonious balance of reason and appetite. A state's laws will therefore have a preamble enunciating the principles on which they are based and persuading the citizens to accept all of the state's statutes as the logical outcome of the principles in which the citizens themselves believe (723A–24B). Law, for Plato, is not so much a force acting upon the individual from without as it is a spirit that the individual must internalize, a spirit inculcated by means of moral education (643E).

Reflecting on history, Plato observes that the kings of Argos and Messene had proved themselves unfaithful to their peoples, their allies, and their laws. The fault lay with the legislators who made laws for the sake of war, not for peace, and who made the additional error of placing all power in the hands of one man. The virtue of self-control – the golden mean – was ignored, and the kingdoms of Argos and Messene perished. Sparta, however, survived because it had observed the mean in at least one crucial respect. Although its laws, like those of Argos and Messene, were defective insofar as they had been designed for a war-state, Sparta's monarchy was never absolute. It was checked from the outset by the provision of a dual kingship, and it was further balanced, as time went on, by the institutions of the ephors (the senior magistrates) and a senate. Historical experience thus strongly suggested that a mixed and balanced constitution succeeded where an unmixed one failed. That was the lesson to be learned from the three Dorian states, and Sparta must therefore serve as the model if legislators wished the state to enjoy stability.

Plato also considers other types of state: Persia, a form of royal absolutism (which Montesquieu later dubbed 'oriental despotism'), and Athens, the model of popular self-government. These examples are polar opposites, which because they are so far from the mean are to be rejected unless each is wisely mixed with the other (693–701C). Pure unmixed or unchecked monarchy, in both its Greek and Persian forms, is condemned by Plato. But he condemns equally the pure and unmixed democracy of Athens. Democracy widens the boundaries of freedom, but its price is ignorance, since every man participates in government regardless of his knowledge and competence to do so. As for monarchy, Plato acknowledges its strong tendency to repress liberty, but he insists that monarchy suggests the rule of wisdom. It followed that one must combine the qualities of monarchy and democracy in order to guarantee wisdom in the ruler (presumably through proper training) and liberty to the ruled. In contrast to the *Republic*, where Plato tried to create philosopher-kings while giving the people no voice in politics, he attempts in the *Laws* to reconcile the principle of monarchy with the principle of popular participation in politics.

Plato's state in the *Laws* is a rather small, self-contained agricultural community, the precise numerical size of which he specifies at 5,040. Just as the state's government must be a monarchy and democracy, so must the society itself be a blend of different elements. Marriage must be a union of diverse characters and classes (773A); property must be a combination of private ownership and public control (740A); and the rich or better off must voluntarily share their wealth with the poor to prevent civil dissension and strife (736D–E). This harks back to the weaver analogy of the *Politicus*, where the warp and the woof were to be properly woven to produce a harmonious social texture (734E–35A). The system of property proposed in the *Laws* thus departs from the communistic ideal of the *Republic*. Still, the best Greek state, for Plato, is one in which the old Greek principle, 'friends' property is common property,' is followed closely. The 'second-best' state being proposed in the *Laws* will, however, fall short of that principle, since land and houses will be private property. Nor will there be any common tilling of the soil, for that is beyond the reach of the individuals born and nurtured under the proposed system (740A). On the other hand, Plato does try to combine private ownership with common use. The right of property is to be used for the common benefit and not to be regarded as an absolute right entitling the individual to do as he likes with it. Moreover, the produce of the land must support common dining halls in which everyone will share (806E). Though ownership is private, consumption will be public and in common fellowship.

In the state of the *Laws* every citizen has his lot, and some citizens are wealthier than others. But Plato severely restricts the citizens' opportunity to develop economic interests. Citizens may not practise any art or craft (846D), nor engage in buying and selling (741E), nor possess gold or silver (742A). Lending and borrowing is permitted, but the taking of interest is forbidden. Lending is at the lender's risk, since the borrower is under no legal obligation to repay (742C). All such ordinances are intended to protect the citizen from the temptation to make the accumulation of wealth his life's aim, and to free him for the pursuit of excellence in body and mind. Plato states outright that vast wealth is the very thing that a bad man would be likely to possess. The immensely rich are not good men, and 'if they are not good, neither are they happy' (742E–43C). All citizens of the *Laws* are a privileged class, since each citizen is assured his allotment of land; each has his lot tilled for him by slaves who pay part of the produce as rent; and each is entirely free of an occupation requiring him to labour. Plato never transcends the traditional Greek view of slavery. He regards the slave as childlike, possessing an imperfectly developed mind (793E, 937A).

In the *Laws*, then, the citizen devotes himself to the art of politics, while the slave tills the soil and the resident alien attends to the economic functions of commerce and industry. Although this three-class system is different from that of the *Republic*, the underlying principle is the same in both works: each individual pursues only a single, specific function. No less than the ideal state of the *Republic*, the 'second-best' state of the *Laws* is also a rigid caste society.

Plato does, however, retain in the *Laws* the *Republic*'s emancipatory approach to the status of women. It is the right and duty of the women to stand side by side with the men in working for the general welfare of the state. It is pure folly, says Plato, to prevent women who are equally qualified from joining men in at least some of the duties of citizenship (805A). Sexual equality will require the institution of universal, compulsory education for both sexes alike. Girls and women, like boys and men, will be trained in gymnastics and participate in the contests and tournaments. Women will also fight in arms and on horseback by the side of men (833–34). Although Plato thus claims the services of the women for the state, he never grants them the right explicitly to vote in the Assembly and to hold political office. There are women officials, but they are exclusively connected with the institution of marriage, which is monogamous, but strictly regulated by the state. It is the duty of husband and wife to breed children for the state; and to that end husband and wife are placed under the supervision of women overseers for the first ten years of marriage (764).

Government in the *Laws*

Law must be sovereign in the 'second-best' state, and government must strive to reconcile monarchy with democracy, the principle of knowledge with the principle of liberty. The first steps in establishing this state on the foundations of mixed government will require special methods. One such method is to join a young, bold, intelligent and high-souled tyrant with the legislator (709E). Plato assures us that 'there is not, nor can there ever be, any better or more rapid way to establish the constitution' (710B). The role of the 'young tyrant' would be to impress the laws upon the people, partly by the power of his personality and example, and partly, when necessary, by means of force. Instead of the philosopher-kings of the *Republic*, there is the single philosopher-legislator joined with a tyrant. It is surprising that Plato, after his disappointing experiences in Syracuse, should still see tyrants in a positive light. In the alternative method proposed by Plato, the founders themselves of the new colony cooperate with the legislator in bringing the new state into being.

Plato explains in considerable detail how the actual governmental institutions will work: the electoral authority is a popular assembly consisting of the whole body of 5,040 citizens, arranged in four classes according to the amount of their property and wealth. Candidates for the executive council are chosen by public vote, but are selected differently from the several classes. The candidates of the first and second classes are to be selected by the citizens of every class, but voting is compulsory for the upper two classes and optional for the lower two. The candidates of the third class are to be selected by the citizens of the first three classes – citizens of the fourth class being free to vote or abstain. In the selection of the candidates of the fourth class, the citizens of the first two classes must vote or pay a fine; but members of the last two classes may either vote or abstain (753–64). Plato has thus put together a carefully calculated combination of class suffrage with universal suffrage. Although Plato speaks of a man's personal and ancestral virtue and of bodily strength and beauty as qualifications for office, the method he actually proposes is based on wealth or poverty (744B–C) – as if the possession of wealth necessarily implied virtue and ability while poverty implied the opposite.

Plato wanted to preserve the monarchical principle on the assumption that monarchy means the rule of intelligence, knowledge, and wisdom. In identifying wisdom with wealth, however, as he does in his class-system, he proposes a state biased in favour of oligarchy. While the rich are compelled to attend the Assembly, the poor are free to stay away. This system gives a clear advantage to wealth, for as Aristotle observed, it is a common device of oligarchies that the rich should be fined and the poor go unpunished for failure to attend the Assembly or to carry out other civic duties (*Politics*, IV, x, 6–8). It is a device, in a word, that is only intended to make a show of popular voice while it actually concentrates power in the hands of the few. Plato's state is not only biased in favour of oligarchy, it is biased against democracy; for his so-called 'mixed' constitution, far from being a real organic mixture in which all elements are active, is rather a combination of popular elements that are mainly passive, with an upper propertied class that is active and directive.

Indeed, Plato unabashedly discloses his real political philosophy in Book XII of the *Laws*, where the traditional Greek institutions of assembly, council, and magistrates, which had appeared in the earlier books, begin to disappear and are replaced by a 'nocturnal council' of philosophical astronomers who guide the state in accordance with their understanding of the heavenly mysteries. The nocturnal council, thus named because it meets between dawn and sunrise, is the supreme executive body of the state. The council's knowledge of the unity of goodness and of the gods comes from the study of astronomy – not the false astronomy that sets matter before mind, but the true astronomy that recognizes the directing mind responsible for the order of the universe. Plato thus ends the *Laws* by returning to the *Republic* with its sovereignty of the philosopher-kings, the members of the nocturnal council being none other than the 'perfect guardians' in another guise. Plato therefore ends the *Laws* not with a firm belief in the 'second-best' mixed constitution, but with an approval of religious persecution in Book X and an affirmation of theocratic rule in Book XII. The state that Plato envisions in the last book of the *Laws* is, in fact, a theocracy – a grey-haired, religious council, acting in the light of a divine truth derived from the study of astronomy.

As Books IX, X, XI, and XII of the *Laws* make clear, the state, under the nocturnal council's rule, will lay down doctrine concerning religion and ultimate reality, and will punish with death those who refuse to accept its creed. If, therefore, Plato granted in the earlier books of the *Laws* some voice to the people – however passive and shadowy it may have been – he eliminates even that voice in the final words of his political philosophy.

Our debt to the *Laws* is nevertheless great, not for its final words, but for the trans-historical insights we have gained from that work. Plato teaches us in the *Laws* that a good society presupposes the sovereignty of the law; and that the constitution of a law-state requires a proper balance of the different social elements that invariably contend for political power in any complex society. The dominant political idea of Plato's final work is therefore this: a state based on law and a mixed constitution is the practical best. And it is this idea that ought to be regarded as a timeless valid principle.

Chapter Two

Aristotle

Human beings are by nature social beings. As such, Aristotle emphasized, they can achieve happiness only in a society rightly organized. Sound political philosophy, therefore, has to discover, first, in what way of life happiness consists and, second, in what form of society and government such a way of life can best be realized. Happiness is not a product of activity, for happiness is activity of a creative and fulfilling kind. Happiness is a supreme good towards which all humans strive, and which renders life worth living. Happiness is pursued and achieved as we strive for excellence in both mind and body. The active exercise of our human faculties, in conformity with standards of excellence, brings us happiness; and we remain happy so long as we are engaged in doing and thinking in accordance with such standards.

In his *Nicomachean Ethics* Aristotle teaches that the highest form of happiness is brought about by the activity of the soul-mind in conformity with the moral virtues; but virtues are not engendered in us by nature. Nature endows us with the capacity to learn the virtues, which are then strengthened by means of habit. We become morally virtuous by forming the good habit of acting rightly. We acquire and perfect the virtues by actually practising them. We become just by doing just acts, temperate by doing temperate acts, brave by doing brave acts. By acting in dangerous situations and forming the habit of confidence or fear, we become either courageous or cowardly. Our moral virtues, in a word, are formed in close correspondence with our patterns of conduct. If, therefore, we want to shape and guide our dispositions in the right direction, we have to control our actions; for it is on the quality of our actions that the quality of our dispositions depends. For Aristotle, then, the training we receive from childhood in one set of habits or another determines our character.

How do we know what set of habits to encourage? Aristotle answers this question by invoking the time-honoured Greek doctrine that was first enunciated by the Delphic Oracle: the golden mean. Moral qualities, Aristotle reminds us, are so constituted as to be destroyed by both excess and deficiency. Strength, for instance, is undermined by either too much or too little exercise, just as health is impaired by too much or too little food and drink. For Aristotle as for Plato, it is the rational part of the soul that must gain the upper hand if we are to form the habit of adhering to the mean. Where the link between emotions and actions is concerned, it is through experience and the rational reflection upon it that we learn to avoid the twin evils of being either too fearful or too bold. To understand, say, the virtue of courage, one must grasp the mean between fear and confidence. He that exceeds in confidence tends to be rash or reckless; he that exceeds in fear tends to be cowardly. Not all actions, however, can be guided by the doctrine of the mean. There are actions that are inherently bad, such as theft, adultery, and murder; so it is not the excess or deficiency that we condemn, but the actions themselves.

For Aristotle, it is the 'Great-Souled Man' who most perfectly embodies the virtues of courage, temperance, and liberality. The great-souled man never courts danger for trifling reasons. He does, however, face danger in a good cause, and while doing so he is even ready to give his life, for he believes that it is not at every price that life is worth living. He is pleased to confer benefits, but ashamed to receive them, because the former is a mark of nobility and the latter of inferiority. He returns a favour with interest, thus putting the original benefactor in his debt in turn. The great-souled man's disposition is to render aid willingly, but to ask help from others never or with reluctance. He is dignified in the presence of men of position and fortune, and courteous towards those of moderate or humble station, for he recognizes in the depth of his soul that it is vulgar to lord it over humble people, or to put forth one's strength against the weak (*Nicomachean Ethics*, IV, iii, 24–28). Recognizing that falsehood is in itself base and reprehensible, and truth noble and praiseworthy, he cares more for the truth than for what people might think. Finally, he understands that justice is a matter of proportion and injustice a violation of proportion – that injustice is a condition in which the perpetrator acquires too much and the sufferer too little of the good in question.

In the *Nicomachean Ethics*, then, we discern clearly what has been called Aristotle's teleological view of nature and life, a view that prompted him to base his philosophy of human conduct on the concept of *Telos*. The Greek concept of *Telos* should be understood not as an end, purpose, or goal in the formal-rational sense, but rather as the continuing process of fulfilment and perfection. The *Telos* of a living being, the final cause of its being, is to realize the potentiality of its nature, to grow into an excellent specimen of its species. As applied to humanity, the *Telos* consists in the full development and exercise in action (*praxis*) of the natural human capacities. True to his calling, Aristotle – like Plato before him – concludes his treatise on ethics by defining the highest human faculty as the theoretic intellect. Contemplation is the human activity most akin to the divine, and is, therefore, the greatest source of happiness. Not that the philosopher can dispense with the lower activities; he is a human being, after all, and must therefore live among human beings, faithfully exercising the highest moral virtues. His calling as a philosopher, however, imposes upon him the special responsibility of providing his non-philosophical fellows with practical knowledge by which to guide their political lives most wisely and prudently. That is the aim of Aristotle's *Politics*.

The *Politics*

Aristotle opens the *Politics* by proposing that the political association called the 'state' is the highest form of association, and that it includes all the other forms, such as the family and village. It is a mistake, he argues, to suppose that the exercise of authority is essentially the same whether it is in the smaller associations or in the state. The difference is not a matter of numbers. To explain the qualitative difference between the smaller associations and the state, Aristotle begins with an analysis of the family, the first coupling of individuals that arises out of necessity. The union of male and female emerges out of the natural attraction they have for one another, and out of the fact that they cannot exist without one another and still continue the species. Originally, the sexual division of labour between man and woman was dictated by the need for the special care that the helpless infant required from the mother. The mother's own need for protection and assistance while caring for the infant required her mate's cooperation. In no real society, however, does the family exist in isolation. From earliest times family-households banded together to form a village community. When neighbouring villages form an association for their common good, aiming for *self-sufficiency*, Aristotle calls this association a *polis*, or city-state. Once the state is thus formed it acquires the characteristics of an organism, of which the family-households and villages are its parts. In these terms the city-state is a 'whole,' for Aristotle, which must necessarily be prior to its parts. The state is therefore also prior to the individual who can never be self-sufficient and who depends for his very survival on the whole.

The impulse to form associations is present in all human beings by nature; and as we learn from Aristotle's *Ethics*, human beings can achieve their good only in a society rightly organized to promote their common welfare. But man, Aristotle sagely observes, is the worst of all animals when sundered from law and justice. The human faculties are such that they can be employed for good or for pernicious ends. When, therefore, humans are devoid of the moral virtues, they are the most destructive of creatures. It follows that law, embodying the fundamental principles of justice, is an essential element of the state, without which there can be no regulation of human conduct in accordance with the virtues.

The Institution of Slavery

The typical household of Aristotle's time included slaves. Given the frequency of war among the Greek city-states, and the captives taken in war, every city had its slave population. Aristotle, like Plato, takes the institution of slavery for granted and cannot imagine a society without it. He recognizes, however, that already in his time there were serious thinkers who challenged the institution of slavery, arguing that it is contrary to nature for one human being to be another's master. It is by force of arms that slavery originated, and it is by force and arbitrary convention that it is perpetuated. There is no difference between master and slave by nature, and therefore slavery is unjust. As we shall see, Aristotle's attitude towards slavery is complex; although he speaks of 'natural salves,' and of slaves as 'living tools,' he also tends to acknowledge the truth of slavery's critics. Having defined the theoretic intellect as the highest human faculty, and the life of the mind the human activity most akin to the divine, Aristotle saw the economic need for human 'assistants' to the inanimate tools: for 'if shuttles wove and quills played harps of themselves, master-craftsmen would have no need of assistants, and masters no need of slaves' (*Politics*, I, ii, 4–6).

Aristotle therefore proposes that the essential quality of a slave is that he belongs to another as an article of property, and that he is an instrument for the use of his owner. Aristotle begins to address the question of whether slavery is natural or contrary to nature by maintaining that authority and subordination are not only inevitable but expedient conditions. Throughout nature, he argues, there is always found a ruling and a subject factor. Even in non-living things there exists a ruling principle, as in the case of a musical scale where each 'mode' is ruled by its keynote. And in living things, the soul rules the body and reason rules the appetite. It follows that all human beings who differ as widely as does the body from the soul are slaves by *nature*. Like his master Plato, Aristotle thus posits a gulf between some humans and others. The slave participates in reason only so far as to apprehend it, but not to possess it. The usefulness of slaves is their bodily service for the necessities of life. Some people are free and others slaves by nature, and in such cases the institution of slavery is both just and expedient.

No sooner has Aristotle made this statement, however, than he is forced to admit that those who assert the opposite are also right, for most individuals become slaves by being taken captive in war. There is a tacit agreement among states that things conquered in war belong to the conquerors. This convention, Aristotle acknowledges, is condemned by many jurists and other learned men who declare it is a monstrous evil when the strong, simply because they have the power to do so, enslave the weak. Learned men also argued that some wars are unjust, and that persons captured in such circumstances neither deserve to be slaves nor really are slaves by nature. Noble, great-souled, and otherwise superior individuals captured in war can hardly be regarded as natural slaves. However, even these learned men were not universally opposed to slavery. It was the Greeks whom they regarded as a superior people. Hence, Greeks, when taken captive, were not natural slaves, but barbarians were. In effect then, says Aristotle, the jurists and learned men agree with him that there are individuals who are slaves everywhere (barbarians) and other individuals (Greeks) who are slaves nowhere – thus recognizing the phenomenon of natural slavery. Apart from this Greek–barbarian dichotomy to which Aristotle apparently subscribed to support the notion of natural slaves, there was the additional question of whether virtue and vice are, respectively, the distinguishing features of master and slave, or noble and base-born. Here Aristotle observes that though nature may intend such an outcome, it frequently fails to bring it about. So Aristotle is compelled to equivocate: the doctrine of natural masters and slaves, he says, is sometimes true and at other times false (*Politics*, I, ii, 18–22).

It appears, then, that for Aristotle there are instances when the master–slave relationship is based, purportedly, on the natural differences between two persons, and other instances when the relationship is simply the result of force and convention. When the master–slave relationship is in fact based on natural differences between two persons then the relationship is mutually advantageous. It is just and proper for the one party to govern and for the other party to be governed by a form of government for which they are by nature fitted. Hence, there is, for Aristotle, a community of interest between master and slave in instances where nature has qualified them for those positions. When, however, the master–slave relationship is the result of coercion and convention pure and simple, there is no such community of interest. Moreover, Aristotle does appear to recognize, at least implicitly, that the roles of master and slave are more a matter of social-class origin than of natural superiority or inferiority in intelligence or any other human capacity. There are, he says, slaves' 'sciences' and masters' 'sciences,' the former consisting of the various branches of domestic work, the latter consisting in the employment of slaves – though the masters' 'science,' he adds, is of no special importance or dignity. It is simply a matter of the master knowing how to direct and supervise the tasks that the slave must know how to carry out. Therefore, all people *wealthy enough* to be able to shun menial tasks employ a servant, while they themselves partake of politics or philosophy (*Politics*, I, ii, 22–iii, 1).

That Aristotle may have recognized the coercive element in *all* master–slave relationships is further suggested by the distinction he drew between mastership on the one hand and the government of free men on the other. For it is in this general context that Aristotle defines republican government as the rule of men who are free and equal. Where the institution of slavery is concerned, it seems to be a fair characterization of Aristotle's position that he remained perplexed by the key issue: Does a slave possess any other excellence besides his skill as a 'vocal tool' and servant? Does he possess, for example, temperance, courage, justice, or any other moral virtues; or has he no virtues besides his bodily service? Aristotle's perplexity is revealed in the way in which he responds to his own questions: 'Either way there is a difficulty; if slaves do possess moral virtue, wherein will they differ from freemen? And if they do not, that is strange, as they are human beings and participate in reason' (*Politics*, I, v, 3–5).

Ideal and Actual Constitutions

The central question of Book II of the *Politics* is this: What form of political community will enable a people to approach the most ideal mode of life? Prompted by the theories set forth by Plato in the *Republic*, Aristotle begins to address this question by considering three possible systems of property: (1) common ownership of all things by all citizens; (2) no common ownership of any kind; (3) common ownership of some things, but not of others. Aristotle asks whether it is really possible to have property, wives, and children in common as Socrates seems to have advocated for the philosopher-guardians in Plato's *Republic*. The aim of Plato's communistic scheme was to achieve the highest degree of social unity. But is such an aim realized when everyone thinks that everything belongs equally to him and to everyone else? It is not at all clear, says Aristotle, why unity would be secured by such a scheme, since no member of the ruling class would develop a personal relationship with either wives, offspring, or things. Common property tends to receive the least attention from the individuals concerned. As a rule, human beings care more for their personal and private possessions, and less for what they own in common. When each citizen has numerous children, and these belong not to him personally but to everyone else equally, all citizens are likely to regard the children with indifference rather than with concern and love. Plato's plan thus undermines the human need for both property and kinship. Indeed, it would be better for a boy to be a nephew in the traditional kinship system than to be a so-called son in Plato's scheme. Moreover, Aristotle insists, it is a near certainty that family likeness would betray the very thing that Plato wished to hide; for it would be impossible to prevent the people concerned from assuming that certain individuals are their real fathers, mothers, siblings, and children.

Moreover, communism of wives and children carries with it the risk of incest; and in situations of conflict, which is inevitable in any group, inadvertent assaults on parents and kin are also likely to occur. Aristotle also questions the possibility of instituting communism in one class of society while leaving intact the family and private property in the other class. But if Plato were to insist on instituting communism in only one class, then it would seem more advantageous to the state, says Aristotle, if communism of wives and children were established in the farmer-producer class. For such a system would generate sexual rivalry, unfriendliness, and dissension, all of which are useful to a state in maintaining a submission to authority in a subject class and in preventing revolution (*Politics*, II, i, 14–16).

As for the philosopher-ruler class, not only kinship but friendship too would inevitably become diluted within it. Expressions such as 'my father,' 'my mother,' 'my son,' 'my daughter,' 'my brother,' 'my sister,' would all lose their meaning and disappear, as would caring for one another as parents, children, and siblings. Plato's ideal, in prohibiting both ownership and stable relationships with kin, would destroy the primary motives that cause humans to care for things and to show love and affection for precious others. Aristotle also underscores the impracticality of Plato's provision for transferring some children from the farmer-producer class to that of the philosopher-rulers and vice versa: the parents who give up their children and the officials who transfer them would be bound to know which children are given to whom.

Private property and family households were left intact in Plato's third class, the tillers of the soil and the artisans; and Plato envisioned unity between this class and the philosopher-rulers. Aristotle insists, however, that there is no reason to infer unity from such an arrangement, since the rebelliousness of the Helots at Sparta suggests the opposite of unity. But, Aristotle asks, what if Plato had left family-households intact but had extended communism of property to the third class? Would that have ensured unity? Judging again from the experience of the Helots, Aristotle replies that even if the members of the third class practised communism of property, there is still no ground for assuming that this would bring about unity either with the rulers or among themselves. Common ownership of property, Aristotle argues, would generate discontent and strife owing to the inequalities in work and consumption: conflicts would arise between those who work little but take much and those who work more and receive less. In general, Aristotle observes, living together and trying to share everything is certainly not easy, which is demonstrated in all conventional groups and communities where people unavoidably quarrel and collide with one another over petty matters and trifles.

What Aristotle himself advocates in the light of these criticisms is the system prevalent in his time of family-households and private property – but regulated by good morals and appropriate legislation. In that way society would gain the advantages of property being both common and private. If all citizens possessed moderate property, there would be little cause for dissension, and the care for property would be ensured because each citizen would apply himself to his own worldly goods. At the same time there would be common property of sorts, as is suggested by the old Greek proverb, 'friends' goods are common goods.' Such a system, Aristotle reminds us, existed in outline among the Greeks of his day: families owned their property privately, but placed their possessions in the service of their neighbours and friends. In Sparta, for instance, citizens used one another's slaves, horses, and hounds, as well as the produce of the fields throughout the country. Improved by the right kind of moral education and legislation, says Aristotle, this system of privately owned possessions being made available for common use would be the best. Property must be private, Aristotle insists, because it brings great pleasure, gratifying the universal and natural love for one-self and one's loved ones. 'Self-love,' however, should not be confused with selfishness, which is a vice; for selfishness is not to love oneself, but to love oneself more than one ought.It violates the principle of living according to the mean. Private property brings additional pleasure because it enables the owner to bestow favours and assistance to friends; communism therefore deprives one of that pleasure and pre-cludes the virtues of generosity and liberality, since the active exercise of liberality presupposes that one possesses things with which one can be liberal.

When someone denounces the evils of private property, Aristotle observes, the notion of communism might take on an attractive and more humane appearance. People might rush to welcome it, thinking that it will result in a new and marvellous friendliness and unity. But the true cause of the evils associated with private property is not the institu-tion itself, but greed and wickedness and not living according to the mean. Besides, it is an unjust procedure to tell us what evils we would lose by adopting communism, but to omit telling us all the good things, too, that we would lose. In a word, life, in the circumstances Plato pre-scribes for the philosopher-guardians, is seen by Aristotle to be utterly impossible. Aristotle finds it strange, moreover, that Plato – the very philosopher who placed so much emphasis on education as the means of making the state morally good – should have imagined that he can improve society by such measures as he proposed, instead of by man-ners, morals, and appropriate laws.

Aristotle makes still another telling criticism: the working of the ideal state as a *whole* was not described at all by Plato. He said virtually noth-ing about the farmer-producer class, which would constitute the vast majority of the people in that state. This prompts Aristotle to ask critical questions: What advantage would the multitude of farmer-producers gain by submitting to the rule of philosopher-rulers? How would the philosopher-rulers ensure the submission of the multitude, if not by clever devices and the threat of force? If the multitude of farmer-produc-ers are to retain family life and private property, as Plato envisioned, would there not be two states in one, antagonistic to each other? For Aristotle, such antagonism would be unavoidable, since Plato makes the philosopher-guardians an armed garrison, while the farmer-producers till the soil and provide the necessities of life. How, then, Aristotle asks, would the dissension and conflict that exists in actual states be prevented in the ideal state? Plato offers no real provision for the regulation of conflict, for he argues that the wisdom of the rulers makes laws superfluous; he designs a detailed educational scheme for the philosopher-guardians, but says nothing about the education of the farmer-producers. Plato expected the farmers, who are the owners of their land, to pay stipends (rent?) to the rulers. So, Aristotle asks, how would the condition of the farmers in Plato's ideal state differ from that of the Helots and serfs in actual states? And why should one assume that Plato's farmers would be less unmanageable or rebellious than the Helots and serfs? For Aristotle, the absence of any adequate discussion of these issues on Plato's part is no small omission, since the multitude's relation to the rulers is crucial in determining the character of the society as a whole and in preserving the rule of the philosopher-guardians (*Politics*, II, ii, 12–14).

Continuing his critique, Aristotle observes that the philosopher-guardians are a ruling caste of sorts, in which for the most part the same individuals and their offspring hold office always. So Aristotle asks: If this type of arrangement occasions conflict and rebellion among those who have not been trained to rule, why would not this arrangement produce an even more pronounced rebelliousness among high-spirited and warlike men? Plato avers that it is the duty of the philosopher-guardians to make the whole society happy. But how can the rulers be happy when they are denied family and property? And if they are unhappy, how can Plato assume that the whole society will be happy? And if the rulers are not happy, what other class is? For it is a near certainty that the farmers and artisans are also far from happy in their subjection to rulers from whom they receive precious little in return for what they give.

Plato's *Laws* is also discussed by Aristotle, who fully recognized that though Plato aimed in that work to propose a constitution suitable for actual states, he concluded by bringing it back to the constitution of the *Republic*. The 'nocturnal council' of the *Laws*, Aristotle observed, is hardly to be distinguished from the philosopher-guardians of the *Republic*. Apart from that, Aristotle views as problematic the life Plato prescribed for the 5,040 male citizens of the *Laws*, who are to be detached from all economic tasks and concerns. To support an unproductive male population of that size together with an equal number of wives and servants would not only require a large territory, but an enormous number of resident aliens – farmers, artisans, and merchants. And although Plato allows a citizen's property to be increased up to five times its original value, he makes no such provision for the expansion of a citizen's allotment of land. The lack of such a provision, Aristotle suggests, would create difficulties in the absence of birth control. On the whole, the constitution of the *Laws*, Aristotle concludes, tends towards oligarchy. This is borne out by the regulations Plato designed for the appointment of magistrates, regulations making it compulsory for the wealthier citizens to attend the Assembly, vote for magistrates, and fill other political offices, while the poorer classes are allowed to stay away. This and other well-known devices are employed in oligarchies to ensure that a majority of the highest offices will be filled by the wealthy classes (*Politics*, II, iii, 11–13).

Other Political Issues

Aristotle recognized that property questions are universally the cause of social strife, and that the regulation of property and wealth is, therefore, an all-important political matter. Having in mind primarily landed property, Aristotle calls attention to an oversight of legislators: they regulate the amount of landed property without regulating the size of the family, thus allowing the population to grow beyond the capacity of the land to support it. The resulting parcellization of the land and impoverishment of the citizenry is politically dangerous, for it is difficult for impoverished people not to be supporters of radical social change. The violent social strife inevitably accompanying the impoverishment of the multitude is as old as Greek history, and precisely what Solon's legislation aimed to moderate. Here as throughout Aristotle's reflections we are reminded of the paramount importance of the mean: when estates are too large they promote prodigality, and when too small, they cause a penurious standard of living. It is therefore insufficient for the legislator to strive to equalize landed property; he must, instead, aim at medium-sized property for all. Aristotle well realized, however, that prescribing moderate property for all would not put an end to social conflict, since levelling the desires of human beings is more important than levelling their properties. The right kind of moral education reinforced by law is therefore essential.

Civil strife is caused not only by inequalities in wealth, but also by inequalities in honour, though the two conditions operate in opposite ways, the masses being resentful when their possessions are unequal, the upper classes turning bitter when their honours are equal. It was clear to Aristotle that it is not primarily for the sake of bare necessities that people commit crimes. People do wrong in order to satisfy a variety of desires having nothing to do with hunger and cold. Indeed, the worst transgressions spring from a desire for superfluities – witness those who become murderous tyrants. Equality of moderate property is therefore one of the fundamental conditions contributing to the diminution of faction and strife, which, however, cannot be entirely eliminated. For the human appetite is by its very nature unlimited and insatiable, and the bulk of humankind lives for the satisfaction of appetite. In the light of this fact it is the beginning of wisdom to cultivate in all citizens the virtue of temperance, and to regulate wealth and property so as to avoid a polarization of society between rich and poor. An extremely unequal distribution of wealth could be observed in sparta, where some citizens owned too much property and others too little and much of the land was concentrated in a few hands.

Aristotle averred that leisure from menial occupations is desirable; but how it was to be achieved was not easy to ascertain. The serfs of Thessaly like the Helots of Sparta rose up repeatedly against their masters and became a potent, internal foe lying in wait for a decisive military disaster to befall their masters. Furthermore, Aristotle observes, the criticism Plato made in the *Laws* of Sparta and Crete as war-states was a valid one. The constitutions of those states having been entirely directed to military valour and the art of warfare, the states began to decline when they gained an empire because they had had no training for the peaceful life.

As he turns his attention from Sparta to the history of Athens, Aristotle considers the accomplishments of Solon, the famous lawgiver, who had put an end to extreme oligarchy and lightened the oppression of the people. Solon's constitution was a skilful blending of elements: the Council on the Areopagus being the oligarchic element, the elective magistracies the aristocratic, and the law courts the democratic. It was especially by constituting the jury courts from all the citizens that Solon laid the foundations for Athenian democracy. Solon was followed by Ephialtes who reduced the oligarchic power of the Council on the Areopagus, while Pericles instituted payment for serving in the law or jury courts, thus making it possible for those engaged in earning their livelihood to participate in politics.

The Nature of a State

In his response to the question of what constitutes a state, Aristotle proposes that it is a collection of citizens. Citizens are the basic elements of a state. What is a citizen, or what is the nature of citizenship? Citizenship, says Aristotle, is the condition that entitles individuals to participate in the government of the state. In Greece, at the time, the definition of citizenship varied with the nature of the constitution of the state in question, and, indeed, in some states the people were subjects rather than citizens. In general, it is the special privilege and responsibility of citizens to concern themselves with the security and well-being of their community. The goodness of a citizen consists in the ability both to rule and to be ruled well. To learn how to rule, one should have had the experience of being ruled. Citizenship therefore implies the knowledge and experience of government by free individuals.

In the non-democratic states of Aristotle's day, property was a prerequisite of citizenship, and the working classes were, therefore, excluded from the privilege. And Aristotle was inclined to agree that the best-ordered state will *not* make an artisan a citizen. Aristotle reasoned that one who is engaged in a menial occupation has neither the knowledge necessary for participation in government, nor the leisure necessary for the acquisition of such knowledge. In oligarchies, where admission to political office was based on high property assessments, artisans – but not hired labourers – were permitted to hold office if they were well off. The presumption was that propertyless working people have no material interest in concerning themselves with the welfare of the state. The existence of Athenian democracy meant, however, that Aristotle had to acknowledge that in a major Greek constitution citizenship necessarily extended to both the artisan and the hired labourer.

The diverse definitions of citizenship led Aristotle to propose that states vary according to the nature of their sovereign. In oligarchies the propertied and otherwise privileged few are supreme; in democracies the people are sovereign. Human beings, Aristotle again reminds us, are social beings; they desire to live together, and they are, in fact, brought together owing to their interdependence and mutual need. Moreover, they share a common interest in creating a good life for all concerned. Even in conditions of extreme inequality, Aristotle argues, as in the master–slave relationship, there is a sense in which the parties to the relationship share a common interest: if the condition of the slave deteriorates, that of the master is also adversely affected. In *all* varieties of states, then, the wise ruler recognizes his interdependence with the ruled. It follows that those constitutions that aim at the common advantage are rightly framed in accordance with justice, while those that aim exclusively at the ruler's own advantage are not only defective, but self-defeating. Whereas the latter are despotic, a just society is a partnership of free and interdependent individuals.

For Aristotle, it is possible, in principle, for the one, the few, or the many to govern in the common interest; in such cases we have 'constitutional government.' When a monarchy rules in the common interest, it is 'kingship'; when the few rule with a view to what is best for the society as a whole, it is 'aristocracy'; and when the multitude governs with a view to the common advantage, it is 'constitutional government' – for, as we shall see, 'democracy,' for Aristotle, is a deviation from such government. There are deviations from each of these constitutional forms, tyranny corresponding to kingship, oligarchy to aristocracy, and democracy to constitutional government. Tyranny is monarchy ruling exclusively in the interest of the monarch; oligarchy, government in the interest of the rich; and democracy, in the interest of the poor – none of them governing with regard for the common good. Aristotle thus wishes to make clear that neither governments of the rich nor governments of the poor are just, for insofar as they rule not in the common interest, but strictly in their own, they are devoid of constitutionality. A decisive factor, then, in assessing the goodness of a political system is not whether the few or the many rule, but whether they rule in the collective interest.

Collective interest is more than sharing a common territory and preventing mutual injury. A just state ruled by constitutional government is a partnership of families and villages living a full, independent, and good life. Hence, the right to rule should rest on the ability to contribute to the good life of all. If, therefore, a government by the poor takes advantage of its greater numbers and confiscates the property of the rich, that is no less unjust than a government of the rich that oppresses the poor due to its control of the most efficient means of violence. However, what is especially interesting in this regard is Aristotle's qualified approval of the view that it is best for the multitude to be sovereign, since it is possible for the many, when they come together, to be better than the few, however virtuous they might be (*Politics*, III, vi, 3–6). Aristotle is not saying that this is true of all multitudes, but that it is true of some, under specific conditions.

Given the sovereignty of the multitude, this question follows: Over what matters should the authority of the mass of citizens extend? Should, for example, the common people be allowed to hold the highest offices? Aristotle's reply reveals his ambivalence towards the people. On the one hand, he fears that owing to their lack of specialized knowledge they would make unjust decisions in some cases and mistakes in others. On the other hand, he realizes that not admitting the people to the highest offices would create a politically dangerous situation. Taking a cue from Solon and other great lawgivers who enabled the common citizens to elect magistrates and call them to audit, but not to hold office as individuals, Aristotle proposes that when the common citizens assemble together they possess sufficient discernment; and by mingling with the upper classes they are more likely to benefit the state – just as mixing bran with flour makes the whole more nourishing than pure flour alone.

In this context (*Politics*, III, vi, 6–8) Aristotle critically examines the Socratic–Platonic doctrine that statesmanship, like the practice of medicine, requires expert knowledge – that, for example, the best judge of whether a physician has prescribed the best treatment is another physician. Here Aristotle departs significantly from his master, for he contends that 'physician' applies not only to the master of the craft and the ordinary practitioner, but also to the individual who has studied medicine as a part of his general education. In almost all the arts, including politics, says Aristotle, there are cultivated amateurs, and we assign the right of judgment to them as we do to experts. In this way, Aristotle strengthens his view that the preponderance of the people in government is best. It is best, he argues, not only because the many, when assembled together, are as good or better judges than the so-called wise and expert few, but also because there are things about which the specialized craftsman is not the only or even the best judge, things about which the knowledge of the layman must come into play: those who live in a house are better judges than the builder of its quality, just as the steersman judges a rudder better than a carpenter, and the diner judges a banquet better than the chef (*Politics*, III, vi, 8–10). It is therefore reasonable and just, Aristotle concludes, that the people should elect and control the magistrates. But Aristotle now qualifies his proposition about the multitude and makes his all-important point: in order for the rule of the many to be good and just, they must be guided by good laws. *Ultimately, the power of the people must be subordinate to the laws.*

Employing the analogy of flute players, Aristotle asks who should be given the finest instruments, individuals of so-called better birth or superior performers? Is it not obvious, Aristotle replies, that the best flutes should be given to the best flute players? It follows that since political office is an instrumentality, the claim to office must necessarily be based on the superiority in such things as go into the making of a good state. It is therefore reasonable that the people should not withhold political office or honours from the wealthy simply because they are wealthy. So long as they contribute substantially, as taxpayers, to the revenue essential for the state's existence, and so long as they participate in the state in accordance with the standards of justice and civic virtue, they are valuable citizens in any form of constitutional government, including a democracy. A state consisting entirely of impoverished people is no more a state than one consisting entirely of slaves. So wealth, breeding, *and* numbers all have their respective claims in the constitution of a good society; but the majority of citizens have a more just claim than the minority, since they are stronger, richer, and better owing to their superior numbers (*Politics*, III, vii, 7–10). For Aristotle, these considerations seemed to demonstrate the fallaciousness of all arguments on the basis of which minorities claim that they themselves should govern while everyone else should be governed. Against such claims of sovereignty on account of either wealth or virtue, the multitude is able to advance a more just claim, since it is quite possible that the multitude may be collectively better and richer than the few (*Politics*, III, vii, 10–13).

Monarchy, Law, and the People

In his analysis of the varieties of monarchical rule Aristotle captures the essence of each type. The Spartan kings, for instance, were guided and controlled by law, and their rule applied primarily to matters relating to war. The power of the kings was also limited by the institutions of the ephors and the senate. In contrast, there was the highly centralized monarchy that existed at the time in Asia, and which Montesquieu later dubbed 'oriental despotism.' The power possessed by such a monarch, says Aristotle, resembles that of a tyrant. Aristotle believed that because Asiatics were more servile than Europeans, the subjects of Asiatic monarchy endured despotic rule with much less resentment (*Politics*, III, ix, 2–3). Another form of monarchical rule Aristotle called 'elective tyranny,' exemplified by the rule of Solon who was elected to mediate between the rich and the poor and to moderate the violent conflict that prevailed between them. Finally, there is absolute monarchy, the form of kingship in which a single ruler is sovereign over all matters. Here we find Aristotle once again underscoring his general principle that good government must be based on law. Although a good ruler must have leeway where exceptional cases not adequately covered by the law are concerned, the law is nevertheless to remain sovereign. Where the law seems ambiguous with respect to special cases, Aristotle asks who is best equipped to decide such cases – the so-called wise ruler or the citizens? In his reply Aristotle again affirms that the educated multitude of citizens judges more wisely than any single person. Furthermore, just as the larger stream of water is purer, the multitude is less corruptible than the one or the few (*Politics*, III, x, 4–6).

For Aristotle, the multitude must, of course, consist of freemen in whom the moral virtues have been inculcated and who respect the law and conduct themselves in accordance with it. And though respect for the law may not be attainable in all citizens, it is possible to achieve it in the majority of citizens. So Aristotle asks, given a majority of good citizens, who would make a better and more incorruptible ruler, an individual or the majority? And he replies, 'the majority, is it not quite evident?' (*Politics*, III, x, 6–8). Aristotle calls this an 'aristocracy,' meaning by that term the rule of the best; but in his recognition of the virtues of an educated and law-abiding majority of citizens, he has, in effect, made an excellent argument for democracy. It is also noteworthy that in contrast to Plato's unhistorical proposition that tyranny emerged out of democracy, Aristotle had an accurate grasp of the actual historical sequence. Following Thucydides, Aristotle observes that as men became baser and began to make money out of the community, oligarchies arose and turned wealth into honour. As power was concentrated in fewer and fewer hands, and as the oppression of the people became more severe, the people won to their side the military support of disaffected strong men from the privileged classes. However, tyranny in Greece endured nowhere for long. After a tyranny accomplished what the disadvantaged classes had expected of it, it disappeared. In that way, oligarchies turned into tyrannies, and tyrannies into democracies. And Aristotle believed that 'now that the states have come to be even greater than they were, perhaps it is not easy for yet another form of constitution beside democracy to come into existence' (*Politics*, III, x, 8–10).

Constitutional government, whatever its form, presupposes sufficient power to safeguard the laws and to enforce compliance with them. Among free and equal individuals, it is unjust for any one person to govern or be governed more than another; and to ensure the equal participation of all in government, law is necessary. For Aristotle, then, again in contrast to Plato, it is always preferable for the law to rule; and in all circumstances, whoever is chosen to govern must be a guardian of the laws and subordinate to them. He who says that men should govern opens the door to the appetites and passions that warp the rule of even the best men; but when men are subordinate to the laws, reason alone governs. When citizens seek justice, they seek for what is impartial; and the essence of law is impartiality.

Laws should be adapted to the constitution of the society in question. The constitution is the body of principles designating the sovereign power in the state and regulating the distribution of governmental offices. The term 'constitution,' for Aristotle, refers not only to a written code of political and legal principles, but also to the socio-political structure of the state: kingship, aristocracy, and constitutional government are, therefore, three distinct constitutions; and the three deviant forms are tyranny, oligarchy, and democracy. Tyranny, being the furthest removed from constitutional government, is the worst; democracy, most closely approximating constitutional government, is the best; and oligarchy stands in the middle. Democracy should be defined not simply as the rule of the majority, but rather as a system in which the free who rule are in the majority. When the law rules in such a system, and all citizens have equal access to political office, this comes quite close to constitutional government and is, therefore, the highest form of democracy. This, the highest form of democracy, stands in sharp contrast to the lower forms in which the multitude is sovereign but not the law. In the lower forms of democracy the majority tends to become despotic and is therefore comparable to a tyranny. So Aristotle again underscores the paramountcy of law.

Aristotle, however, being no democrat, rejects even the highest form of democracy in favour of a blend of oligarchy and democracy; for constitutional government is precisely such a mixture. Wealth is the defining characteristic of oligarchy, just as freedom is of democracy. Therefore, it is only by means of a mixture of the two elements that a properly constituted balance of rich and poor can be achieved. But balance and social stability require something more. Here Aristotle introduces a principle that possesses a trans-historical validity. Invoking again the doctrine of the mean, Aristotle proposes that this doctrine must serve as the criterion by which the goodness or badness of a state and its constitution is assessed. In every society, says Aristotle, one can distinguish three divisions: the very rich, the very poor, and those who are between the two extremes. If we imagine a society polarized between the very rich and the very poor, it is evident that a society of that kind is fundamentally unstable, torn by tension and strife, and fluctuating between revolution and despotism. If we now imagine a society in which the middle class is the majority and stronger than either pole, we can easily see how it becomes an essential stabilizing element. Aristotle accordingly argues not only that the middle amount of all good things is the best amount to possess, but that the best state consists as much as possible of persons who are equal in the good things. It is in the middle class in which such likeness or equality is most likely to be found. The existence of a middle class that constitutes the majority in any given society provides a state's greatest security; for by applying its weight as necessary, the middle class maintains the social balance and prevents the extreme deviations from coming to power (*Politics*, IV, ix, 3–8).

Where the middle classes are numerous, states are freer from factional strife; and Aristotle candidly acknowledges that democracies are more secure and long lived than oligarchies owing to the existence of a large middle class and its mediating role in politics. Moreover, it is significant, Aristotle observes, that all the great lawgivers – notably Solon, Lycurgus, and Charondas – came from the middle classes. Every wise lawgiver, then, will be guided by the doctrine of the mean in forming a constitution and will strive to increase the numbers of the middle class so that it exceeds by far the extremes of very rich and very poor. Only thus can a lasting constitutional government be established. Those who aim to establish oligarchies therefore make a great mistake not only in granting too much power to the wealthy, but also in cheating the people; for history demonstrates that it is the encroachments of the rich, more than those of the people, that ruin constitutional government (*Politics*, IV, x, 3–6).

A definite class structure is therefore a prerequisite of Aristotle's best form of mixed and constitutional government. In addition, Aristotle speaks of the three elements of government itself. And although he does not fully anticipate the theories of Locke and Montesquieu on the division of powers, Aristotle's elements are roughly equivalent to what the modern thinkers referred to as the executive, legislative, and judicial branches of government (*Politics*, IV, x, 11–xi, 1).

Revolution

Aristotle understood that social conflict is everywhere due to inequality, a condition in which classes are unequal in power and in access to material and other goods. As a rule, the cause of factional and class conflict is the desire for equality. In considering, therefore, how to form the best constitution, Aristotle reflected on the two basic political regimes of his time, regimes that had contended with one another in the course of the Peloponnesian War. Democracy, he maintains, is safer and freer from civil strife than oligarchies; for in oligarchies there are two kinds of civil strife, struggles between different factions of the oligarchy and struggles between the oligarchs and the people. In democracies, on the other hand, there is only strife between the people and the oligarchical party, while struggles between different sections of the people are so rare as to be hardly worth mentioning.

In Book V of the *Politics* Aristotle returns to stress the fundamental role of the middle classes. A government formed on the basis of the middle classes is nearer to the people than to the few, and it is the safest kind of constitution. It is safest because a society lacking a large middle class and thus divided by very rich on the one side and very poor on the other must vacillate between insurrection and despotism. Where the few have aggrandized to themselves great wealth while the vast majority of the populace is impoverished, there can be no social peace. Where, in contrast, a society is constituted by a large middle class, and the extremes of wealth and poverty are negligible, the likelihood of violent social conflict and despotism is minimal. Conflict is also caused by the excessive predominance of an individual or group. A good constitution must therefore provide that no persons or groups can aggrandize to themselves so much power that they can tyrannize over others.

Anticipating Machiavelli, Aristotle observes that the means employed to cause and to prevent revolution are sometimes force and sometimes fraud. Where the safety and the interests of the people are concerned, Aristotle alerts us to the dangers inherent in both revolution and counter-revolution. After the revolutionary leaders have seized power by force with the aid of the people, they often resort to fraud, deceiving the people and altering the constitution with their consent. At a later stage when they have alienated the people, the leaders hold on to the government by force, against the people's will. Whenever the same individual becomes both supreme military commander and leader of the people, he successfully erects a tyranny. The largest number of tyrants in Greek history had begun, purportedly, as friends and leaders of the people. Aristotle thus observed a pattern that became strikingly evident in the nineteenth and twentieth centuries. The fertile economic soil for the emergence of tyranny is the polarization of classes. So again Aristotle underscores the principle that only when moderate differences of wealth characterize the vast majority of citizens is there but little likelihood of either revolution or despotism.

In his discussion of revolution and the ways to forestall it, Aristotle continues to stress that social stability presupposes certain political safeguards such as mixed, constitutional government. Also important is the fostering of an atmosphere in which citizens relate to one another in a democratic spirit. For 'the equality which men of the democratic spirit seek for in the multitude is not only just, but also expedient in the case of their compeers' (*Politics*, V, vii, 2–4).

No less prescient is Aristotle's analysis of the ways in which tyrants strive to preserve their power. What he has to say about Periander of Corinth applies with equal force to the murderous tyrannies of the twentieth century. Here Aristotle relies on the famous account in Herodotus. 'To begin with,' wrote Herodotus,

> Periander was less violent than his father [Cypselus], but soon surpassed him in bloody-mindedness and savagery. This was the result of a correspondence which he entered into with Thrasybulus, the master of Miletus. He sent a representative to the court of this despot, to ask his opinion on how best and most safely to govern his city. Thrasybulus invited the man to walk with him from the city to a field where corn was growing. As he passed through this cornfield, continually asking questions about why the messenger had come to him from Corinth, he kept cutting off all the tallest ears of wheat which he could see, and throwing them away, until the finest and best-grown part of the crop was ruined. In this way he went right through the field, and then sent the messenger away without a word. On his return to Corinth, Periander was eager to hear what advice Thrasybulus had given and the man replied that he had not given any at all, adding that he was surprised at being sent to visit such a person, who was evidently mad and a wanton destroyer of his own property – and then he described what he had seen Thrasybulus do. Periander seized the point at once; it was perfectly plain to him that Thrasybulus recommended the murder of all the people in the city who were outstanding in influence or ability. Moreover, he took the advice, and from that time forward there was no crime against the Corinthians that he did not commit; indeed, anything that Cypselus has left undone in the way of killing or banishing, Periander completed for him. (*The Histories*, V, 92E–G)[1]

In all times tyrants seek to preserve their power by murdering, banishing, or incarcerating outstanding individuals who might oppose them, and also by prohibiting all gatherings and clubs where political opposition might be generated. The tyrant's police agents, says Aristotle, keep close watch upon and prevent the formation of study-circles, debating societies, and even gatherings of the kind one observed in Plato's academy or among the peripatetic philosophers of Aristotle's own Lyceum. The tyrant's agents, alert to the possible organization of resistance, employ spies and provocateurs who infiltrate all potential resistance groups. And it is a key device of tyranny to prevent the people from arming themselves and becoming a challenge to the tyrant's forces. Furthermore, the people are kept so busy with their daily affairs that they have no leisure to plot against the ruler. Instances of this are the various colossal building projects from the time of the pyramids to the temple of the Olympian Zeus begun by Pisistratus. It is also the mark of a tyrant to be extremely distrustful of the members of his entourage who possess the influence or power to do him in. Distrusting their subordinates and fearing the dignified and courageous, free-spirited individuals, tyrants do not sleep well. So the tyrant's devices are designed to prevent mutual confidence among the subjects, to make them as servile and humble-spirited as possible, and to eliminate their ability to resist effectively. Nevertheless, the tyrant who, typically, had seized power with substantial popular support, soon found that his days as ruler were numbered. He had alienated himself from the people, thus destroying the ultimate source of his power.

In the closing pages of Book V of the *Politics* Aristotle observes, in a proto-Machiavellian spirit, that a ruler who wishes to avoid even the appearance of being a tyrant should inspire respect rather than fear. Not only must he himself be known to have perpetrated no outrage against any of his subjects, so also must it be known about everybody in his circle. The ruler must care for his city and adorn it as its loyal trustee; and he must always be seen to be exceptionally zealous as regards religious observances.

For Aristotle, to govern free men is, of course, nobler and more virtuous than to rule despotically. Where safeguards of democracy are concerned, Aristotle advises against the dole, since that way of helping the poor simply perpetuates their dependence. The wise democratic statesman must learn how to save the multitude from extreme poverty; for it is the growth of extreme poverty that gives rise to massive discontent and rebellious activity threatening not only the interests of the wealthy, but the general social order. The statesman must therefore bring home to

the wealthy and privileged that it is in their interest to contribute gener-
ously to a fund to be distributed to the needy not as a dole, but as a sum
large enough to serve as capital for trade or husbandry or for any other
means by which they might earn their own livelihood. Aristotle
acknowledges, however, that until such a time as this policy is fully
implemented, the democratic statesman must retain the goodwill of the
needy by instituting a temporary system of poor-relief (*Politics*, VI, iii, 5–
iv, 2).

The Best Constitution

The best constitution must be guided by the principles laid down in the
Nicomachean Ethics: pursue the mean in all things and recognize that it is
virtue and wisdom that bring happiness. Indeed, the best life for both
individuals and states is a life furnished with the material conditions
sufficient for taking part in virtuous and just actions. In Book VII Aristotle speaks out against imperialism – the policy of striving for the conquest and domination of neighbouring peoples. An imperialist policy is
contrary to good constitutional government, since an imperialist state
treats other states in a manner that it regards as unjust for itself. A good
state cannot be a war-state – a state designed for offensive warfare and
conquest. The military function of a good state must be strictly limited
to defending itself and avoiding enslavement by others.

For Aristotle, it was self-evident that all human beings aim at the
good life and at happiness. Some individuals, however, possess the
means of attaining the good life, while others do not, owing to some
adverse condition of either fortune or nature. Even those who possess
the means often go wrong from the start, because they treat wealth and
power as ends rather than means. So Aristotle reminds us of the definition of happiness he proposed in the *Ethics* – that happiness is the development and active employment of one's excellences or virtues. To the
question of how one becomes virtuous, Aristotle replies that there are
three means by which humans are made virtuous: nature, habit, and
reason; and since good habits and reason require nurturing, it is clear
that a primary responsibility of the good state is the proper education of
its citizens. Social life as a whole consists of business and leisure, war
and peace, things useful and things noble. So war must be for the sake of
peace, business for the sake of leisure, things necessary and useful for
the sake of things noble. The stateman must therefore legislate with
these principles in view.

Like Plato, Aristotle proposes in Book VIII that the appetite must be trained for the sake of the intellect, and the body for the sake of the soul. And like Plato, Aristotle also introduces a eugenic element in the state's policy: the government must take measures to ensure that deformed offspring shall not be reared. Aristotle also makes certain sensible and unobjectionable proposals such as seeing that children should drink milk, not wine, and get plenty of exercise and opportunity for play; but children's games should be imitations of the serious occupations of later life.

In many ways, then, Aristotle's *Ethics* and *Politics* have fulfilled his aim of helping us to think through two fundamental questions: In what way of life does happiness consist? In what form of society can that way of life best be realized? In his consideration of these questions, Aristotle has made no small contribution to our understanding of the human condition.

Chapter Three

Machiavelli

Niccolo Machiavelli was the first modern thinker to study history as the basis for theorizing about power. Indeed, the historically grounded nature of his reflections is evident throughout his works – *The Prince, Discourses on the First Ten Books of Titus Livy, The History of Florence,* and *The Art of War*. In the preface to the *Discourses* he bemoans the fact that neither prince nor republic learns from the experience of antiquity. They lack a proper appreciation of history. The great bulk of those who read history take pleasure, perhaps, in hearing of the various occurrences contained in it, but they never think of learning from them. The reason, apparently, is that they somehow believe that the human species as a whole has become different from what it used to be. Insisting that one may speak of 'recurring events,' Machiavelli argues that if we compare the present with the past, it is easy to see that in all societies and peoples the same desires and passions have always existed and continue to exist today. It follows that if one reflects diligently on the past, one may anticipate future troubles and apply the tried and tested remedies that were used of old. But since history is rarely studied with this aim in view, the result is that similar troubles continue to beset us.[1]

What is the nature of Machiavelli's reasoning that allows him to speak of 'recurring events'? Did he somehow believe, literally, that history repeats itself? It is certain that he believed no such thing. Machiavelli understood that 'history' – the actual course of human events – is a unique and unrepeatable constellation of events and circumstances. Unique, because whether the event in question was the battle of Marathon, the Peloponnesian War, or Caesar's crossing of the Rubicon, they are all events that occurred only once and never will recur. Similarly in modern history, whether it is, say, the seizure of power by Napoleon,

Mussolini, Hitler, or Stalin, they too are unique events. Machiavelli understood that the notion that 'history repeats itself' is more metaphorical than real. But he also grasped the essential insight embedded in that epigram and the sound basis for it.

According to Machiavelli, human beings, everywhere and always, are primarily driven by self-interest and ruled by the insatiable desire for gain, whether it be in the form of wealth, power, or honour. Selfishness or egoism is an eternal trait of human nature, a nature constant and immutable. However, this rather unfavourable view of human nature leads, paradoxically, to a positive assessment of human possibilities through the study of history. For if human actions are primarily motivated by a self-seeking nature, and if that nature tends to produce similar and recurring patterns of action, then the actions of the past, as recorded in history, may be studied as a basis for anticipating future patterns. Hindsight thus provides a serviceable degree of foresight. The study of history supplies us with a vast reservoir of guidelines as we step into the uncertain future. Machiavelli's conception of human nature therefore allows for no utopias envisioning a future radically different from the past.

Machiavelli's historically grounded theorizing did not, however, lead him to propose – as some popularizations of his theory have suggested – that the end justifies the means. He certainly did not propose that *all* means are justified in the pursuit of any end; nor did he separate moral standards from political actions. What he did maintain is that the employment of evil means, such as violence, is often necessary. When violence is clearly in the public interest, the prince should not shy away from employing it. Force, as a last resort, is essential in some circumstances if the prince is to fulfil his two primary responsibilities of ensuring the state's internal stability and external independence.

Machiavelli proposed that violent conflict, invasions, and war are permanent attributes of the human condition. But he stressed again and again that conflict can produce beneficial results if it is dealt with by a properly organized and stable government. It was precisely the social strife between the patricians and plebians that contributed to the liberty and greatness of ancient Rome. For Machiavelli, those who regret and criticize the incessant quarrels between the nobles and the plebs condemn the very condition that enabled Rome to retain its freedom. Critics see only the tumult and commotion that resulted from the strife, but miss altogether the good effects. They fail, moreover, to recognize that in every republic there are two dispositions, that of the populace and that of the upper classes, and that all institutions favourable to liberty are brought about by the clash between them (*Discourses*, I, 4).

In the *Discourses*, more clearly than in *The Prince*, Machiavelli displays a pro-republican inclination that is both moral and political. Every state wisely ruled, he insists, should provide ways and means by which the populace may find an outlet for its ambitions, especially a state that hopes to enlist the support and participation of the populace in important undertakings. The demands of a free populace are rarely harmful to liberty, for they are most often a result of actual oppression or the anticipation of it. If one asks what the upper classes are after and what the common people want, it is undoubtedly true, says Machiavelli, that the upper classes strive to dominate while the people wish merely to prevent their being oppressed. As a rule, then, it is the people who are most keen on widening the boundaries of their freedom. It follows that if the people are made the guardians of freedom, it is reasonable to suppose that they will take better care of it than the upper classes.

On the virtues of a republic, Machiavelli observes that when Rome got rid of its kings the dangers entailed by the accession of a bad ruler were vastly diminished; for the sovereign power was now vested in consuls who acquired it by the free votes of the people and not by heredity or trickery (*Discourses*, I, 19–20). Machiavelli goes further: the lessons of history teach us that the faults one may discern in the people are due to their rulers. A prince should never complain of failings in the people whom he governs, for such failings result either from his own negligence or from his being himself stained with similar defects (*Discourses*, III, 29). Now, what is truly interesting and striking about this pro-republican, pro-populace position is that it is being espoused by Machiavelli, not Rousseau. Indeed, many centuries before Rousseau advocated the 'sovereignty of the people,' Machiavelli highlighted the advantages of political systems in which, in his words, the 'populace is the prince' (*Discourses*, I, 58).

From Machiavelli's hard-headed, historically grounded approach to politics, it was obvious that social conflict is here to stay, and that all attempts to suppress it produce only apparent harmony and stability. Wise government will therefore strive to create a dynamic equilibrium among the diverse and competing social forces of society. However, it is noteworthy that in the struggle between the 'haves' and the 'have-nots,' Machiavelli sees the main source of disequilibrium in the 'haves,' because they fear that they cannot secure what is at hand without gaining more at the expense of others (*Discourses*, I, 5–6). We shall return to this pro-populace, pro-republican disposition and give it the fuller attention it deserves; but first we need to survey *The Prince* to determine whether there are significant differences between that work and the *Discourses*.

The Prince

Scholars are in general agreement that Machiavelli started work on *The Prince* after he had written a part of the *Discourses*; and although he writes in the latter from the standpoint of an ardent republican, and appears to be less explicitly pro-republican in *The Prince*, the difference in that respect between the two works has been exaggerated. For it is doubtful that Machiavelli's outlook in *The Prince* was fundamentally different from that in the *Discourses*. Indeed, he states in the opening sentence of the second chapter of *The Prince*: 'I shall leave out any discussion of republics, since I discussed them at length on another occasion.' Some students of Machiavelli's thought have suggested that in *The Prince* he advocated the rule of an amoral autocrat, ruthless and efficient. As we shall see, however, *The Prince* no less than the *Discourses* proposes that the ruler must build the state on the goodwill of the people. It is also misleading to suggest that in *The Prince* the question whether an action is evil or not can only be decided pragmatically – that is, in the light of what it is designed to achieve and whether it achieves it successfully. In *The Prince* as in the *Discourses* the criterion is prudence, expedience, *and* morality all at once: it is in the wise prince's interest to maintain the state by the force *of* the people, not over the people; and it is also morally the right way to rule.

Aristotle, as we have seen, called attention to the fundamental difference between the Persian regime, a form of Asiatic despotism, and the mixed and constitutional form of government that he advocated. Similarly, Machiavelli, as he looks back at the Persian empire, asks why the kingdom conquered by Alexander the Great did not rebel against his successors after his death. The point for Machiavelli, as it was for Aristotle, is to compare the socio-political structures of two systems and thereby to show why one is unavoidably despotic while the other offers considerable freedom. Machiavelli proposes that all states known to history are governed in one of two ways. In the first, the prince is sovereign over the people, and his ministers are also subservient, having no real power of their own. This is a highly centralized, hierarchical, and bureaucratic order in which all power is concentrated in the hands of the ruling individual or party. The second and contrasting way is one in which the prince rules not alone, but together with a class of autonomous nobles, who have subjects of their own. A nobility of this kind has definite responsibilities towards its subjects, providing, for example, protection and the administration of justice. What we have here, in effect, is the contrast between the centralized agrarian empires of Asia and the feudal orders of western Europe. Anticipating Montesquieu, Machiavelli thus recognizes that although landlords in all agrarian societies strive for independence from the political power above them, success in this endeavour was achieved only under feudalism. Feudalism was a decentralized and polycentric political system in which the prince's officials were either forbidden access to the lord's domain or, if allowed, had to obtain permission directly from the lord himself for the performance of their duties on behalf of the prince, such as the collection of feudal dues or the serving of military summons.

Machiavelli thus understood that feudalism was a 'division of powers,' a multiplicity of comparatively autonomous domains, a political system that made possible the emergence in western Europe of republican and other forms of constitutional government. Machiavelli cites Turkey and France as the contemporary examples of the two contrasting forms of government. The Turkish empire was ruled by one man to whom everyone, the people, landlords, and ministers alike, was subservient. The king of France, in contrast, was surrounded by a long-established order of nobles with subjects of their own and with definite authority and prerogatives that the king dared not try to take away from them. (Of course, this was the period prior to the emergence in Europe of royal absolutism, a regime in which monarchs such as Louis XIV of France not only dared but succeeded in reducing the power of the nobles and turning them into appendages of the throne.) The centralized, hierarchical nature of the Persian and Turkish empires explains, for Machiavelli, why it is difficult to gain control of such an empire, and why, once it has been conquered, it can be held with ease. For it is only the ruler at the top that is changed, while everything else in the governing structure remains intact. On the other hand, the territory of the French state or a portion of it may be more easily seized, but it can be held only with great difficulty, since the invader's conquest of an area in no way precludes opposition to him on the part of many autonomous warrior-lords and their retinues.

In both the Persian and Turkish systems, the local satraps are mere officials in the imperial bureaucracy, bound in loyalty to the ruler. Not only do they lack any real power of their own, their relationship to the people is so oppressive that they are unable to draw the people after them. Whoever attacks an empire of the Turkish type should therefore expect to find it totally united. In such an attack one would have to rely entirely on one's superior forces and not on any disunity in the enemy's ranks. The opposite, however, is true in the French type of kingdom: one can easily invade by winning over one of the powerful and disgruntled barons, but then countless difficulties emerge. There being no real centre of power, it is not enough to destroy the ruler and his family because there still remain numerous nobles who can mobilize opposition. So in response to the original question, since Darius's empire was a form of centralized despotism, Alexander had to utterly crush his forces in order to seize his territory, and that was sufficient after Darius's death to ensure that the state would rest securely in the hands of Alexander's successors. And, in fact, there were no serious disturbances in the empire other than such as they themselves had provoked. As for states constituted like that of France, it is impossible for all the reasons previously given to rule them with so little difficulty. In concluding his comparative analysis of the two contrasting systems, Machiavelli emphasizes that it is not so much the skill of the conquerors that accounts for the ease or difficulty in holding a territory; rather, the ease or difficulty depends 'on the kind of state they conquer.'[2]

Machiavelli's close attention to the socio-political structure of states does not mean that he fails to recognize the role of the outstanding individual in history. Citing Moses, Cyrus, Romulus, and Theseus, he remarks that perhaps Moses should not be considered in this regard, since he merely executed what God had commanded. But as he examines the careers of Cyrus and the others who acquired or founded kingdoms, he suggests that their actions and the institutions they formed do not seem to differ from those of Moses who had such a mighty teacher. These outstanding individuals, with their extraordinary prowess, received nothing from fortune except opportunity. Fortune provided the material, as it were, but they gave the material its form; for 'without opportunity,' writes Machiavelli, 'their prowess would have been extinguished, and without such prowess the opportunity would have come in vain' (The Prince, VI, 50). Moses's opportunity was finding the Israelites enslaved and oppressed in Egypt; Cyrus's was the rebelliousness of the Persians against the empire of the Medes, who had grown lax through the long years of peace. Outstanding individuals who innovate are bound to encounter difficulties and dangers, for there is nothing more dangerous than initiating changes in a state's governing structure. The innovator is greeted with hostility by all the established interests and powers who prospered under the old order, but he receives only lukewarm support from those who are uncertain they will prosper under the new. The innovating prince who relies on persuasion alone will always come to grief. The prince, however, who controls the means of forcing the issue is seldom endangered: 'That is why armed prophets have conquered, and unarmed prophets have come to grief' (*The Prince*, VI, 52). Neither Moses, nor Cyrus, nor Romulus would have realized their will had they been unarmed. These considerations – the diversity of governing structures, the role of the outstanding individual in history, and the need for force as a last resort – bring Machiavelli to the subject that best demonstrates his commitment to constitutional government.

The Constitutional Principality

When a private citizen becomes the ruler of his society neither by crime nor by violence, but by the will and consent of his fellow citizens, Machiavelli regards this as constitutional government. To achieve the position of a constitutional ruler, it is astuteness that one needs, not good fortune or prowess. The fellow citizens with whose will and consent one becomes the ruler may be either the people or the nobles. In every city the people are disposed to avoid being oppressed, while the upper classes are equally disposed to dominate and oppress. The opposition between the nobility and the people tends to produce one of three results: a principality (a state under the authority of a prince), a free city, or anarchy.

A principality may be created by either the nobility or the people, depending on which of them acquires the opportunity. When the nobles find they cannot withstand the power of the people, they recruit a strong man from among themselves and raise him to the status of a prince to attain their ends under his protection. Similarly, the people, finding they cannot effectively resist the will of the nobles, will raise an individual from their own ranks to the status of a prince and seek protection under his authority. A prince who has attained his power with the favour of the nobles will find it more difficult to maintain his position than will the prince who has been chosen by the people. In terms reminiscent of Aristotle's analysis of oligarchy, Machiavelli describes the principality of nobles as one in which the prince, surrounded by men who regard themselves as his peers, cannot command or govern effectively. Dissension and rivalry in the ranks of the nobles is characteristic. In a principality of the people, however, the prince, finding none or a few who are unwilling to obey, governs with greater freedom. It is impossible in an oligarchy to satisfy the interests of the nobles without violating the interests of the people, for the nobles want only to exploit the people. Once the people become opposed to the prince owing to his oppressive regime, his power is no longer secure; for at the first opportunity they will surely desert him. And although the nobles tend to be more astute in defending their interests and siding with those in their ranks, a wise prince should remember this: he must always live with the people, and if he has their support, he can well do without that of the nobles.

Where the nobles are concerned, either they tie their fortunes to that of the prince, or they do not. Those who become totally dependent upon him, the prince should honour and love. Those, however, who out of ambition remain deliberately aloof, the prince should recognize as potential adversaries who would join his enemies and help to destroy him. The man who is made a prince by the will of the people must do all he can to retain their friendship, an easy task since the people seek only freedom from oppression. If a man has become a prince with the support of the nobles and against the people's will, his first mission must be to win the people over by taking them under his wing. By doing so, they will become all the more favourably disposed towards him, since they expected him to offer them ill, and instead he has offered them protection. In all circumstances the friendship of the people is essential, for if they desert the prince he is defenceless in times of adversity.

For Machiavelli, the foundations of every state are good laws and good arms – good laws to defend the rights of the citizens and the interests of the people, and good arms to enforce the laws and defend the state against external aggression. The wise prince will never rely on mercenaries for the defence of the state, for the mercenaries' sole incentive is their pay, which is never enough to make them ready to die for him. The prince must mobilize his own forces, either an army of subjects or an army of citizens. Indeed, it is a prince's primary responsibility to acquire outstanding prowess in the art of war, its organization, strategy, tactics, and discipline. Acquiring such prowess demands not only rigorous physical training, but intellectual training as well, the best form of the latter being the study of history, and especially the history of the great strategists of the past. The prince should learn from them just as Alexander the Great emulated Achilles, Caesar emulated Alexander, and Scipio took Cyrus as his model.

In ruling a state constitutionally, a prince will inevitably face the question of how to avoid a reputation for cruelty and gain a reputation for compassion. The prince should, of course, prefer a reputation for compassion, but not make a bad use of it. Keeping his citizens united and loyal is his main responsibility, which means that on occasion he might have to employ extreme measures to curb the actions of individuals and groups who threaten the integrity of the state with their disorders, murder, and rapine. Addressing the question of whether it is better for a prince to be loved or feared, Machiavelli replies that it would be best to be both loved and feared, but because it is difficult to combine them, it is better to be feared. Still, the prince should make himself feared in such a manner as to avoid being hated. Fear and the absence of hatred are quite compatible, if harsh measures such as execution are carried out only when the offence is evident, and only in accordance with the law.

A prince should honour his word and be straightforward in his dealings. He should nevertheless be sufficiently astute to understand that there are times when he must resort to deception or to force. Machiavelli has no respect for governments that fail to defend their societies with resoluteness and boldness. In one of the most famous passages of *The Prince* (XVII, 99) he maintains that the internal stability and external independence of a state demand from the prince that 'he should learn from the fox and the lion; because the lion is defenseless against traps and a fox is defenseless against wolves. Therefore one must be a fox to recognize traps, and a lion to frighten off wolves. Those who simply act like lions are stupid.' They are stupid in light of the fact that princes 'who have known how to imitate the fox have come off best' (ibid.). History has demonstrated that the successful prince must be a skilful pretender. It is best if he actually possesses the virtues of compassion, good faith, charity, kindness, and piety; but given the cruel, dishonest, and hypocritical nature of many of his adversaries, he is bound to be ruined if he always conducts himself in accordance with the virtues. So the model prince should not deviate from what is good so long as good means are effective; but he should know when and how to employ evil means when that proves necessary. As a lion he must be prepared to use force, for as Machiavelli remarks in the *Discourses*, 'it is the man who uses violence to spoil things, not the man who uses it to mend them, that is blameworthy' (I, 9). The prince's judicious use of force may be, in effect, more merciful than clemency; for while the former injures only a few and restrains the rest by fear, the latter breeds disorder and rebellion, which injures the entire body politic.

The incidence of force can never be radically lessened in the international arena because it lacks a prince – or a leviathan as Hobbes later argued. Domestic violence can, however, be reduced by means of law, the appropriate political institutions, and the cultivation of civility. In the category of such institutions Machiavelli cites the parliament, which serves to mediate between the nobles and the people. Well-organized states possess such institutions that enable the wise prince to satisfy the people without alienating the upper classes. In France, for example, the parliament saved the prince from being reproached by the nobles for favouring the people, and by the people for favouring the nobles. The founder of the French state had thus instituted an independent arbiter to control the avarice of the nobles and defend the weak without bringing reproach on the king.

For Machiavelli, a chief criterion of the strength and solidity of a prince's rule is the diminishing need to resort to cruel and violent measures. Increased cruelty shows that the prince has lost the consent of the governed. The wise, bold, and self-confident prince who rules with the consent of the governed will never disarm the citizenry. On the contrary, he will arm them if he finds them unarmed, since by arming the citizens he arms himself. The aim of the wise prince, then, should be the maintenance of his rule by the force *of* the people, not over the people. This is best accomplished by ensuring that the people's material needs are met; by protecting them and their possessions; and by striving to eliminate dangerous social and economic inequalities. The existence of competing groups and conflicting classes being inevitable, the prince must wisely mediate between them so that order and justice and the overarching interests of the commonwealth as a whole are maintained. It is the well-being of the general community and not merely of individuals and factions that makes a state great. In pursuing these ends a government should never suppose that it can adopt perfectly safe courses of action; rather, it should regard all possible courses of action as risky. For it is the nature of reality that whenever one seeks to avoid one danger, one runs into another. Prudence, therefore, an essential element of wise government, 'consists in being able to assess the nature of a particular threat and in accepting the lesser evil' (*The Prince*, XXI, 123). Equally important for the wise prince is that he should show esteem for political aptitude and actively encourage able individuals to join him, thus ensuring to his government a continual supply of fresh political talent. The selection of individuals for his administrative staff is, after all, a matter of no small importance for a prince; and the first impression formed of his intelligence and sagacity is based on the quality of the persons he has around him. When his officials are competent and loyal, he is respected and considered wise; but when they are otherwise, he is open to adverse criticism. The wise prince will solicit the opinions of his ministers, demanding they speak the truth on the matters on which he has consulted them, and showing his wrath to those who hold back the truth. But he must make up his own mind.

In *The Prince*, then, we can see that although Machiavelli wrote this slender volume in response to the conditions of his time, as an exhortation to liberate Italy from foreign occupation, he has given us insights of lasting validity. As we return to the *Discourses*, we shall see that it is no less rich in insight.

The *Discourses*

The full title of this work is *Discourses on the First Ten Books of Titus Livy*. Livy had devoted his long life to writing his *History of Rome*, comprising 142 volumes (thirty-five are extant), covering the foundation of Rome to 9 BC. Machiavelli carefully studied the first ten volumes and treated the history of Rome and other ancient societies as a major source on which to base his reflections on political affairs. He compares ancient with contemporary events so that his readers may more easily learn practical, political lessons. History being the great record of human experiences, it is Machiavelli's view that a proper appreciation of that record has been lacking. Neither prince nor republic has turned to antiquity for what can be learned about creating a republic, preserving a state, governing a kingdom, conducting war, dealing with subjects, or maintaining an empire. Machiavelli's aim in the *Discourses*, therefore, is to fill the gap.

Machiavelli follows Plato and Aristotle in distinguishing types of government and degenerative deviations from them: a principality may easily degenerate into a tyranny, an aristocracy into an oligarchy, and a democracy into anarchy. He also follows them in reconstructing the process by which societies and governments came into being, and in doing so he anticipates the later 'state of nature' and 'social-contract' theorists. In primordial times, Machiavelli speculates, when the human population was small, human beings lived scattered like the beasts. Then with the growth of population they came together, and in order better to defend themselves they selected the strongest and boldest man among them as their leader. They had learned to distinguish good from evil, for the sight of someone injuring one's kin or one's friends evoked sympathy for the injured and hatred for the aggressor. To prevent evil, rules and laws were made to assign punishments to offenders, and the notion of justice thus came into being. Accordingly, when it came time to choose a prince, it was no longer simply the strongest who was chosen, but rather the one who had distinguished himself for his wisdom, prudence, and justice. At a still later stage when the prince's rule became hereditary, the heirs began to degenerate, believing that a prince has nothing to do except to indulge himself in luxury, lasciviousness, and licentiousness. The prince thus came to be hated and, being hated, came to be afraid and launched offensive actions against the populace out of fear. Circumstances of this kind led to tyranny and to the downfall of tyrants. The people, at the behest of wealthy, able, and powerful leaders, took up arms against the tyrant and, having liquidated him, submitted to the authority of government based not on the rule of men, but on the rule of law designed to subordinate private interests to the common advantage.

In time, however, avarice and ambition caused this government by an aristocracy to degenerate into an oligarchy in which civic duties to the society as a whole were entirely disregarded. The reaction to oligarchy was not unlike the rebellion against tyranny: the popular masses, disgusted with the existing rulers, turned to a strong man willing to lead them in destroying the oligarchical regime. Since the memory of the tyrannical prince and the oppressive oligarchy was still fresh, the people demanded a democratic form of government in which authority was no longer vested in either a single prince or a few rich and powerful men. Democracy, however, soon transformed itself into anarchy as everyone began to act as if everything was permitted, constantly committing all sorts of outrages. In reaction to this state of affairs, the people called for a strong man who would bring order out of this chaos, and a prince was once again placed at the helm. With this deliberately schematic sketch of the history of government, Machiavelli proposes that the 'cycle' from principality to anarchy begins once more. It is not literally a cycle, however, since no state has sufficient vitality to endure such changes repeatedly while still remaining in being. Typically, a state in the throes of tumultuous change becomes easy prey for conquest by a better organized and more powerful state.

For Machiavelli, the key point of his sketch is that all these forms of government are unsatisfactory: the three good ones – principality, aristocracy, and democracy – because they are so short-lived; and the three bad ones – tyranny, oligarchy, and anarchy – because they are inherently evil. Prudent legislators of the past, having observed these defects, refrained from adopting any of these forms and chose instead to create a *mixed constitution*. Such legislators recognized that government would be stronger, more stable, and more just if all three elements (principality, aristocracy, and democracy) were built into the constitution of one and the same state.

Like Aristotle, who also favoured mixed constitutional government, Machiavelli cites the great lawgiver Lycurgus, whose constitution assigned to the kings, to the aristocracy, and to the people their distinct and respective functions, thus introducing a form of government that lasted more than 800 years. If longevity is the criterion, then Lycurgus was a greater lawgiver than Solon; for though the latter had tried to mediate between the nobles and the people, he gave to the people more power in the law courts, thus failing to blend with this democratic element either princely or aristocratic power. The result was that even after the expulsion of the last tyrants from Athens, that city succeeded in retaining its liberty less than a hundred years. As for Rome, though it had no Lycurgus, strife between the patricians and the plebeians eventually brought about unexpectedly what had been provided in Sparta by a lawgiver.

As the aim of the founders of Rome was to establish a kingdom, not a republic, they overlooked the need to provide for institutions essential to the preservation of liberty. Even after the kings were deposed, those who expelled them appointed at once two consuls in their place. In the new republic that thus arose there were the consuls and the senate – the elements of principality and aristocracy – but no provision as yet for democracy. How, then, did the democratic element emerge? This came about later, Machiavelli explains, as the Roman nobility became so oppressive that the people rose up against them. The nobility, fearing that they would lose everything, granted the people a share in government. The tribunes were thus instituted to defend the interests of the people, and it was the institution of the tribunes that added the democratic element to that of the senate and the consuls, thus enhancing the stability of the republican form of government. It was the blending of the three elements, or principles, that made a more perfect commonwealth. And it was Machiavelli's original contribution to recognize that this desirable result was brought about as a consequence of the strife between the patricians and the plebs.

Machiavelli does not say that all men are wicked, but he does say that legislators would be wise to act as if that were true. In the history of

Rome, so long as the kings were in power, harmony seemed to prevail between the nobles and the plebs. The nobles, fearing that if they behaved harshly towards the people they would make common cause with the kings, treated the plebs with consideration. But as soon as the kings were expelled, the nobles revealed their true colours and began to oppress the people in every way imaginable. For Machiavelli, this chain of events tended to bear out his view of human nature as self-seeking – the view that men will seek their own good at the expense of others as soon as the opportunity presents itself. With the collapse of the monarchical regime of the Tarquins, the nobility was no longer kept in check by fear of them. It was therefore necessary to devise a new institution that would achieve the same effect as did the Tarquins. That institution was the *tribunes* appointed for the protection of the people and invested with the authority to curb the extremes of the nobility. Hence, it was the conflict between the nobles and the plebs that contributed substantially to the creation of laws and institutions that made Rome both free and powerful. In the 300 years from the reign of the Tarquins to that of the Gracchi, there was comparatively little social discord thanks to the new institutions and laws. Generalizing from this and other historical evidence, Machiavelli proposes that in every republic it is the clash between the people and the upper classes that brings about legislation favourable to liberty.

Indeed, Machiavelli has no doubt that where the protection of liberty is concerned, it can be more safely entrusted to the have-nots than to the haves. The upper class, by its very nature, wants to dominate and exploit the people, while the people, in contrast, want merely to avoid being dominated and exploited. The 'haves,' moreover, strive to enlarge their privileges, for they fear that they cannot retain the privileges they already have without gaining more at the expense of the people. It is therefore reasonable to suppose that the people have the strongest interest in preserving liberty (*Discourses*, I, 5).

The Role of Religion

For Machiavelli, the observance of divine worship is the cause of greatness in republics, while the neglect of it is the cause of their ruin. Religion is essential for the maintenance of a civilized state. In the history of Rome it was religion that facilitated the great exploits of the people as a whole. Citizens had more fear of breaking an oath than of breaking a law because they held in higher esteem the power of God than the power of man. Prudent and wise legislators recognized the role of religion in controlling the armies, in encouraging the people, in bringing out the good in men and in curbing the bad. Where there is religion it is easier to teach men to use arms for the common good; where, however, there are armed men but religion is absent, the common good is achieved with the greatest difficulty, if at all.

So if it is a question of the ruler to whom Rome was more indebted, Romulus or Numa, it is Numa, for Machiavelli, who deserves the highest honour. In establishing the senate and other civic and military institutions, Romulus deemed it unnecessary to appeal to divine authority; but for Numa it was so necessary that he pretended to consult privately with a deity who advised him how to lead the people. Numa, wanting to introduce new institutions with which the city had no experience, recognized that his own authority would not suffice. And as one examines the careers of other great legislators, it becomes quite evident that none of them attempted to introduce new or extraordinary laws to the people without recourse to the Divine. This was necessary because it would have been impossible to persuade the people of the benefits to be gained from such laws by means of reason alone. The observance of divine worship is therefore essential, Machiavelli insists, because where there is no fear of God, people tend to believe that everything is permitted; and fear of the prince alone is insufficient to hold the evil impulses in check.

Furthermore, inasmuch as any prince, even the most virtuous, can rule only for a lifetime, it may very well happen that when a state loses its prince, it will lose the virtue of its prince as well. It follows that the lasting security of a republic depends not on its ruler governing prudently during his lifetime, but upon his so ordering the state that after he is gone it will maintain itself for the common weal. For that the institution of religion is indispensable.

The Prince and the Populace

Machiavelli recognized that in a people's transition from servitude to freedom, there are special problems that the legislator must take into account. He is bound to encounter hostility from the 'haves' as he tries to introduce free institutions. His first task, then, is to make the populace his friend; and the best way to achieve this is to learn what the people desire and need. The prince will always find that the people want (1) to avenge themselves upon those who have tried to keep them in servitude, and (2) to regain their freedom. The first of these demands the prince can satisfy entirely. Machiavelli cites cases in which a prince found himself between an arrogant upper class and a raving populace that greatly resented threats to its freedom. In such instances, the prince found it expedient to free himself from the vexations caused by the upper class by inflicting severe wounds upon it, and thus satisfying the people's demand for vengeance. As for the people's second demand – the restoration of freedom or the enlargement of its boundaries – the prince should determine the grounds on which this demand is based. As a rule, says Machiavelli, the prince will find that only a small section of the populace wants freedom in order to lord it over others; but the vast majority of those who demand freedom want nothing more than to live their lives securely.

The prince who therefore wishes to mediate wisely and prudently between the classes should know that in all states, whatever their form of government, the real holders of extraordinary wealth and power are a small minority. And since they are a small minority, it should be an easy task for the prince to secure himself against it. Here Machiavelli returns implicitly to the alternate metaphors of the lion and the fox: the prince may either reduce the powerful minority by means of force, or he may win them over by granting them appropriate offices and honours. As for the people, the prince can easily win them over simply by introducing such laws and institutions as will heighten their security and enhance their material well-being.

Although Machiavelli stresses repeatedly that the well-being of the populace is the foundation of a free, just, and stable society, he also calls attention to the circumstances in which the people become corrupt and reform proves to be impossible. Machiavelli supports his contention by comparing and contrasting two epochs in the history of Rome. When the Tarquins were expelled, Rome was able forthwith to constitute itself as a republic and thus to acquire and maintain its liberty. Yet when Caesar was assassinated and Gaius Caligula and Nero were also killed, Rome found itself unable to restore the republic. In the earlier era the populace possessed enough integrity and understanding to strengthen its resolve never to consent to any king or despot ruling in Rome. By the time of Caesar, however, the masses had become so effectively blinded by his personality and by the state's policy of 'bread and circuses' that they were unaware of the yoke they themselves had placed on their necks. When the people are corrupted by false concessions, they are more easily induced by deceit to go along with measures that spell their own ruin. The reconstitution of a healthy republic in such circumstances is extremely difficult. Machiavelli therefore proposes that in a crisis of this kind it is necessary to introduce a form of government akin rather to monarchy than to democracy, for it is impossible by legal processes alone to restrain the arrogant men of power and to create republican government afresh. Machiavelli's solution in this regard, which he calls 'quasi-regal power,' is a temporary dictatorship, an expedient reminiscent of Aristotle's 'elective tyranny.'

Machiavelli explores the origin of the expedient in ancient Rome. As the Roman republic expanded its power and dominion, some forty peoples formed a league against Rome. Recognizing the danger of laxity in the face of the league, the Romans resorted to the appointment of a dictator who was invested with absolute authority. The Romans responsible for instituting the dictatorship came under heavy criticism by certain Roman writers who alleged that it was the dictatorship that eventually led to tyranny in Rome. They pointed out that the individual who became Rome's first tyrant had acquired his authority by virtue of his title as dictator; and they argued that had it not been for this institution, Caesar would have failed to cloak his tyranny with the semblance of legality. Machiavelli counters this view by maintaining that it was not the institution itself that made Rome servile, but rather the length of the dictator's rule that deprived the citizens of authority for too long a time. If Rome had not invented this rank and title, a decision-maker of such authority would have arisen anyway out of the need for one. So long as the dictatorship was bestowed in a constitutional manner and not acquired by the individual's own force, it was always of benefit to the state. Furthermore, Machiavelli insists, no dictator in Rome's history ever did anything but good for the republic. Although the term 'dictatorship' has an ominous ring for twentieth-century ears, we need to recognize the validity of Machiavelli's contention that some such institution is necessary in all constitutional governments – the 'emergency powers,' for example, that were granted to the executive branches of government during the Second World War.

The concept of 'emergency powers' captures nicely what Machiavelli had in mind: the dictator was appointed for a limited period and for dealing with the critical matters that had led to the appointment. He had authority to make decisions that responded to definite and extreme dangers, and he could act quickly without extensive consultation. He could not, however, do anything to reduce the constitutional position of the government. He could not, for example, abolish the authority of the senate or the people or the other ancient institutions of the city. So given the temporary nature of the appointment, the limited authority vested in him, and the heightened loyalty of the people to the constitution in the face of the external threat, it proved to be impossible for the dictator to overstep his bounds and do the state harm.

As we listen to Machiavelli making his case, we can see the logic in it. He ranks this institution very high among those to which Rome's greatness is due, for without it republics would have great difficulty in coping with emergencies. The constitutional institutions normally used by republics for decision-making are necessarily slow in their functioning. There was, after all, a certain rudimentary division of powers that had already existed in the Roman republic: neither the assembly nor any magistrate could act alone without mutual consultation and a reconciliation of differences, all of which took considerable time. In situations requiring a quick response or remedy, a reliance on the normal constitutional procedures would therefore have been dangerous. Machiavelli is convincing, then, when he maintains that some sort of device for the granting of emergency powers is necessary in all republics. A healthy republican constitution should provide for such powers, for otherwise it would be necessary either to stand by the constitution and be ruined by responding too late to imminent dangers or to violate the constitution in order to meet the dangers. And if a republic were to resort to the latter option, it would set a very bad precedent: sanctioning the abrogation of constitutional procedures for a good purpose would make it likely that, on some pretext, those procedures would be abrogated for a bad purpose. So a sound republican constitution must provide for all contingencies and determine in advance the method by which to meet national emergencies (*Discourses*, I, 34).

Other Lessons of History

In his discussion of the Agrarian Law in Rome and the troubles to which it led, Machiavelli opens with a paragraph on human nature. Even when there is no other need to fight, says Machiavelli, men fight for ambition's sake. So powerful is ambition that it never leaves men no matter how high they have risen. The reason is that human nature is so constituted that all things are objects of desire, but all things are not attainable. As desire always exceeds the means of attaining its objects, men are chronically ill-content with what they have. Since some individuals desire more than they have and other individuals fear losing what they have already acquired, this gives rise to enmity and war, which bring about the ruin of a state.

The Agrarian Law, which in the end caused the destruction of the Roman republic, illustrates this process well. Under the provisions of that law (1) no citizen was allowed to possess more than a stipulated amount of land, and (2) all lands taken from an enemy were to be divided among the people. This law outraged the nobility, for it was they who possessed more land than the law permitted and who, therefore, were to be deprived of the excess. The fact that captured land was to be shared with the people meant that there was an additional curb on the patricians' ability to enrich themselves. Although the law itself gave offence to the powerful nobles, it was not put into effect until the time of the Gracchi. By that time, however, the power of the law's opponents was twice as great, and the mutual enmity between the patricians and the plebeians had become so intense that it led to armed conflict and much bloodshed. As the magistrates found themselves helpless to mediate, each side to the conflict sought a strong man to head and defend it. The people took the initiative and threw in their lot with Marius, making him consul four times. Soon, however, he was able on his own power to appoint himself consul on three other occasions. The nobility, in turn, backed Sulla, appointing him head of their party. In the savage civil war that ensued, the nobles got the upper hand, but the tensions between them and the plebeians lay beneath the surface until the time of Caesar and Pompey. Caesar became the head of the Marian party and Pompey the head of Sulla's, and open war between the parties erupted again. With Caesar's victory he became Rome's first tyrant, and Rome never again regained its freedoms.

Machiavelli recognizes that his interpretation of this chain of events appears to contradict his original proposition that the strife between the patricians and plebeians kept Rome free, since it was due to their mutual hostility that laws were made to preserve liberty. Although the consequences of the Agrarian Law seem to be incompatible with that proposition, Machiavelli defends its validity on the following ground: the ambition of the rich and powerful is so insatiable that unless a city finds ways and means to keep them in check, that city will soon be brought to ruin. Moreover, since it was a full 300 years before the Agrarian Law led to Rome's servitude, Machiavelli believes that the republic might have fallen victim to tyranny much earlier had not the people by means of this law and other demands held the ambition of the nobles in check (*Discourses*, I, 37). Machiavelli's analysis of the causes of tyranny is reminiscent of Aristotle's. The root cause, Machiavelli avers, is the excessive demand of the nobles to dominate and the excessive demand of the people for freedom. When mediation between the two classes fails, and one or the other supports a strong man called upon to defend its interests by force, tyranny at once emerges.

Machiavelli provides another historical illustration of this process with the events following the appointment of the Decemvirate, or the ten. In the course of the intense conflict between the senate and the people of Rome, it was decided that new laws were required to ensure the freedom and stability of the state. Accordingly, three distinguished citizens were sent to Athens to obtain copies of the laws that Solon had given to that city, so that the Roman laws might be based upon them. When they returned it was decided that for the purpose of codifying the new laws ten citizens would be appointed for a year, among them Appius Claudius, a sagacious but ambitious man. Under the conditions of their appointment, in order that the ten should begin with a new slate, so to speak, all other magistrates, including the tribunes and consuls, were suspended. The people's right to appeal was also suspended so that Appius's magistracy became, in effect, a princedom in Rome. Before his appointment with the backing of the patricians, Appius had gained notoriety as a cruel persecutor of the plebs; but after his appointment his conduct was such as to make him appear a partisan of the people. When the ten eventually wrote down the laws on ten tables, they set them before the public so that all citizens might discuss them, call attention to defects, and propose changes before the laws were ratified.

At this juncture Appius let it be known throughout the city that if two more tables were added to the ten, the codex would be complete, a project requiring the election of a new Decemvirate. The plebs, now believing that Appius was their friend, supported his proposal of electing ten new members of the Decemvirate for another year. The patricians, with Appius among the foremost, were, of course, eager to gain those positions of power. During the election campaign, however, Appius's pronouncements displayed such goodwill towards the plebs that his colleagues became suspicious of him. Reluctant to oppose him openly, they decided to do so by means of a stratagem: they authorized him to propose the future ten to the people, thinking he would have to observe the well-established convention in which the nominator never proposed himself. Appius, however, seizing the opportunity, placed his name at the head of the list, and after it, the names of nine of his partisans.

The retention of the ten for another year soon revealed to both the nobility and the people that they had been deceived. To intimidate the people and the senate, the ten now appointed 120 lictors instead of the usual twelve. Then the ten began to play up to the senate and abuse the plebs who, realizing their mistake, appealed to the nobles in the hope of regaining a breath of liberty, but to no avail. At the end of the second year the two additional tables of laws were ready, but not yet published. With this pretext for continuing their magistracy, the ten now responded to opposition with violence, confiscating the property of opponents and turning it over to partisans of Appius and his colleagues.

At this time the Sabines and the Volsci started to make war against the Romans, which demonstrated to the ten the weakness of their position, for no adequate preparations for war could be made without the senate. And if the senate were summoned, the ten feared they would lose their position altogether. The external threat drove them to adopt the latter course, and the senate resolved to mobilize for war. In the course of the war the ten were forced to relinquish their power, and the institutions of tribunes and consuls were reinstated.

For Machiavelli, there are important lessons to be learned from this experience. The people and the nobility had originally agreed to appoint the ten because each party believed it would gain real advantages from it. The people believed they would get rid of the consuls, and the patricians believed they would rid themselves of the tribunes. The people, wholly deceived by Appius's demagoguery, lent him support to put down the nobility. But, says Machiavelli, when a people throws its weight behind a strong man simply because he appears to be down on those whom they detest, that is a big mistake that will always lead to tyranny. For the general pattern revealed by historical experience is this: the strong man, with the support of the populace, will first intimidate and weaken the upper class; and when he has made them compliant, he will turn against the people, afflicting and enslaving them.

In cold, analytical terms Machiavelli observes that Appius might have prolonged his tyranny had he acted more wisely. His major error was to try to hold on to his power by making an enemy of the people, who had given him the power, and who were able to maintain him in it. As for the nobility, it seems axiomatic that though the nobles desire to tyrannize, those left out of the tyrannical regime always become enemies of the tyrant. Hence, Appius, in turning against the populace and courting the nobles, made an obvious mistake. It follows, for Machiavelli, 'that those who have the public as a whole for their friends and the great ones for their enemies are the more secure, in that their violence is backed by a greater force than it is in the case of those who have the populace for an enemy and the nobility for a friend' (*Discourses*, I, 40).

The Multitude

Like Aristotle, Machiavelli proposes that the multitude can be wiser than a prince – not the 'masses' as an agglomeration of disconnected and undisciplined atoms, but rather the people, guided and regulated by laws. When the multitude is thus guided, says Machiavelli, they are more knowing and more constant than kings, and in them will be found more goodness than in kings. The people no less than a prince can make mistakes; but when the populace is in power and well ordered by laws and institutions, it is stable and prudent. If one asks whether one is better than the other, it is unquestionably the populace that is better owing to the greater respect it has for the laws. Reflecting on the role of the Roman populace Machiavelli observes that for 400 years they stalwartly opposed the very notion of monarchy, dedicating themselves to the common good of the republic. The populace had proved itself to be more prudent, more constant, and of sounder judgment than any prince. It is with good reason that the *vox populi* is likened to the voice of God. Public opinion is remarkably accurate in its perceptions and prognoses.

Contrary to Plato's view of a gullible multitude easily swayed by a sophisticated demagogue, Machiavelli asserts that when two speakers of equal skill are heard advocating alternative options, it is very rare that the populace fails to adopt the better view, or fails to grasp the truth of what it hears. In the election of officials too, the people make better choices than a prince, since a prince is more likely to be swayed by selfish interests to appoint to office a notoriously corrupt individual. This is the context in which Machiavelli employs the striking phrase cited in the opening paragraphs of this chapter: 'One finds that cities in which the *populace is the prince*, in a very short time extend vastly their dominions much more than do those which have always been under a prince; as Rome did after the expulsion of the kings, and Athens after it was free of Pisistratus' (*Discourses*, I, 58, italics added).

Government by the populace, Machiavelli avers, is better than government by princes, for in goodness and in glory the populace is far superior. History has shown that both princely and republican forms of government have been long-lived, and that what was essential for the enduring quality of both forms was their regulation by laws. If, however, it is a question of a prince or a populace subservient to the laws, more virtue will be found in the populace than in the prince; and if it is a question of either of them being released from the guidance and control of laws, it will be found that the populace makes fewer errors than a prince and, indeed, errors of lesser moment and much easier to correct. For when a good man can obtain a hearing, even a licentious and turbulent populace can be calmed and prompted to conduct itself properly. No one, however, can reason with a bad prince, for whom the only remedy is the sword.

Nothing in what Machiavelli has to say here should be construed as a contradiction of what he had to say in his analysis of the ten. He underscores that when the tensions and strife between the upper classes and the people reach crisis proportions, and the people make a mistake, it is not the people's actions that are to be feared, but rather what will follow, for out of the tumult a tyrant will surely emerge. Since the people are the vast majority of the society, their well-being and fortunes can hardly be opposed to the common good. If the masses act brutally, then, it is directed against those whom they suspect of conspiring against the common good; when a prince acts brutally, however, it is often against those whom he suspects of conspiring against his own good.

Characteristically relying on the experience of history, Machiavelli insists that states never increase in power and wealth unless they are free of both internal tyranny and external domination. Hence, Athens attained its greatness in the space of a hundred years after it had liberated itself from the tyranny of Pisistratus; and even more striking was the greatness Rome achieved after freeing itself from its kings. The reason is clear:

> It is not the well-being of individuals that makes cities great, but the well-being of the community; and it is beyond question that it is only in republics that the common good is looked to properly in that all that promotes it is carried out; and however much this or that private person may be the loser on this account, there are so many who benefit thereby that the common good can be realized in spite of those few who suffer in consequence. (*Discourses*, II, 2)

It is noteworthy that, contrary to the opinion prevalent at the time, Machiavelli's conception of a republic was not that of a small city-state, but rather that of an open society allowing for the growth of a large population. There are two ways of acquiring a large population – by force or by friendliness – and Machiavelli advises, of course, that it be done by friendliness as 'when the road is kept open and safe for foreigners who propose to come and dwell there so that everybody is glad to do so' (*Discourses*, II, 2–3).

International Relations, Revolution, and Other Issues

Like Hobbes after him, Machiavelli recognized that the international arena is a 'state of nature.' No state can expect to remain forever in the peaceful enjoyment of its liberties; for though it may refrain from aggressing against other states, it will be harassed and attacked by them. And when thus provoked, there will arise in it the need for war. The right way to make a republic great, therefore, is to attend with the utmost care to the military training of its citizens, and to give due consideration to the security and defence of the republic. To achieve this aim the republic should strive to make other states its allies, not its subjects. For if one learns well the lessons of the past, one sees that the greater the liberality one displays towards one's neighbours, and the more averse one is to seize their lands, the more readily will they submit if necessary. The only token of *imperium* exercised by the Romans, for example, was the imposition of certain conditions that, if they were observed, enabled the defeated people to retain their form of government, their culture, and their self-esteem. This policy contributed significantly to the growth of Rome's power. As a rule, the vanquished are more inclined to submit to the victor, the more humane and easy-going is the victor's treatment of them.

Where the internal structure of a state is concerned, republics that are so constituted as to make desirable renovations in accordance with original principles, are healthier and have a longer life. In the history of Rome the institutions that enabled the republic to return to its principles were the introduction of the tribunes and the laws that put a check on the ambition and arrogance of the patricians. Such institutions were essential for order and justice. As we reflect on history, we see that some social and political changes were accompanied by violence while others were not. What is the explanation for the fact that in the many revolutions of history involving a transition from tyranny to freedom or the other way about, some were attended by bloodshed and others were peaceful? Machiavelli's answer is simple and to the point: whether a revolutionary change in government will be peaceful or not depends on whether it is or is not brought about by violence. Violence begets violence. Those who in their defeat have experienced death and injury in their ranks will inevitably seek revenge. It is the desire for vengeance that leads to the violent, protracted struggles in which large numbers of human beings are killed and maimed. When a change in government is introduced by the common consent of the people, there is no reason why anyone should be harmed, except the head of the old order. That was the case in Rome with the expulsion of the Tarquins. In a republic it is highly unlikely that any strong men could seize supreme power and impose a tyranny unless it has become disordered by massive discontent. To avoid this dangerous state of affairs, a republic must adapt itself to changing conditions to ensure the continuing liberty and well-being of the populace.

Even the long-lived Roman republic did not last forever. For Machiavelli, there were two causes of its dissolution. The first was the continuing strife following the passage of the Agrarian Law, and the second was the prolongation of public office and military commands. Having already discussed the long-term effects of the Agrarian Law, we may confine our attention to the harm done to the republic by the granting of prolonged military commands to certain citizens. The first citizen to have his military command prolonged was Publius Philo. His consulate came to an end just as he was besieging the town of Paleopolis. The senate, believing he was on the verge of winning a victory, decided not to appoint a successor and made him proconsul. Although this decision was motivated by the public interest, it was this bad precedent that led ultimately to the destruction of the republic. As the armies went farther and farther afield, the prolongation of commands, appearing to be necessary, became a frequent phenomenon. This produced two undesirable results. First, only a small number of men acquired the experience of military command, and only a few acquired a famous reputation for it. Second, when such a citizen held his command for an extended period, he won the army over to his person and made it his partisan. Increasingly the soldiers ignored the authority of the senate and felt allegiance to the commander alone. This explains why Marius and Sulla were able to gain the support of their troops for actions contrary to the public good; and why Caesar was later able to aggrandize so much power to himself.

A most useful policy of a republic is one that keeps its citizens 'poor' – by which Machiavelli means not impoverished but possessing enough land to live on. Being poor in that sense barred no Roman citizen from any office or honour. When Minucius was consul and his army was surrounded on all sides by the Aequi, Rome was so afraid the army would be destroyed that it had recourse, in this emergency, to the appointment of a dictator. It was Lucius Quintius Cincinnatus, who was found on his small farm, ploughing with his own hands, to whom the appointment was given. When the messenger from the senate arrived to inform him of his appointment to the dictatorship, Cincinnatus put on his toga, travelled to Rome, mobilized an army, and went to the rescue of Minucius (*Discourses*, III, 25). Having defeated the enemy and relieved Minucius, Cincinnatus refused to let the army, which had allowed itself to be surrounded, share in the spoils.

Machiavelli's point, then, is that poor men could gain honour in Rome, and that their greatness of spirit, when in command of an army, rose above that of any prince. And when men like Cincinnatus returned to private life, they became humble, frugal, careful of their small properties, obedient to the laws, and respectful to the magistrates. When Machiavelli speaks of such men as 'poor,' he should be interpreted to mean what Aristotle meant by owners of 'moderate' property.

As noted earlier, Machiavelli proposed that the faults of peoples are due to their princes. The faults of a people governed by a prince are the result either of his negligence or of his being tainted with the same defects. Whether it is robbery, murder, or other evil deeds, it is not the wickedness of human nature, but the wickedness or failings of the prince that are the cause. It is important to note that although Machiavelli recognizes the self-seeking nature of human beings, he nevertheless understands that one's conduct has much to do with the kind of education one has received and the examples set by the leaders and notables of the society in question. Therein lies the central significance, for Machiavelli, of good laws and good leaders. Human beings may be self-seeking, but they are prone not merely to evil, but also to good. Which of these inclinations is brought out in human beings is largely contingent upon the way they are brought up and upon the nature of their associates. Hence, says Machiavelli, when it comes to choosing between candidates for government in a republic, citizens should look for those who are known 'to associate with seriously-minded persons, of good habits, and whom everybody esteems as prudent men. For nothing indicates more plainly what a man is than the company he keeps' (*Discourses*, III, 34).

As we conclude this survey of Machiavelli, we see clearly why he rooted his political philosophy in the study of history. If one wishes to foresee the range of consequences following from one's action, one needs to study the past, since everything that happens at any given time bears a genuine resemblance to what has happened before. The reason for this is that human beings have always had the same passions, and from the same passions very similar effects are produced. We also see that Machiavelli explicitly favoured republican and constitutional governments because they offer more freedom than other forms. Given his commitment to liberty as the highest human value, we can safely say that what Machiavelli has imparted to us, far from being an amoral pragmatism, is a highly realistic theory that helps us to gain clarity where the moral consequences of our political actions are concerned.

Chapter Four

Thomas Hobbes

In Hobbes's earliest statement of his political theory, *The Elements of Law*, he argued that the rights disputed by the Short Parliament were an inseparable part of the king's sovereignty. Political tension was high in the land, and this 'little treatise in English' was dated 9 May 1640, just four days after the parliament had been dissolved. *De Cive*, or *On Society*, published in Paris in 1642, is a revised and expanded Latin version of *The Elements of Law*, which reflects Hobbes's central and lifelong political and theoretical concerns with the rights of sovereignty and the obedience due from subjects.

Behemoth or the Long Parliament, completed in manuscript in 1668, when Hobbes was almost eighty years of age, is his final treatment of sovereignty and obedience. The biblical creature Behemoth appears in the book of Job, chapter 40, just before the famous passage about that frightening sea beast, Leviathan, 'King over all the children of pride' (Job 41:34). It is, of course, Yahweh and Yahweh alone who can control both beasts. Hobbes, as we shall see, employed Leviathan as a symbol of the mortal God under the immortal God that is essential for social peace and Behemoth as a symbol for rebellion and civil war. It requires one monster to subdue another: Leviathan is the only possible antidote to Behemoth.

Leviathan

The violence and bloodshed of the English civil war prompted Hobbes to reflect on this question: How may a society ensure a level of internal order that will enable its members to attend to their vital affairs and go about their business peacefully? The tumult, strife, and general insecurity that prevailed during that civil upheaval had made it painfully evident that social order cannot be taken for granted. Hobbes produced the *Leviathan* (1651)[1] to propose that there are definite preconditions for the establishment and maintenance of order. Let us follow his rigorously constructed argument, beginning with his discussion of the all-important concept of 'power.'

Power, for Hobbes, refers to an individual's present means to obtain some future apparent good. 'Natural powers,' such as the outstanding faculties of body and mind, and 'instrumental powers,' such as riches, reputation, and friends, become the means of obtaining more power than one already possesses. Power is generated whenever an individual is either loved or feared by many, who out of love or fear give that individual their support, assistance, or service. Indeed, the reputation alone, without the reality, of possessing certain qualities may suffice to produce the same result. The greatest human power emerges out of the combined powers of a multitude of individuals united by consent, as in a commonwealth. 'I put for a generall inclination of all mankind,' Hobbes writes, 'a perpetuall and restlesse desire of Power after power, that ceaseth onely in Death' (ch. 11, 70). How does Hobbes account for the restless desire for more and more power? Humans desire infinite increments of power not only for the good things power can bring, but also out of fear that the power they already have cannot be secured without acquiring more. The resulting competition for riches, honour, command, or other forms of power leads to contention, enmity, and war, as each competitor seeks to attain his object by supplanting, repelling, subduing, or even killing his rival.

It is Hobbes's basic premise that in nature human beings are so equal in their physical and mental capacities that though one individual may be stronger than another, no individual is so strong as to be able to claim for himself certain benefits that another cannot claim as well as he. For where bodily strength is concerned the weakest has sufficient strength to kill the strongest, either by stealth or by collaboration with others who face the same danger. And where mental faculties are concerned, Hobbes finds an even greater equality, since foresight and sound judgment are largely the fruit of experience, which all individuals can acquire if they devote equal time and energy to the things that concern them. Hobbes adds, sardonically, that what makes such equality unbelievable 'is but a vain conceit of one's owne wisdome, which almost all men think they have in a greater degree than the Vulgar' (ch. 13, 87).

From this natural equality there arises equality of hope in attaining our ends. Therefore, if any two individuals desire the same thing that nevertheless they cannot both have, they become enemies and in pursuit of their goal strive to subdue or destroy one another. In this natural condition of mankind, or 'state of nature,' the only reasonable way for an individual to secure himself in the face of such mutual distrust and vulnerability is to resort to force or wiles in order to master those who constitute a danger to him. That is simply what self-preservation requires. If dominion over others is necessary for one's preservation, it ought to be allowed him. In this state of nature, Hobbes maintains, human beings can take no pleasure in keeping company with others. On the contrary, they are always fearful of one another due to the three principal causes of quarrel: competition, diffidence, and glory. The first prompts individuals to invade for gain, the second for safety, and the third for reputation. Violence or the threat of violence is the result of all three causes of quarrel. For Hobbes, then, the natural condition of mankind is one in which there prevails a war of everyone against everyone. In his words: 'Hereby it is manifest, that during the time men live without a common Power to keep them all in awe, they are in that condition which is called Warre; and such a warre, as is of every man, against every man' (ch. 13, 88).

When Hobbes says that in the absence of a common power war prevails, his meaning is not that fighting is incessant. He explains that the notion of time is as relevant to war as it is to weather: 'For as the nature of Foule weather, lyeth not in a showre or two of rain; but in an inclination thereto of many dayes together: So the nature of War, consisteth not in actual fighting; but in the known disposition thereto, during all the time there is no assurance to the contrary. All other times is Peace' (ch. 13, 89). In the state of nature which is a state of war, all vitally necessary and worthwhile human activities are uncertain – industry, agriculture, commerce, science, art, and literature. Indeed, where there is no common power to keep us all in awe, there is no society. Worst of all, says Hobbes, there is the ever-present fear and danger of violent death; and the life of human beings is 'solitary, poore, nasty, brutish, and short' (ibid.).

Hobbes anticipates that some of his readers might question whether there ever was a time or condition of war such as the one he describes. He acknowledges that it never existed generally, over the entire world; but he insists that there were many places in the world of his time where people did in fact live in such a condition. The examples he gives of the native tribes of America are not good ones, since he ignores the role of the common power of each tribe in maintaining intratribal peace. There were, of course, tribal wars, but Hobbes should have considered that state of affairs as analogous, in his conceptual scheme, to the 'international arena,' which as we shall see is forever in a state of nature and war. However, in order to appreciate fully that Hobbes's 'war of each against all' is no mere hypothetical concept, we need to give a few examples of this condition from our own time.

The disintegration of the Soviet Union and the breakdown of central authority in Yugoslavia, to take only those two European cases, have led to massively destructive wars between national, ethnic, and tribal groups, resulting in a death toll of many thousands. And in Africa the tribal and civil wars in Sudan, Rwanda, Somalia, and other places have also yielded a large number of mutilated and dead victims. Throughout West Africa we have witnessed the withering away of central governments, the rise of tribal and regional domains, the growing pervasiveness of war. West Africa now appears to consist of a series of coastal trading ports, such as Freetown and Conakry, and an interior that due to violence, volatility, and disease is becoming intractable. Oil-rich Nigeria, whose population of roughly ninety million equals the population of all the other West African states combined, is becoming increasingly ungovernable. Ethnic and regional splits are deepening, a situation aggravated by an increase in the number of 'states' within it from nineteen to thirty and a doubling in the number of local government authorities. Add to this serious religious cleavages between Muslim fundamentalists and evangelical Christians, and we can readily see that the power to keep Nigeria from disintegrating is becoming progressively weaker. These examples from the last decade of the twentiethth century should convince us that what Hobbes proposes as the precondition of civil peace should be taken quite seriously as a proposition of trans-historical or lasting validity.

When Hobbes speaks of the state of nature as one in which every man is against every man, he means civil war, not literally a time when individuals are 'in a condition of warre one against another.' But Hobbes's state of nature also refers to the international arena, which is forever destined to remain in a 'condition of war.' In all times independent states are continually jealous of one another and in the 'posture of gladiators,' which is a 'posture of war.' In Hobbes's state of nature, the notions of right and wrong, just and unjust, therefore have no place, for morality and justice presuppose a common power to fear. Where there is no common power, there is no law; and where there is no law, there is no injustice. Justice and injustice are qualities that emerge in society, not in the state of nature where the only cardinal virtues are force and fraud. This is the 'ill condition' that human beings by mere nature are actually placed in. The possibility exists, however, of coming out of that ill condition, a possibility resting partly on passions and partly on reason. The passions that incline us to seek peace are a fear of death and a desire for all such things as contribute to our well-being. And reason suggests what needs to be done to establish the conditions of peace.

In Hobbes's state of nature or 'natural condition of mankind,' it is the natural right of every individual to use his own power for self-preservation; and it is a general, natural law, discovered by reason, that an individual is forbidden to do what is destructive of his own life. Every individual has a right to employ any and every means – including the body of another – of preserving his life against his enemies. Given this natural right, there can be no security for any individual. A general rule of reason follows that if individuals want security, they ought to seek peace. From this first and fundamental law of nature a second law is derived: that an individual be willing – so long as others are too – to lay down his right to all things for the sake of peace, and rest content with as much liberty against others as he would allow others against himself. For so long as every individual retains the right to do anything he likes, every individual remains in the condition of war. If others will not forfeit this right, there is no reason for anyone to divest himself of his, for if he were to do so he would thereby 'expose himself to prey, (which no man is bound to do) rather than to dispose himself to peace. This is that Law of the Gospell; *Whatsoever you require that others should do to you, that do ye to them*' (ch. 14, 92).

Hobbes next distinguishes between simply renouncing a right, which is tantamount to not caring who will benefit from it, and transferring a right, when one intends the benefit thereof to redound to a certain person or persons. The point Hobbes wants to underscore is that once one has voluntarily abandoned one's right and transferred it to another, one is obliged to do nothing to hinder its use, such hindrance being injustice and injury. A person transfers a right by making a declaration to that effect with words and actions, which become the bonds by which he is bound and obliged. These bonds derive their binding power not from the words and actions themselves – for a man's word is easily broken – but from the fear of some severe consequence upon failure to fulfil one's obligation. When one transfers a right, it is in exchange for another right reciprocally transferred to himself, or for some good he hopes to gain thereby. And as there can be no security in the state of nature, the end for which the transferring of a right takes place is nothing other than the security of an individual's person and the means of preserving his life. Such mutual transferring of right is called a contract or covenant.

If in such a contract neither of the parties performs presently, but trusts one another, this is the condition of mere nature, which is a condition of war of everyone against everyone. The contract is therefore void. If, however, the contract is made where a common power exists with the right and force to compel the fulfilment of its terms, the contract is valid and binding. In transferring to the common power the right to govern, we also transfer the means to govern: we give that person the right to levy taxes for the maintenance of soldiers and to appoint magistrates for the administration of justice.

For Hobbes, as we have seen, in order for justice or injustice to have any reality there must exist a common coercive power capable of compelling individuals to fulfil the terms of their covenants. The existence of such a power makes it possible to instill fear in the contracting parties that the punishment will be greater than the benefit they expect from the breach of their agreement. Hobbes briefly considers the view of the nihilist fool who says in his heart that there is no such thing as justice; one may keep or not keep contracts according to one's interest. In an argument reminiscent of that used by Callicles against Socrates, Hobbes's nihilist fool (who also says in his heart there is no God) implies that injustice may be reasonable when it conduces to one's own benefit. Rejecting this reasoning as specious and false, Hobbes shows that if everyone acted in accordance with the nihilist's view, it would lead right back to a war of each against all. Only the fear of the common power can prevent the descent into the state of nature and war.

We have seen that for Hobbes all human beings are equal in the condition of nature. Inequality emerges with the common power and the civil laws. If, however, nature has made human beings equal, human equality is to be acknowledged in civil society. Hobbes therefore posits as a 'Law of Nature' that as individuals enter the condition of peace, everyone acknowledge the other as his equal; and no one reserve to himself any right that he is not content to have all others reserve for themselves. It is noteworthy that in this context (ch. 15) Hobbes speaks of a Law of Nature that he calls 'compleasance,' that is, 'that everyman strive to accommodate himselfe to the rest' (106). These are individuals, Hobbes observes, who, owing to the asperity of their nature, strive to retain things which to themselves are superfluous, but to others necessary; if such individuals cannot be corrected, they should be cast out of society.

Why? Because their conduct creates a fertile soil for civil war. In Hobbes's words: 'For seeing every man, not only by Right, but also by necessity of Nature, is supposed to endeavour all he can, to obtain that which is necessary for his conservation; He that shall oppose himselfe against it, for things superfluous, is guilty of the warre that thereupon is to follow; and therefore doth that, which is contrary to the fundamentall Law of Nature, which commandeth *to seek Peace*' (ch. 15, 106).

In the making of peace, those who try to take for themselves things they would not grant to others act contrary to the Law of Nature commanding the acknowledgment of natural equality. The violators of this law are arrogant, says Hobbes, and he cites the Greeks who called the violation of this law *pleonexia*: a desire for more than one's share. The nature of human equality also commands that such things as cannot be divided be enjoyed in common without stint, if the quantity of the thing permits, otherwise in proportion to the number of individuals who have the right. In all, Hobbes proposes nineteen such laws of nature that dictate peace and indicate the means of preserving a multitude of human beings in civil society. The essence of these laws, says Hobbes, may be summed up in a variation on the Golden Rule: '*Do not that to another which thou wouldest not have done to thy selfe*' (ch. 15, 109).

For Hobbes, the knowledge or science of these laws is the only true moral philosophy; for moral philosophy is nothing but the knowledge of what is good and evil in the conservation of society. Good and evil are terms signifying appetites and aversions that vary according to the diverse human customs and doctrines. Humans differ not only in their judgment of what is pleasant and unpleasant to their senses, but also what is reasonable and unreasonable with respect to common life. Such differences of judgment are the ultimate source of controversies, disputes, and finally war. So long, therefore, as private appetite is the sole criterion of good and evil, humanity remains in the state of mere nature, which is a state of war. It follows that all have to agree that peace is good; and that practising the moral virtues, which are the Laws of Nature – for example, justice, equity, gratitude, modesty, mercy – are, together with the establishment of the common power, the means of achieving peace.

Preparing himself for a fuller discussion of the nature of a commonwealth, Hobbes proposes that a multitude of individuals can be made one 'Person,' so to speak, when they are represented by one person, and when the representative is agreed to by every individual of the multitude *in particular*. It is the unity of the representer, Hobbes insists, not of the represented, that makes the person one. Hobbes's point here, which acquires enormous significance in the unfolding of his argument, is that because the multitude is in reality not one, but many, they cannot constitute a corporate entity from which the authority of the common power is derived. Instead, the multitude may only be regarded as the many individual authors of everything their representative says or does in their name. It is every individual, *in particular* – not the 'general will' of the multitude, as Rousseau will later argue – who gives the representative authority. Finally, Hobbes lays down a majoritarian criterion when the representative is an assembly: the decision of the greater number must be considered the decision of them all.

Of Commonwealth

For Hobbes, then, the miserable and destructive condition of civil war is a necessary consequence of the natural passions of human beings when no visible power is present to keep them in awe and bind them by fear of punishment to the performance of their contractual obligations. And although Hobbes has deduced from his axiom of human equality certain laws of nature enjoining justice, equity, modesty, and mercy – summed up in the Golden Rule – he recognizes that these laws by themselves, without a common power to fear, are helpless to bring the state of war to an end. For 'Covenants, without the Sword, are but Words, and of no strength to secure a man at all' (ch. 17, 117). If anyone still questions the validity of this proposition, believing that a multitude of human beings would observe justice and the other laws of nature without a common power to hold them in awe, he might as well believe that all humanity would do the same. Hobbes rightly argues that a rejection of his proposition implies that there is no need for civil government or commonwealth at all, and that peace may be achieved without subjection. Aware that other creatures such as bees and ants live in societies without any coercive power, Hobbes explains why the human species cannot do the same:

1 Human beings compete for honour and dignity, while other creatures do not; consequently there arises among human beings envy and hatred and, ultimately, war.
2 Among other creatures the common and the private good coincide. Though each individual by nature is inclined to satisfy its own needs, this redounds to the benefit of all. Humans, in contrast, derive their

joy from comparing themselves with others, relishing nothing more than feeling themselves eminent.

3 Other creatures, lacking the faculty of reason, see no fault in the administration of their common affairs. Among humans, however, there are always many who think themselves wiser and better than the rest where governing the public is concerned. Those who think themselves better strive to change and innovate, pulling this way and that, and thus bring society into distraction and civil war.

4 Though other creatures possess the ability to make known to one another their desires, they lack the art of words with which some men can distort meanings, presenting the good as if it were evil, and evil as if it were good. They employ rhetoric to stir the emotions of many others, causing discontent among them and troubling their peace.

5 Other creatures, as long as they are left at ease, are not offended by their fellows. The human individual, in contrast, is often most troublesome when he is most at ease, for it is then that he loves to show his wisdom, seeking to control those who govern the commonwealth.

6 Finally, the mode of agreement of other creatures is natural, whereas that of humans is by covenant only. It is therefore not to be wondered at that something else besides covenant is required to make their agreement binding. This 'something else' is, of course, a common power to keep them in awe and to direct their actions to the common weal.

For Hobbes, there is only one way to establish a common power that will have the capacity to protect us from both foreign invaders and internal warfare: we must confer all our power and strength on one individual or assembly, thereby reducing all our wills to one will. In appointing one individual or assembly to represent us, each and every one of us acknowledges himself to be the author of whatever the representative shall decide in all matters that concern our common peace and safety. We thus submit our wills and judgments to the will of the representative. 'This is more,' writes Hobbes,

> than Consent, or Concord; it is a reall Unitie of them all, in one and the same Person, made by covenant of every man with every man, in such a manner, as if every man shall say to every man, *I authorize and give up my Right of Governing my selfe, to this Man, or to this Assembly of men, on this condition, that thou give up thy Right to him and Authorize all his actions in like manner.* This done, the Multitude so united in one Person, is called a Com-

mon-wealth, in latine Civitas. This is the Generation of the great LEVIA-
THAN, or rather (to speake more reverently) of that *Mortall God*, to which
we owe under the *Immortal God*, our peace and defence. For by this Author-
itie, given him by every particular man in the Common-wealth, he hath the
use of so much Power and Strength Conferred on him, that by terror
thereof, he is inabled to conforme the wills of them all, to peace at home,
and mutual ayd against their enemies abroad ...

   And he that carryeth this Person, is called Soveraigne, and said to have
Soveraigne Power, and every one besides, his Subject. (120–21)

We need to alert ourselves once again to a special feature of this for-
mulation: the authority conferred on the Leviathan by which he
becomes sovereign is conferred not by the multitude as a collectivity or
corporate entity, but by *every particular man*. This is fundamental in Hobbes's conception of the covenant. The right to represent the multitude
and act on its behalf is conferred upon one person or assembly by a covenant of every individual with every individual, and *not* between the
sovereign and any of the individuals. Hence, there can occur no breach
of covenant on the part of the sovereign. Every particular individual, by
his own voluntary act, has willed himself to become a subject. Therefore,
none of the sovereign's subjects, on any pretence of forfeiture, can be
freed from his subjection. That the sovereign has made no covenant with
his subjects beforehand is evident, Hobbes avers, because either he must
make it with the entire multitude, as one party to the covenant, or he
must make a multiplicity of covenants with every individual. But making it with the whole, as one party, is impossible because they are not yet
one person. And if we suppose that the sovereign has made as many
covenants as there are individuals in the multitude, those covenants,
after he has the sovereignty, are void, because 'what act soever can be
pretended by any one of them for breach thereof, is the act both of himselfe, and of all the rest, because done in the Person, and by the Right of
every one of them in particular' (ch. 18, 123).

   It is in that way – by means of a covenant solely of one individual
with another, but not of the sovereign with any of them – that the sovereign power is conferred by the consent of the people assembled. Therefore, according to Hobbes, they have voluntarily become subjects to a
monarch, and cannot, without his permission, reject monarchy and
return to the condition of a 'disunited Multitude.' The individual members of the multitude have, in effect, transferred their person to the monarch, and may not, therefore, transfer their person from him to another

person or assembly. The individuals who have thus transferred their person to the monarch are bound, every one to every one, to acknowledge that they are the author of all that he, who is already their sovereign, shall do and judge fit to be done. And if any one individual dissents from the sovereign's policy, that is the same as all the rest breaking the covenant with him, which is, for Hobbes, injustice. Moreover, if one of the covenantors attempts to depose his sovereign, and is killed or otherwise punished for the attempt, he is, for Hobbes, the author of his own punishment, since he has agreed that he and all the other covenantors are the author of all the sovereign shall do.

Hobbes further provides that if a majority has, by consenting voices, declared a sovereign, the minority must consent with the rest, or else be justly destroyed by the rest. Hobbes is so intent upon providing a solid foundation for the absolute and undivided sovereignty of the monarch that he can say, 'It is true that they that have the Soveraigne power, may commit Iniquity; but not Injustice, or Injury as the proper signification' (ch. 18, 124). Hobbes saw the chief cause of the civil war in the division of powers between the king, the lords, and the House of Commons. If the opinion that such a division is good had not prevailed in England, the people would never have been divided and fallen into the misery of civil strife. As for the objection that the condition of subjects is miserable, Hobbes replies that the pain suffered by subjects under a sovereign with unlimited power is nothing compared with the miseries and calamities of civil war, a condition in which dissolute, violent, and masterless men are subject neither to a common power nor to laws.

Indeed, for Hobbes, government in any form is better than none. Denying the reality of tyranny, Hobbes asserts that 'tyranny' is simply monarchy disliked, just as 'oligarchy' and 'anarchy' are terms, respectively, for aristocracy and democracy disliked. Hobbes sees no fundamental difference between the three forms of commonwealth where sovereignty is concerned. He prefers monarchy over the others because in monarchy, he believes, the private and the public interest are more nearly one. In denying that the absolute power of the sovereign can corrupt him, or turn him into a tyrant in the classical sense, Hobbes argues that 'the riches, power, and honour of a Monarch arise onely from the riches, strength and reputation of his Subjects. For no king can be rich, nor glorious, nor secure; whose subjects are either poore, or contemptible, or too weak through want, or dissention, to maintain a war against their enemies' (ch. 19, 131). Monarchy is superior to aristocracy and democracy because the resolutions of a monarch are subject to no other inconstancy than that of human nature. In assemblies there arises the additional inconstancy of number; for the absence of a few or the deliberate attendance of a few can make a big difference. It is an 'inconvenience,' Hobbes admits, that a sovereign can impoverish any subject in order to enrich a favourite or a flatterer. But the same can happen, he insists, where the sovereign power is an assembly. Furthermore, an assembly can not only become subject to evil counsel as can a monarch, it can also be seduced by clever orators, as is evident when assembly members become one another's flatterers, serving one another's covetousness and ambition. And whereas a monarch has only a few favourites who have no one else to advance but their own kin, an assembly has many favourites, and their kin are much more numerous.

Hobbes distinguishes, in chapter 20, a commonwealth by *acquisition*, where the sovereign power is acquired by force, from sovereignty by *institution*. In the latter people choose their sovereign out of fear of one another, while in the former out of fear of the sovereign himself. The rights of the sovereign are the same in both cases, Hobbes maintains. A commonwealth by acquisition refers to dominion acquired by conquest or victory in war. The victor acquires dominion when the vanquished, to avoid the danger of death, covenant each with the other, that so long as his life is spared the victor shall have the use of the vanquished at his pleasure. Following such a covenant, the vanquished becomes a subject or 'servant,' which Hobbes distinguishes from a captive or slave. Slaves have no obligation at all. They may justly break their bonds, escape from prison, kill or carry away their captor or master. It is not the victory, but the consent of the vanquished by his own covenant that gives the victor the right of dominion. Without thus consenting, the conquered has no obligation to submit to the conqueror; and the victor, on his part, has no obligation to spare the vanquished's life, unless he, the victor, has promised to do so. In a word, the rights and consequences of sovereignty by acquisition are the same as those in sovereignty by institution.

In chapter 20 Hobbes employs both reason and Scripture to argue that whether the sovereign power is placed in one man, as in a monarch, or in an assembly, as in aristocratic and democratic commonwealths, the sovereign power ought to be absolute. And those who fear the evil consequences of absolute power must come to recognize that the want of it, resulting in the war of every man against his neighbour, is far worse. A subject may, however, disobey his sovereign under certain circumstances.

When May a Subject Disobey His Sovereign?

A subject may defend himself even against those who lawfully want to injure him. If a sovereign commands a justly condemned individual to kill, wound, or mutilate himself, or to refrain from resisting those who intend to kill or harm him, or to deny himself food, water, air, medicine, or anything else without which he cannot live, that individual has the right to disobey. If a subject is interrogated by the sovereign or his agents concerning a crime allegedly committed by him, he is not obliged, without assurance of pardon, to accuse himself. No individual is bound by his covenant either to kill himself or any other person. If the sovereign commands a subject to undertake a dangerous or dishonourable mission, his obligation depends on the goal of the mission. Sovereignty was instituted to establish and maintain civil peace. If, therefore, disobedience prevents the goal, for which sovereignty was instituted, from being accomplished, there is no liberty to disobey; otherwise, there is.

Similarly, a subject commanded as a soldier to fight an enemy, though his sovereign has the right to punish refusal with death, may in some cases refuse without injustice. One example is when the soldier who has received the command finds a suitable substitute to take his place. But Hobbes also allows for natural timorousness. In the face of an upcoming battle and even in the battle itself, there are always those who run away or try to do so. When this is done not out of treachery, but out of fear, it is dishonourable but not unjust – unless the soldier in question has voluntarily enlisted or accepted conscription, in which case the excuse of a timorous nature loses its validity. Nor would this excuse be valid when the survival of the commonwealth is at stake, requiring at once the participation of all who are able to bear arms. In such a case everyone is obliged, for otherwise the institution of the commonwealth was in vain.

No subject has the liberty to resist the sword of the sovereign in defence of another subject, innocent or guilty, since such resistance deprives the sovereign of the means of protecting the commonwealth as a whole. Interestingly, however, Hobbes allows this liberty to those who have already resisted the sovereign power unjustly, or who have committed some capital crime. They have that liberty because they are now simply defending their lives, and defence is a fundamental liberty of the guilty as well as the innocent. And if, Hobbes writes, 'a man be held in prison, or bonds, or is not trusted with the liberty of his bodie; he cannot be understood to be bound by Covenant to subjection; and therefore may, if he can, make his escape by any means whatsoever' (ch. 21, 154).

In this regard, Hobbes's view is the precise opposite of the one defended by Plato in the *Crito*: obey the law even when your own life is at stake; disobey it only when your conscience is at issue.

Civil Laws

Law, in general, is command, not counsel. Civil law refers to the rules that the commonwealth has commanded the subject to obey, rules distinguishing right from wrong. For Hobbes, the Laws of Nature and the civil laws embody each other. What Hobbes has called 'Laws of Nature' (justice, equity, mercy, and other implications of the Golden Rule) are, properly speaking, not laws but moral qualities that dispose us to peace. In a state of nature there is no way to ensure that these qualities or virtues will be practised. It is therefore only when a commonwealth is established that these virtues actually become civil laws, because a sovereign power now exists that can compel men to obey them. Just civil laws must embody the moral principles of the 'Laws of Nature.' Civil law nevertheless abridges and restrains the natural liberty of the human being. Indeed, a primary aim of civil laws is to impose certain restraints, without which there can be no civil peace. Law was brought into the world to limit the natural liberty of individuals, so that instead of injuring one another they would engage in mutual aid and join together against a common enemy.

It is the sovereign power who ensures that the 'Laws of Nature' will become civil laws. Hobbes underscores that a commonwealth, as he conceives it, cannot justifiably make a civil law contrary to a natural law. It is, for example, certainly against the Law of Nature to punish an innocent individual. Suppose then, that a man has been accused of a capital crime, and having become aware of the malice and power of some personal enemy, and the frequent partiality and corruption of the judges, flees out of fear, but is apprehended, brought to trial, and exonerated. A judge nevertheless condemns him and confiscates his property. There 'is no place in the world,' Hobbes writes, '[in] which this can be an interpretation of a Law of Nature, or be made a Law by the Sentences of precedent Judges, that had done the same. For he that judged it first, judged unjustly; and no Injustice can be a pattern of Judgment to succeeding Judges' (ch. 26, 192). It must always be the intention of the sovereign legislator to adhere to the principle of equity. If, therefore, the words of the civil law do not fully authorize a just and equitable sentence, the judge should provide it from the principal Law of Nature, called equity. A good judge or interpreter of the civil laws is, first, one who has a firm grasp of that principal law, a grasp that depends on the goodness of one's own natural reason. A good judge is, second, one who disdains excess wealth, and who, third, divests himself of all those emotions that might impair his impartiality.

We have seen that the Laws of Nature are, for Hobbes, fundamental moral principles, eternal and universal, and recognized by human reason as essential for social peace, though a common power is required to ensure they will be obeyed. The Laws of Nature are also divine, being the commandments of God. *Positive*, or civil laws, are those that have been written down or otherwise conveyed to subjects by the sovereign power. Finally, there are what Hobbes calls 'Divine Positive Laws,' laws declared to be divine by those who claim authority from God to so declare them. But how, Hobbes asks, can one be sure that those who make such claims have actually received revelation? Sanctity may be feigned, and what are often called miracles are no more than the result of natural and ordinary causes. No one, Hobbes reminds us, can infallibly know by natural reason that another has had a supernatural revelation of God's will. The question therefore arises whether subjects are bound to obey so-called 'divine positive laws.' Hobbes offers an infallible criterion by which one may decide whether or not to obey. 'I conclude,' he writes, 'that in all things not contrary to the Moral Law, (that is to say, to the Law of Nature,) all Subjects are bound to obey that for divine Law, which is declared to be so, by the Lawes of the Commonwealth' (ch. 26, 199). In other words if the divine positive law in question is not against the Law of Nature, and a subject has undertaken in his covenant with others to obey it, he is obliged by his own voluntary act. He is obliged to obey, but not necessarily to believe. The beliefs of individuals, their interior cogitations, are not subject to the sovereign power.

It is clear that Hobbes is no nihilist or moral relativist. The 'Laws of Nature' are eternal and universal, and ignorance of them excuses no one because every individual who has attained the use of reason knows the Golden Rule. Hobbes despises those who espouse false principles of right and wrong, and who argue that justice is but a meaningless word, that whatever an individual can get by his own effort is his. Such nihilists from the time of Callicles and Thrasymachus have held up the practice of all nation-states as a good argument for individuals behaving likewise. The proponents of these false principles have observed that in all places and ages unjust actions have been authorized by those who have possessed the means of imposing their domination by force and oppressing the weak. It is quite common, Hobbes observes, that those who value themselves by the greatness of their wealth commit crimes and strive to escape punishment by corrupting public justice. Popular men, who have gained a reputation with the multitude, also violate the laws, hoping to overturn the legitimate authority; just as those men who have an inflated and false opinion of their own wisdom try, with their public discourse, to call into question the legitimacy of those who govern. Of these presumptuous men who become the first movers in the disturbance of the commonwealth leading to civil war, few are left alive long enough to see their schemes realized.

The 'Laws of Nature' are the criterion by which an individual may decide, in extraordinary circumstances, whether a specific positive law of his commonwealth is to be obeyed. If, for example, a man has been taken captive in war and is in the power of the enemy, the binding nature of his commonwealth's positive law ceases: he must obey the enemy or die. Such obedience to the enemy is no crime, for everyone is obliged – when the protection of his own commonwealth has failed him – to preserve his life by the best means available. Whenever an individual is faced with the threat of imminent death, and thus compelled to act against the positive law of his commonwealth, he is totally excused for the same reason: no positive law can oblige an individual to abandon his own preservation. If an individual is destitute of food or any of the other necessities of life, and cannot preserve himself except by breaking the law and taking food by stealth or force, he is also totally excused. Finally, Hobbes proposes that if an individual, high in civil authority, orders a subordinate to act against the law, he is excused – except when a third person is thereby injured. When the law is violated in such cases, both the author and the actor are criminals.

Punishment is also to be determined by its compatibility with the Laws of Nature. Punishment is inflicted by the public authority on those who have transgressed the positive laws, the aim being to incline subjects to obedience and, ultimately, to preserve the peace and integrity of the commonwealth. Again Hobbes stresses that the sovereign's policies are to be guided by the Laws of Nature. No good can come to a commonwealth by inflicting pain on innocent subjects. If, however, innocent people are harmed in a defensive war of the commonwealth, there is no breach of the Laws of Nature; just as there is no breach when innocent persons are harmed in the course of the sovereign's effort to suppress armed rebellion. In renouncing subjection, individuals relapse into the condition of war, and when those who so offend against the common power suffer harm, they suffer not as subjects, but as enemies: 'For *Rebellion*,' says Hobbes, 'is but warre renewed' (ch. 28, 219). Rebellion comes about due to certain internal weaknesses and diseases of the body politic.

Things That Weaken or Tend to Dissolve a Commonwealth

Like Machiavelli, Hobbes observed that a sovereign (prince) sometimes rests content with less power than is required for the internal peace and external defence of a commonwealth. When a sovereign belatedly recognizes his error and endeavours to exercise the power necessary, it is perceived as an unjust act, prompting large numbers of men to rebel. In denying themselves the power required, and in assuming that they can recover it as the need arises, sovereigns make a big mistake; for their internal opponents will surely be supported by foreign states that miss no opportunity to weaken the condition of their neighbours.

Another weakness of a commonwealth stems from the seditious doctrine that every private individual is the judge of what is good and evil. Proponents of this false doctrine, inclined to dispute the commands of the commonwealth, decide on the basis of their private opinions whether to obey or disobey. A related doctrine repugnant to civil society is that whatever an individual does against his conscience is sinful. This doctrine also rests on the presumption of making oneself the judge of good and evil. For Hobbes, it is true only in a state of nature that one sins by acting against one's conscience, there being no other rule to follow in that condition but one's own reason. But this cannot be true for an individual in a commonwealth, because the law is the public conscience – ideally embodying the Laws of Nature and moral virtues by which the individual has already covenanted to be guided. Given the diversity of private consciences in any society, the foundations of a commonwealth are bound to be undermined when no individual will obey the sovereign power beyond that which seems good in his own eyes. No less pernicious is the common notion that supernatural inspiration, not reason, is the way to attain faith and piety.

Especially repugnant to the nature of a commonwealth is the opinion that the sovereign power is subject to the civil laws. A sovereign, Hobbes reaffirms, is subject to the eternal and universal Laws of Nature; but the civil laws are those that the sovereign himself – that is, the commonwealth – has made. To say, then, the sovereign is subject to the civil laws is to say the sovereign is subject to himself. Hobbes is defending his principle that the sovereign power must be absolute and undivided, for a division of powers leads inevitably to faction, strife, and civil upheavals. It is this principle that Locke and Montesquieu will attack. The very division of powers that they came to regard as the key to the prevention of tyranny Hobbes had rejected as an internal defect leading inexorably to civil war and the dissolution of society. 'Tyranny,' for Hobbes, being merely monarchy disliked, he cannot help seeing an egregious error in the doctrine that sets the civil laws above the sovereign himself, thus setting above him a judge and a power to punish him, 'which is to make a new Soveraigne; and again for the same reason a third, to punish the second; and so continually without end, to the Confusion, and Dissolution of the common-wealth' (ch. 29, 224).

Hobbes believed that the recent historical experience of England supported his view; but he also invokes the historical evidence of antiquity. As a translator of Thucydides' *Peloponnesian War*, he knew very well that the cities of Greece were continually torn by the strife and sedition of the aristocratic and democratic factions, one party desiring to imitate the Lacedaemonians (Spartans), the other party, the Athenians. Indeed, Hobbes believed that one of the most frequent causes of rebellion against monarchy was the reading by young men of the histories of ancient Greece and Rome. From the reading of such books by Greek and Latin writers, men have learned, says Hobbes, that it is lawful and laudable to kill their kings, provided that before doing so they call him a tyrant. From the same books men who live under a monarch derive the opinion 'that the Subjects in a Popular Commonwealth enjoy liberty; but that in a Monarchy they are all slaves. I say, they that live under a Monarchy conceive such an opinion; not they that live under a Popular Government: for they find no such matter' (ch. 29, 226).

In these terms Hobbes expressly opposes the principles of his great predecessors – Aristotle and Machiavelli – that *mixed* government prevents tyranny (the unlawful usurpation of power) and promotes liberty. For Hobbes, mixed government is no government at all, but rather a division of the commonwealth into three independent warring factions that are bound to dissolve the commonwealth. The well-being of a people ruled by an aristocratic or democratic assembly comes not from the nature of those regimes, but from the obedience of the subjects.

Rejecting mixed government as an invitation to factional warfare, Hobbes proposes that the safety and well-being of a people can be assured by the undivided sovereign power if justice is administered equally to all classes of people, the rich and mighty as well as the poor and weak. This is equity, the cardinal Law of Nature to which the sovereign is as much subject as the humblest of his people. Guided by the Laws of Nature, the sovereign will make good laws, that is, laws that are necessary for the commonwealth.

A good law cannot be one that is for the benefit of the sovereign, but not for the people. The good of the sovereign and the people cannot be separated. Hobbes avers that it is the leaders of commotion and sedition, not the poor seduced people, who should be punished. In almost the precise language Machiavelli used to counsel the prince, Hobbes writes: 'To be severe to the People, is to punish that ignorance, which may in great part be imputed to the Soveraigne, whose fault it was, they were no better instructed' (ch. 30, 241). The best counsel is to be taken from the people themselves, 'who are best acquainted with their own wants, and ought therefore, when they demand nothing in derogation of the essential Rights of Soveraignty, to be diligently taken notice of' (243). And when by attending diligently to the needs of the people the sovereign himself is popular, 'that is, reverenced and beloved of his people, there is no danger at all from the Popularity of a Subject' (244). In thus closing part II, 'Of Commonwealth,' Hobbes expresses the hope that his writings will fall into the hands of a sovereign who will know how to translate Hobbes's theory into the 'utility of practice' (254).

Of a Christian Commonwealth

Hobbes's primary aim in part III of the *Leviathan* is to reaffirm the principles laid down in the earlier parts, and to apply them to a Christian commonwealth. His method is a rational-critical analysis of Scripture, and in employing that method he shows himself to be among the most brilliant pioneers in biblical criticism. In parts I and II it was Hobbes's intention to derive the rights of sovereign power solely from human nature and historical experience. There he also sought to demonstrate, however, that the Laws of Nature, or moral virtues, were the Natural Word of God, as it were, epitomized in the Golden Rule. Even in the state of nature and war human beings know that there would be peace among them if they followed that rule; but they soon come to realize that there is only one way to bring the war of each against all to an end, and to ensure that men will conduct themselves according to the natural laws of justice and equity. They therefore covenant with one another to give up the right of governing themselves and to transfer that right to a sovereign, common power.

As we have seen, the term 'sovereign' means, for Hobbes, that the person or assembly authorized to represent and protect us is supreme in any form of commonwealth, the power of the sovereign being absolute and undivided. What does this imply for the relation of church and state? In Britain at the time the issue was still alive as to whether a Christian monarch was subordinate to the Pope: Was a Christian king the supreme authority in his commonwealth, or was he subject to papal authority in ecclesiastical and theological matters, if not in temporal ones? Another issue, stemming from Protestant theology, was whether individuals such as the Puritans could justifiably disobey the sovereign on the grounds of conscience and religious principles. Hobbes's entire effort in his analysis of the principles of Christian politics is therefore aimed at demonstrating that the sovereign is literally sovereign in all matters including religion. Hobbes sets the stage for his meticulously constructed argument by proposing that the age of both miracles and prophets has ceased, leaving only Scripture and natural reason to provide the rules for Christian life. It is true, he grants, that Scripture does not stipulate what laws every Christian king shall enact in his own dominions; but Scripture does determine what laws he may *not* enact. Supernatural revelation having ceased, the will of God cannot be known except by that *natural reason* that had guided the multitude to the condition of peace and justice, through obedience to their lawful sovereign in all matters not contrary to the Laws of Nature.

Hobbes agrees that the histories and prophecies of the Hebrew Bible and the Gospels and Epistles of the New Testament have had one and the same purpose, to convert men to the obedience of God. But the question of what it means to obey God was much disputed among the diverse Christian sects. There being no general answer acceptable to all, Hobbes argues that the truly important question is this: By what authority are the Scriptures, or certain scriptural principles, to be made into law? Hobbes replies that insofar as scriptural principles 'differ not from the Laws of Nature, there is no doubt, but they are the Law of God, and carry their authority with them, legible to all men that have the use of natural reason: but this is no other Authority, than that of all other Moral Doctrine consonant to Reason; the Dictates whereof are Laws, not *made*, but *Eternall*' (ch. 33, 268). And, not surprisingly, it is the sovereign power, motivated and guided by the Laws of Nature, who shall determine what is to be given the force of law in religious as in secular matters. To defend this proposition, Hobbes had to provide an adequate rebuttal to the Catholic view, which denied that Christian monarchs or sovereign assemblies in Christian commonwealths possessed absolute power in their own territories, subject only to God.

The first point Hobbes makes in the unfolding of a long and complex argument is that in the Hebrew Bible the word 'kingdom,' in the phrase 'kingdom of God,' is meant literally, not metaphorically. 'Kingdom' refers to God's sovereign power over his Israelite subjects, acquired by their own consent. A covenant was first made between God and Abraham, by which he obliged himself and posterity to be subject to God's law; later the covenant was renewed with Moses (Exod. 19:5) where the Lord commands him to speak to the people and say that if they will obey God's voice and keep his covenant, they will become a 'peculiar' people to Him. Hobbes explains the meaning of 'peculiar' in this context: all the nations of the world are God's, but the Israelites or Jews are his in a *special manner*. All nations of the world are God's by reason of His power, but the Jews are His by reason of their own consent and covenant. So the 'kingdom of God' in the Hebrew Bible (the so-called Old Testament) is to be properly understood as God's civil sovereignty over a peculiar people, by pact.

The meaning of 'kingdom of God' is the same in the New Testament, Hobbes insists. He cites Luke 1:32–33, where the angel Gabriel says of Jesus, 'He shall be great, and be called the Son of the most High, and the Lord shall give him the throne of his father David; and he shall reign over the house of Jacob forever; and of his kingdom there shall be no end.' To support further his contention that the reference here is to a kingdom on Earth, Hobbes cites the texts in the Gospels according to which Jesus was executed as an enemy of Caesar: the title over the cross stated, 'Jesus of Nazareth, King of the Jews.' Likewise, in the book of Acts, 17:7, it is said of the disciples 'that they did all of them contrary to the decrees of Caesar, saying there was another king, one Jesus.' Hobbes thus argues that the 'kingdom of God' is a civil kingdom, which was first established with the obligation of the people of Israel to the laws Moses brought from Mount Sinai; and it is this worldly, civil kingdom, the restoration of which one prays for in the Lord's Prayer. Given this understanding of the concept 'kingdom,' Hobbes proceeds to clarify the concept of ecclesia or church.

Hobbes defines a church as *'a company of men professing Christian Religion, united in the person of one Soveraign; at whose command they ought to assemble, and without whose authority they ought not to assemble'* (ch. 39, 321). This formal definition suits Hobbes's purpose, emphasizing as it does that in all commonwealths assemblies are lawful or unlawful according to the authority of the civil sovereign. Hence, a church, which has assembled in any commonwealth without warrant from the civil sovereign, is an unlawful assembly. Moreover, there exists on Earth no such thing as a universal church that all Christians are obliged to obey, because there is no sovereign civil power in the international arena to which all commonwealths are subject. It follows that a Christian commonwealth and church are one, for though there are Christians in the dominions of many princes and states, every Christian is subject to the commonwealth of which he himself is a member.

The distinctions, temporal and spiritual, carry no weight in this regard, for there is no other government in this life but the temporal; and it is the governor of both the state and the church that rightfully decides whether the teaching of any doctrine to his subjects is lawful or not. The governor must be one, for otherwise there will inevitably follow faction and civil war between church and state and the diverse sects. In matters of religion as in all other matters, the authority of the sovereign power in any commonwealth must be grounded on the consent of the people and their promise to obey him. Hobbes provides abundant scriptural evidence to support this principle. After reviewing the narratives in Exodus and Numbers in some detail, Hobbes concludes that 'neither Aaron, nor the People, nor any Aristocracy of chief princes of the People, but Moses alone had next under God the Soveraignty over the Israelites: And not only in causes of Civill Policy, but also of Religion' (ch. 40, 326). And in a much later era, when in response to the Philistine menace the people came to Samuel saying, 'Make us a king to judge us, like all the nations,' (1 Sam. 8:5–20), the entire government of civil affairs was placed in the hands of King Saul. For Hobbes, then, there can be no doubt that 'from the first institution of God's Kingdome, to the Captivity, the Supremacy of Religion, was in the same hand with that of the Civill Soveraignty; and the Priests office after the election of Saul, was not Magisteriall, but Ministeriall' (ch. 40, 329).

Turning to the ecclesiastical power in Christendom, and basing himself on the New Testament, Hobbes argues that the kingdom of Christ is not of this world; and that his ministers, unless they are also princes, can require no obedience in Christ's name. For if Christ, the supreme king, has no regal power in this world, by what authority can his officers require obedience? This means that the Pope of Rome is certainly no sovereign with coercive powers, and that the ecclesiastical power of the Pope is simply the power to teach – to proclaim the kingdom of Christ, and to persuade men to submit themselves to it. Like all ministers of the

Gospel, the Pope, too, teaches those who have submitted what they are to do, in order to be received into the kingdom of God, when it comes. All ministers of the Gospel are teachers, not commanders, and their precepts are counsel, not laws.

The question arose whether the Pope, or any other minister of the church, had the power to excommunicate. It followed from Hobbes's premises that he who believes Jesus to be Christ is free from all dangers of excommunication. The power to excommunicate cannot be extended beyond the end for which the apostles and pastors of the church received their commission from Christ, which is not to rule and command, but to teach and guide men in the way of salvation in the world to come. Excommunication, then, when it is done without the authority of the sovereign civil power, is without effect and ought not to be feared. The civil sovereign is the supreme pastor, and it is from him that all ecclesiastical powers are derived. All pastors are but his ministers in quite the same way as 'Magistrates of towns, Judges in courts of Justice, and Commanders of Armies, are all but ministers of him that is the Magistrate of the whole Common-wealth, Judge of all Causes, and Commander of the whole Militia, which is alwaies the Civill Soveraign' (ch. 42, 373). The civil sovereign, if a Christian, is head of the church in his own dominion. If it pleases Christian sovereigns, they may turn over the supervision of their subjects, in matters of religion, to the Pope; 'but then the pope is in that point Subordinate to them [to Christian sovereigns], and exercises that Charge in another's Dominion *Iure Civili*, in the Right of the Civill Soveraign; not *Iure Divino*, in God's Right; and may therefore be discharged of that Office, when the Soveraign for the good of his Subjects shall think it necessary' (ch. 42, 378). In response, therefore, to Cardinal Bellarmines's question – Which is the best government of the church? – Hobbes replies that outside the Pope's own dominions he has no say in such matters: 'For in all other Common-wealths his Power (if hee have any at all) is that of the Schoolmaster onely' (379).

All that is necessary for salvation, Hobbes avers, is faith in Christ and obedience to the laws. Which laws? Are they the laws given to the Jews by the hand of Moses, the commandments of God? If so, why are Christians not taught to obey them? And if not those laws, then what others are there? 'For our Saviour Christ,' Hobbes replies,

hath not given us new Laws, but Counsell to observe those wee are subject to; that is to say, the Laws of Nature, and the laws of our several

Soveraigns: Nor did he make any new laws to the Jews in his Sermon on
the Mount, but merely expounded the Laws of Moses, to which they were
subject before. The Laws of God therefore are none but the Laws of Nature,
whereof the principall is, that we should not violate our Faith, that is, a
commandment to obey our civill soveraigns, which we constituted over us,
by mutual pact with one another. (ch. 43, 404)

There is no inconsistency in a Christian's obeying God *and* the civil
sovereign. For what is to be understood throughout in Hobbes's argument is that the sovereign's civil laws embody the Laws of Nature,
which are the Laws of God. That is the reason why a Christian owes
obedience even to a non-Christian, civil sovereign; for disobedience is a
sin against the Laws of Nature, which are synonymous with the Laws of
God; and disobedience is also a rejection of the counsel of the apostles
who admonished all Christians to obey their princes.

Of the Kingdome of Darknesse

In the fourth and final part of the *Leviathan*, Hobbes continues his critical
analysis of the Bible to demonstrate that certain dark and erroneous
doctrines have emerged from a misinterpretation of Scripture, and that
such doctrines tend to dominate men's minds, extinguishing in them the
light of both Nature and the Gospel. The greatest abuse of Scripture
leading to 'spiritual darkness' is the view that the kingdom of God,
mentioned so often in the Scriptures, is the present church, the great
mass of Christians living or dead, who will rise again on the last day.
This was the view with which the Catholic Church had set forth the
claim that the Pope was the one and only sovereign in Christendom. In
his rebuttal of this view Hobbes restates his thesis that the kingdom of
God was first instituted by Moses over the Jews only; that the kingdom
afterwards ceased with the election of Saul, when the people demanded
a king like that of other nations; and that though this had God's consent,
it meant, effectively, that in their temporal affairs the people were no
longer ruled by the priests. After that event, then, there was no other
kingdom of God on Earth, except in the obvious sense of God being the
king of all creation 'by his infinite power.' And though the prophets
promised that God's government on Earth will be restored, that has
not yet occurred, so we are not now under any other kings by covenant
but our civil sovereigns.

From the gross error of regarding the present church as the kingdom of God came the distinction between civil and canon law: the civil law being the authority of sovereigns in their own commonwealths, and the canon law the authority of the Pope in the same commonwealths. At first these canons were in the nature of counsel voluntarily received by Christian princes; but as the power of the Pope increased, canons became commands as the princes themselves passed them into laws, to avoid the greater troubles which the people, blinded by false doctrine, might be led into. Hence, there prevailed an ironic state of affairs: in all commonwealths in which the Pope's ecclesiastical power was established, Jews, Muslims, and pagans were tolerated where their religion was concerned, so long as they offended not against the civil power, while non-Catholic Christians were persecuted.

Hobbes also rejects and ridicules the church's turning of consecration into a vain and impious conjuring trick. Strongly committed to both rationality and a respect for sensory experience, Hobbes calls it a 'conjuration' when the priests would have people believe a change of nature contrary to the experience of the senses. Instead of consecrating the bread and wine to God's peculiar service in the sacrament of the Lord's Supper,

> (which is but a separation of it from common use, to signifie, that is, to put men in mind of their Redemption, by the passion of Christ, whose body was broken, and blood shed upon the Crosse for our transgressions,) [the priest] pretends, that by saying of the words of our Saviour, *This is my Body*, and *This is my Blood*, the nature of Bread is no more there, but his very Body; notwithstanding there appeareth not to the Sight, or other Sense of the Receiver, any thing that appeared not before the Consecration. (ch. 44, 422)

The priest, becoming an enchanter of sorts, thus turns words into a charm and bread into a man, 'nay more; into a God; and require[s] men to worship it, as if it were our Saviour himself present God and Man, and thereby to commit most grosse Idolatry' (423).

In general, Hobbes finds repugnant all notions of the devil, of demons, of purgatory, of literal exorcism, and other such fantasies that originated not in the Hebrew Bible but in Hellenistic and other polytheistic religions. As an extraordinarily well educated man committed to a rational and empirical approach to knowledge, Hobbes also recognized the Hellenistic origin of the doctrine of the eternity of separated souls, on which the belief in purgatory is based. 'For supposing Eternall Life by Grace onely,' he writes, 'there is no Life, but the Life of the Body; and no Immortality till the Resurrection' (ch. 44, 433). Other vestiges of polytheism, such as the worship of images, fetishes, saints, and relics practised in the Church of Rome, Hobbes regarded as idolatry pure and simple. Such beliefs and practices were partly deposited in early Christianity with the first conversion of the Gentiles, and afterwards 'countenanced, and confirmed, and augmented by the Bishops of Rome' (ch. 45, 453). So one of Hobbes's targets is Roman Catholicism, which has imported into men's minds a host of spiritually dark notions, and which has also challenged the sovereignty of the Christian prince in his own commonwealth.

Hobbes's other target is Aristotle's *Politics*. For Aristotle, as we have seen, the experience of history left no doubt that tyranny and oligarchy were realities and not mere epithets hurled at regimes disliked. Aristotle recognized that in addition to the structural prerequisites of a well-ordered commonwealth, it is not men who should govern, but the laws. For Hobbes, however, this is a hopelessly naïve notion. For what individual, he asks, who possesses his senses believes the 'Law can hurt him; that is, Words, and paper, without the Hands and Swords of Men?' – as if Aristotle had failed to realize that the rule of law presupposes a common power that inspires awe in the multitude. Hobbes thus deliberately refuses to see Aristotle's point: that it is only by means of law and, naturally, the material means of enforcing it, that the power of the prince can be defined and kept from becoming arbitrary. For Hobbes, however, there is no such thing as non-arbitrary government:

> That which offendeth the People, is no other thing, but that they are governed, not as every one of them would himselfe, but as the Publique Representant, be it one Man, or an Assembly of men thinks fit; that is, by an Arbitrary government: for which they give evill names to their Superiors; never knowing (till perhaps a little after a Civill Warre) that without such Arbitrary government, such Warre must be Perpetuall; and that it is Men and Arms, not Words and Promises, that make the Force and Power of the Laws. (ch. 46, 471)

This is the note on which Hobbes ends his discourse on the mutual relation between civil peace and obedience to authority. And as we proceed to review the political thought of subsequent thinkers, we shall give special attention to the question of whether civil peace and the protection of subjects requires arbitrary government, as Hobbes claimed.

Epilogue: Hobbes and Democracy

Individual members of the original multitude recognized that they had to covenant with one another to institute a common power in order to bring the state of war to an end. This fact suggests that, far from being totally disunited, they had risen to a certain level of organization. If every individual in that multitude covenanted with every other individual, that necessarily implies they were able, at least temporarily, to free themselves from the insecurity of the war of each against all. They were able to declare a truce, so to speak, and affirm their *disinclination* to fight for the duration of the covenanting. A careful reading of the *Leviathan* and Hobbes's other writings makes it clear that Hobbes's fundamental doctrine – that sovereignty must be absolute and undivided – applies not only to monarchy, but to aristocracy and democracy as well. And it is from Hobbes's earliest work, *The Elements of Law*,[2] that we gain the greatest clarity concerning the democratic option of the original multitude.

In *The Elements of Law*, Hobbes states that of the three types of government, 'the first in order of time ... is democracy, and it must be so of necessity, because an aristocracy and a monarchy, require nominations of persons agreed upon.' A democracy exists 'where the votes of the major part involve the votes of the rest' (*EL*, II, 2, 1). When a group of individuals covenant together to be bound by majority decisions, we have the creation of a commonwealth in which the people possess the sovereign power. If the people continue in this condition, they remain a democracy; but if, for any reason, they find this unsatisfactory, they can choose an individual or assembly to take over the responsibility of ruling them. Evidently, that is what Hobbes imagined in the *Leviathan*, where he posits that the people transferred their sovereignty to a monarch or aristocratic assembly. Hobbes there assumed that *if* the people have retained no method of making their will known, the transfer of sovereignty is to be considered as having been made in perpetuity.

In *The Elements of Law*, however, Hobbes specifies the mechanism by which the multitude would continue as a democracy, if they so wished. The original democracy need not have forfeited all authority once and for all. If the people have prearranged to meet again in order to choose a successor to the leader whom they had first elected, they have not actually surrendered their sovereignty. 'For it is to be understood,' Hobbes writes, 'when a man receiveth anything from the authority of the people, he receiveth it not from the people his subjects, but the people his sovereign' (*EL*, II, 2, 9). The people, having thus retained their sovereignty, can go even further and recall the elected leader any time they see fit. Under popular sovereignty, the people 'reserve unto themselves the right of assembling at certain times and places limited and made known' (*EL*, II, 2, 10). We need to underscore the centrality for Hobbes of this provision: the criterion of whether the people have retained sovereignty is their agreement in advance upon a time and place of assembly to call the leader to account. This prior arrangement may sound like a merely formal or technical requirement; but if we think of it as a constitutional requirement, we have the rule of law, which from the time of the Greeks was considered an essential element of good government – though Hobbes, in the *Leviathan*, chides Aristotle for his insistence on it.

When Hobbes applies his doctrine of absolute sovereignty to democracy, he is right, since citizens owe obedience to their elected leaders for the duration of their terms of office. Minorities and dissenters also owe obedience; for if they disobey and/or organize resistance and rebellion, that is not only unjust, but also presents the danger to the society as a whole that it will revert to a state of civil war.

For Hobbes, therefore, sovereignty began with an original democracy, with the people; and sovereignty would remain with the people so long as they have not failed to arrange in advance a time and place of assembly to demand accountability from their elected leaders. Although the people thus entrust their sovereignty to their chosen leaders, the fact that the people will be voting again at an appointed time means that their pressure is continuously felt by the leaders, so that in a sense the people never disband or dissolve between elections. In these terms it may be said that though Hobbes was no democrat, he anticipated Rousseau in suggesting how popular sovereignty may be established and maintained.

Chapter Five

John Locke

To understand the chain of events in Britain from the outbreak of the civil war to the Glorious Revolution, it is necessary to analyse the structure of the parliament and the source of its conflict with Charles I. The parliamentary party consisted of two factions, the Presbyterians and the Independents. The former desired to preserve a state church but to abolish the episcopacy, while the latter, although agreeing on the matter of the episcopacy, insisted that each congregation should be free to choose its own religious doctrines without the interference of any central ecclesiastical government. The Presbyterians, being generally of a higher social class than the Independents, and also more moderate, were more conciliatory towards the king. They strove to weaken him just enough so that he would come to terms with them. The king, however, refused to abolish the episcopacy; and the military forces at his disposal were such that weakening or defeating him proved impossible until it was accomplished by Oliver Cromwell's New Model Army. Although the king's military resistance was broken, he still refused to come to terms, and the Presbyterians lost their preponderance in the parliamentary armies. The defence of constitutional government had thus thrown power into the hands of a minority that showed a total disregard for constitutional government.

Cromwell first dismissed about a hundred Presbyterian members from parliament, making it a Rump effectively subservient to him; and then, finally, he dismissed the parliament altogether. The government of England had become a military dictatorship, hated by a growing majority of the nation, but impossible to throw off so long as Cromwell's followers remained militarily dominant. With Cromwell's death, however, his son Richard ruled in his place, and power was slowly restored first to the Rump, and then to the Long Parliament and the restoration of the monarchy in the person of Charles II. He agreed to impose no taxes not approved by parliament, and he assented to the Habeas Corpus Act, which deprived the Crown of the power of arbitrary arrest. Although he occasionally got around the fiscal power of parliament through subsidies from Louis XIV, he conducted himself in the main as a constitutional monarch.

James II, however, a Catholic, managed to unite against himself the Anglicans and the Nonconformists, though he had tried to conciliate the latter by granting them tolerance in defiance of parliament. Foreign policy also contributed to the growing disaffection with the Stuarts who, to avoid fiscal dependence on parliament, aligned themselves first with Spain and then with France. The latter's expanding power caused English concern, while the revocation of the Edict of Nantes (the Edict that had granted tolerance to the Huguenots) roused bitter opposition to Louis XIV among English Protestants. Soon a majority of the English people wished to rid themselves of James II, but they intended to accomplish this without a return to civil war. As there was no constitutional way to depose James, there had to be a 'revolution,' but one that was quick, leaving no opportunity for violent conflict. The aim was to depose the present king, but to preserve the monarchy, not as a monarchy of divine right, but as one dependent upon the legislative power of the parliament. Through the combined efforts of the aristocracy and the large commercial interests, a constitutional monarchy was established without violence. This was the so-called 'Glorious Revolution.'

The new king, William, being Dutch, brought with him the commercial and theological wisdom for which his country was noted. In his reign the Bank of England was created and the national debt was made into a secure investment, no longer subject to repudiation by the monarch. And the Act of Toleration, though it left Catholics and Nonconformists subject to various forms of discrimination, put an end to actual persecution. This, then, was the general context in which Locke set forth his theory of government.

It is with good reason, as we have seen, that Thomas Hobbes is regarded as the most brilliant man of the seventeenth century to have written about politics in Britain. As a defence of absolute sovereignty, the *Leviathan* remains the outstanding philosophical essay of that century, unsurpassed for its intellectual rigour and logical consistency. And although Hobbes had stated repeatedly that his theory of sovereignty applied equally to monarchy, aristocracy, and democracy, the view prevailed among his contemporaries that the *Leviathan* was an apologia for royal absolutism. Indeed, the term 'Hobbist' was soon applied to writers who defended the divine right of kings.

One such writer who is important for our understanding of Locke's *First Treatise of Government* was Sir Robert Filmer, who advocated in his *Patriarcha* an extreme royalism. Monarchy, he alleged, was intended by divine right to be absolute, and the attempt to impose limitations upon it was sacrilege. Filmer denied that a prince can ever be obliged by contracts, concessions, or coronation oaths to abstain from the lives, liberties, or properties of his subjects. One of the earliest and best-known responses to Filmer was a substantial little volume called *Patriarcha non Monarcha, or The Patriarch Unmonarch'd*, published in 1681. The author was James Tyrrell, who argued that human beings are naturally endowed with freedom from subjection and at liberty to choose whatever form of government they please; and that the power that any individual has over others was originally bestowed by a multitude, according to its discretion. Against Filmer's view that the authority of a king over his people is founded on a father's authority over his children, and thus instituted by God, Tyrrell upheld a social-contract theory of the origin of government. Proposing that the authority of a father over his children, far from being absolute, is subject to moral laws, Tyrrell went on to argue that even if paternal authority were absolute, royal absolutism could not be derived from it, because a king's relationship to his people is not a natural one, as is that of a father to his children. A king, Tyrrell maintained, is therefore as much under the law as are his subjects, for his power was bestowed conditionally in the original covenant with the multitude.

It is known that Locke had purchased a copy of Tyrrell's book in June 1681; and scholars have long recognized that it anticipates many of the key ideas in Locke's political writings. David Wootton has observed in this regard that Tyrrell himself believed that his *Patriarcha non Monarcha* had inspired Locke's *Two Treatises* and that Locke's political theory was much more influenced by Tyrrell's work than the *Treatises* readily acknowledged. For although Locke had made a favourable reference to *Patriarcha non Monarcha* in the *First Treatise*, he made no acknowledgment of his substantial debt to it in the *Second*.[1]

It is not known with certainty when Locke's treatises on government were composed. For generations scholars had relied on Locke's *Preface* to propose that the treatises were written after 1688 to justify the Glorious Revolution. This view was questioned in the 1960s by Peter Laslett, who suggested that the bulk of the *Second Treatise* was written in 1679–80. This implied that its aim was to advocate a revolution for the near future and not to defend one that had already taken place. But a critical scrutiny of Laslett's thesis has shown that it is not entirely convincing. What is beyond dispute, however, and most important for our purposes, is that whether the *Second Treatise* was written before or after 1688 it was definitely composed in defence of the *right* of revolution.

Another debated question is whether Locke wrote his treatises as a reply to the political theory of Hobbes. Scholars appear to be largely in agreement that the first of Locke's treatises was intended as a detailed refutation of Filmer, and the second as an alternative political philosophy to Filmer's. The argument that Locke wrote in response to Filmer, not Hobbes, is made on the following grounds: Hobbes was almost as much disliked by the Tories as by the Whigs; and his theory took too dark and 'Machiavellian' a view of human nature to be popular. Hobbes had frankly avowed that human beings are driven by fear and self-interest, while Filmer posited nobler motives of human conduct. So although Filmer was intellectually inferior to Hobbes in all respects, Filmer, in saying what people listened to and wished to believe, was much more influential. It was therefore more urgent for Locke to refute Filmer.

It is true that 'Hobbism' is derided in Locke's *Second Treatise* only two or three times, and then only in passing and without any apparent sign of concern that there may be Hobbesian sympathies among his readers. And yet, one suspects that a thinker of Locke's stature would have recognized Hobbes as his worthiest adversary. We may therefore assume that however ghostly his appearance may be on Locke's pages, Hobbes is nevertheless there as a formidable foil. Besides, for the heuristic purpose of deriving the most valuable insights from Locke's *Second Treatise* – his most important essay on government – it will surely enlighten us most if we contrast his views with those of Hobbes in the *Leviathan*.

The State of Nature

Locke's primary aim in *The Second Treatise of Government* is to define political power and, in particular, the power of a magistrate over a subject. Like Hobbes, Locke maintains that a right understanding of political power requires a consideration of the original condition of human beings in a state of nature – a hypothetical state in which they are perfectly free to order their lives and dispose of their belongings as they think fit. This state, for Locke as for Hobbes, is one in which humans are fundamentally equal. It is a condition in which no individual possesses more power than another, in which subjection is an unknown phenomenon, and in which obligations are reciprocal. Relying on the theological writings of Richard Hooker, Locke cites Hooker's postulation of human equality as the foundation of the reciprocal duties humans owe one another. It is in the nature of being human, Hooker proposed, that every individual should wish to receive good; but no one can hope to satisfy that desire unless he is careful to satisfy the like desire in others. If I act towards others in a manner repugnant to their desire for good, if I do them harm, I must be ready to suffer; for there is no reason that others should show me a greater measure of love than I have shown to them. Therefore, wrote Hooker, 'my desire to be loved by my equals in nature, as much as possible may be, imposeth upon me a natural duty of bearing to themward fully the like affection; from which relation of equality between ourselves and them that are as ourselves, what several rules and canons natural reason hath drawn for direction of life, no man is ignorant' (*Ecclesiastical Polity*, lib. 1).

Locke makes this elaboration of the Golden Rule the foundation of his conception of the state of nature and of natural liberty. Although every individual in that state is free to govern himself and his possessions, he is not free to destroy either himself or others. Locke's state of nature, far from being a state of war, is governed by a law of nature, which becomes known to humans through their natural reason, and which obliges everyone. Being equal and independent, no one may harm another in his life, health, liberty, or belongings. For Locke, human equality and liberty are truths derived from the moral principles of the Bible: all human beings are creatures of the omnipotent and infinitely wise maker; as such they are the servants of one sovereign master, brought into the world to live according to his commandments. In contrast to Hobbes, then, whose postulate of human equality leads to diffidence, competition, and war, Locke's premise of a common and equal nature precludes any such condition among us 'that may authorize us to destroy one another.' (264).

However, even Locke's comparatively benign state of nature allows that one's preservation may be threatened by offensive competition, and that in order to administer justice to an offender it may become necessary to 'take away or impair the life, or what tends to the preservation of the life, liberty, health, limb, or goods of another' (264). The law of nature and reason, designed to further the peace and preservation of all humanity, places into the hands of every individual the right to punish transgressors of that law and to prevent the violation of it. Like all laws concerning human relations, the law of nature would be ineffectual if no one in the state of nature had the power to execute that law and thereby to protect the innocent and restrain the offender. Everyone in the state of nature has a right to punish another for any evil he has done; for in this state of perfect equality, where superiority or jurisdiction over one another is nonexistent, what anyone may do in prosecution of the law of nature, everyone may do.

In Locke's state of nature, individuals do, therefore, gain power over another; not an absolute or arbitrary power, but a limited one – only so much power as is necessary to punish the offender. Punishment, guided by reason and conscience, is to be proportionate to the transgression, so that the damage may be repaired, the offender restrained, and further offences deterred. In Locke's state of nature it is solely for the purpose of punishment that one individual may lawfully do harm to another. For in transgressing the law of nature, the offender has flouted the rule of reason and common equity, the divine rule without which human beings cannot ensure their mutual security. As the offender has become dangerous to humanity, he has effectively broken the ties with his fellows, which would have secured him against injury and violence. Hence, every individual has a right to serve as the prosecutor of the law of nature, and to punish an offender. Moreover, the individual who is personally injured, or whose belongings are damaged by an offender, possesses not only the common right to punish, but the additional right to seek reparation from him.

For Locke, then, there are two distinct rights in the state of nature: (1) the right to punish an offender, which everyone possesses; and (2) the right to take reparation, which the injured party alone possesses. In a commonwealth the common right to punish is placed in the hands of a magistrate who can – by his own authority and where the public good demands it – refrain from punishing an offender; but the magistrate has no authority to remit the satisfaction due to any individual for the damage done to him. It is solely the individual to whom damage has been done who has the right to demand or to remit restitution. These distinct rights are equally in effect in the state of nature. The injured party, by the right of self-preservation, has the authority to appropriate to himself the goods or services of the offender. However, *all* individuals in the state of nature have the authority to kill a murderer, since his action is an act of war against all humanity. This 'great law of nature' is based, for Locke, on Genesis 9:6: 'Who so sheddeth man's blood, by men shall his blood be shed.'

By the same great law every individual in the state of nature may punish lesser offences. Each crime may be punished with a severity that will suffice to make it a poor bargain to an offender, allow him to repent, and deter others. In this respect there is no difference between the state of nature and a commonwealth; for Locke avers that the existence of the 'great law of nature' is no less evident to a rational individual than are the positive or civil laws of the commonwealth. Indeed, the positive laws partake of right only insofar as they are founded on the law of nature, by which they are to be interpreted and applied.

Locke recognizes the objection that can be raised against his doctrine, that every individual in the state of nature possesses executive authority where the law of nature is concerned: when, for instance, individuals become judges in their own cases, self-love will most often, if not always, make them partial towards themselves, their families, and their friends; and the human passion for revenge is such that injured parties would be inclined to impose cruel and unusual punishment. Acknowledging the existence of such natural human tendencies and the disorder that would follow from them in the state of nature, Locke grants that only civil government can effectively restrain partiality and violence. In this respect Locke appears to be making an implicit concession to Hobbes. For although Locke's state of nature is not a state of war of each against all, he nevertheless grants that where individuals are judges in their own cases, as they are in his conception of the state of nature, it is naïve to suppose that violators of the law of nature would condemn themselves. But Locke then immediately urges us to remember that absolute monarchs are only human.

In his repudiation of royal absolutism, Locke asks this question: If disorder and other evils in the state of nature result from the condition in which every individual is a judge in his own case, how much better is absolute monarchy, a government in which one man commands, and everyone else obeys? Absolute monarchy is, after all, a regime in which one man has the freedom to judge in his own case and rule the multitude in whatever manner he chooses, while no one but the monarch has the least liberty to question or control those who execute his commands. And regardless whether those commands are prompted by reason, blind passion, or error, they have to be obeyed. 'Much better it is in the state of nature,' Locke argues, 'wherein men are not bound to submit to the unjust will of another, and if he that judges judges amiss in his own or any other case, he is answerable for it to the rest of mankind' (268).

Locke's state of nature is distinct from a 'state of war,' to which he devotes a separate chapter. We should observe, however, that if in his state of nature each individual is inclined to be partial towards himself and likely to be excessive in punishing others, and if each who judges 'amiss' is 'answerable for it to the rest of mankind,' this begins strongly to resemble the Hobbesian state of nature as a state of war. Locke's reply to the question of whether and where a state of nature has ever existed, strengthens the impression that it is also a state of war. The primary example Locke offers as proof of the existence of a state of nature is the same as it is for Hobbes, namely, the international arena, though for Hobbes the state of nature is at one and the same time a state of war. All princes and rulers of independent governments throughout the world, writes Locke, are in a state of nature, so it is beyond dispute that the world never was and never will be without large numbers of human beings in that state. Locke proposes that some princes of independent commonwealths emerge from the state of nature as they form compacts agreeing to form one community or body politic; but surely Locke would have to acknowledge that the international arena as a whole always remains in a Hobbesian state of war, since a 'community' formed from several independent commonwealths finds itself in potential or actual conflict with other such alliances and, indeed, with other independent states. Up to this point, therefore, in the unfolding of Locke's argument, it appears that he has failed to distinguish his state of nature from a Hobbesian state of war.

Locke strives to salvage the distinction by again citing Hooker, who had posited a fundamental interdependence of humans in the state of nature. Inasmuch as 'we are not by ourselves sufficient to furnish ourselves with competent store of things needful for such a life as our nature doth desire, a life fit for the dignity of man, therefore to supply those defects and imperfections which are in us, as living singly and solely by ourselves, we are naturally induced to seek communion and fellowship with others: this was the cause of men's uniting themselves at first in politic societies' (268). Hooker's observation is, of course, true as a general proposition: human beings are never literally independent individuals and must cooperate, engage in mutual aid, and form political societies in order to survive. But, alas, this general proposition obscures another equally valid one, that in the formation of political societies, that is, independent states, human beings also unite *against* one another. So it would seem that Locke's endeavour to separate the state of nature from the state of war is not aided by his reliance on Hooker.

Of the State of War

For Locke, this is a condition in which enmity and destruction prevail. When any individual by word or deed shows the intention of threatening the life of another, he thereby exposes his own life to the power of the other and to anyone else who joins him in his defence. It is only reasonable, says Locke, that an individual should have the right to destroy that which threatens him with destruction. It is a fundamental law of nature that human life should be preserved as much as possible; and when everyone cannot be preserved, the lives of the innocent are to be preferred.

Locke's understanding of the threat to one's life extends to include the threat to one's freedom. It follows that if one attempts to place me under his absolute power without my consent, he thereby enters into a state of war with me, since his primary aim is to use me as he pleases, and even destroy me if he so chooses. My freedom being the sole means of preserving myself, reason dictates that I should regard as a deadly enemy anyone who would deny me my freedom. In the state of nature freedom is the foundation of everything else; he, therefore, who would take away my freedom may be supposed to have the intention of taking from me everything else. There is no difference in this respect between the state of nature and the state of society; in both cases the threat to an individual's freedom must be seen as a design on everything else the individual possesses.

In contrast to Hobbes, for whom the state of nature and the state of war are one, Locke proposes that they are two distinct realms, the former characterized by peace, goodwill, mutual assistance, and preservation, the latter by malice, enmity, violence, and mutual destruction. For Locke, the state of nature becomes a state of war when force or the threat of it is aimed at another and there is no common superior power to whom to appeal for relief or protection. It is the absence of such a common power that gives an individual the right of war against an aggressor even in society. If, for example, the government and law that were made for my preservation cannot intervene in time to save my life from an aggressor, I am permitted in my own defence to exercise the right of war. I have the right in such circumstances to kill the aggressor if necessary, because he allows me no time to appeal to the common, superior authority. Hence, the absence 'of a common judge with authority puts all men in a state of nature; force without right upon a man's person makes a state of war, both where there is and is not a common judge' (270–71).

It is a near certainty that Hobbes would have found Locke's separation of the two states unconvincing; and although Locke is determined to preserve his distinction between the state of nature and the state of war, his further discussion of the matter appears to make an implicit concession to Hobbes's view. For Locke writes that where there is no common superior judge to whom to appeal, as in the state of nature, 'the state of war, once begun, continues' (#20, 271). And in the next paragraph he states: 'To avoid this state of war ... is one great reason of men's putting themselves into society, and quitting the state of nature. For where there is an authority, a power on earth from which relief can be had by appeal, there the continuance of the state of war is excluded, and the controversy is decided by that power' (#21, 271). These passages implicitly acknowledge the validity of Hobbes's proposition, that the state of nature and the state of war are one and the same.

Moreover, if we return, for the moment, to paragraph #14, where the international arena is Locke's example of an actually existing state of nature, it becomes even clearer why his distinction between the two states is highly problematic. As we reflect on international relations from earliest times to the present, it is easy to see that the rulers of independent governments always have been and continue to be in a Hobbesian state of war: a mutually known disposition to fight, which manifests itself periodically in actual fighting. Indeed, Locke's own biblical example makes Hobbes's point. Had there been, Locke writes, 'any superior jurisdiction on earth to determine the right between Jephtha and the Ammonites, they had never come to a state of war' (271). In this respect it appears that Hobbes's conception of the state of nature as a state of war captures the reality of international relations more adequately than does Locke's attempt to separate the two states. Fortunately, however, Locke's problematic separation of the two states has no necessary implications for the validity of his argument about government.

Liberty in Nature and in Society

The next step in Locke's argument is to clarify the difference between liberty in a state of nature and liberty in a state of society. Natural liberty, for Locke, refers to a condition in which the adult human being is free from any superior power on Earth and, hence, not subject to the will of any other human being. If human beings are thus free in a state of nature, it follows for Locke that only such power may be placed over them in society that they themselves have established by their own consent. Locke speaks of a commonwealth's legislative power being established in that manner, and he maintains that human liberty in society means that no individual is to be under the dominion of any will or restraint that has not been enacted by the legislative power, duly consented to by the governed. Freedom in society is not freedom from any and all constraints; it is not freedom for everyone to do as he or she pleases. Freedom in society is freedom under government, and government means rules to live by, which are common to everyone and which have been enacted by the legislative power. In all matters on which the rules are silent, neither prescribing nor proscribing, the individual is free to follow his own will, and hence free from subjection to the arbitrary will of another.

Earlier we observed that for Locke the human individual, being the workmanship and property of the divine architect, has no power over his own life: humans are enjoined by both God and nature to preserve themselves. Since it is not the individual but God who has the authority over human life, no one may, by his own consent, agree to place himself under the absolute and arbitrary power of another who may then take away one's life when he pleases. 'Nobody,' writes Locke, 'can give more power than he has himself; and he that cannot take away his own life cannot give another power over it' (#23, 272).

Of Property

Just as earlier Locke sought the ground for human equality in both reason and the Bible, he now argues that whether it is from the standpoint of natural reason or revelation, humans have a right to their preservation and, hence, to their subsistence. What about property? If, as the Bible states, God 'has given the Earth to humanity' (Psalm 115:16), and this implies that the Earth was given to humanity *in common*, how can one justify the institution of private property? In addressing this question Locke begins with the biblical premise that the fruit of the Earth and the animal life it sustains were at first the spontaneous product of nature and, hence, the common property of the human species. Originally no individual had the right of private dominion over any part of the Earth and its yield. So how did private dominion come about and how, according to Locke, may it be justified?

Every individual, says Locke, possesses a property in his own person, to which no one but he has any right. A human individual's person includes the capacity *to labour*. The work of one's hands and one's body are properly one's own. Whatever the individual has removed from the original condition of nature and reworked with his labour becomes, therefore, something of his own, his private property. Because he has removed from the common store of nature some part of it with which he has mixed his labour, he has thereby also removed it from the common right of other individuals. Labour being the indisputable property of the labourer, no one but he can have a right to whatever he has appropriated and transformed with his labour – although Locke adds the proviso, 'at least where there is enough and as good left in common for others' (#27, 274). When does the right of an individual who has laboured upon nature begin? If he gathered up acorns that fell from an oak, or picked apples from a tree in the wood, when did they become his? Locke replies that if the first gathering failed to give the individual the right of possession, then nothing else could. It is the labour of gathering or picking that added something more than nature to the fruit of the Earth; and it is the adding of that something more that makes the acorns and apples the individual's private property by right. And would anyone contend, Locke asks, that the individual in question had no right to the acorns and apples without the prior consent of all humanity? The very asking of the question, Locke avers, shows how unreasonable it would be to demand the prior, express consent of all the so-called common owners. For Locke there can be no doubt, then, that one's labour makes anything one acts upon and removes from the common condition of nature one's own private property.

Locke, however, recognizes that a serious objection may be raised against his proposition: if gathering and other forms of labour give one a right to the fruits of the Earth, does not that imply that one may accumulate as much as one can? No, says Locke, for although 'God has given us all things richly' (1 Tim. 6:17), he has given it to us to enjoy. As much, therefore, as anyone can use 'to any advantage of life before it spoils, so much he may by his labour fix a property in. Whatever is beyond this, is more than his share, and belongs to others' (#31, 276). In imagining the origins of private appropriation, Locke hypothesizes a nature so bountiful that no individual could accumulate the fruits of the Earth at another's expense; and in invoking reason as the faculty that would have defined the limits on what might serve for an individual's use, Locke posits a rather benign condition in which there would be little room for quarrels over property.

If it were by means of labour that human beings originally acquired property in the fruits of the Earth and the animals that subsist on them, then the same principle applies to the Earth itself. The individual is entitled to as much land as he can till and cultivate. By means of his labour, he encloses it, as it were, from the common. Again Locke considers whether this individual's right is invalidated if he has enclosed without the consent of all his fellow commoners, all of humanity. Arguing from Scripture, Locke denies that an individual's right can be thus invalidated. When God gave the Earth in common to all human beings, he commanded them to labour upon it for the benefit of life; and since labour is one's own property, he who in obedience to God's command tills and sows any part of the Earth thereby appropriates it as his rightful property, to which no one else may have title. Can such an appropriation be at the expense of others? Locke replies in the negative, positing, in effect, that land was limitless in quality and quantity: 'For he that leaves as much as another can make use of, does as good as take nothing at all. Nobody could think himself injured by the drinking of another man, though he took a good draught, who had a whole river of the same water left him to quench his thirst. And the case of land and water, where there is enough of both, is perfectly the same' (#33, 277). In that way Locke constructs an originally bountiful and benign state of nature that precludes social strife over property.

Although the state of nature is an original condition that, of course, no longer prevails, Locke nevertheless proposes that the same principles would hold in the world of his time, were it not for the intrusion of money and other spoiling developments. To defend his view Locke must explain why in England, though the land is held in common, the law stipulates that no one may enclose or appropriate any portion of the land without the consent of his fellow commoners. The reasoning behind the law was that often with an enclosure of a part, the remainder might not be as good to the fellow commoners as was the whole when all could make use of it. In the beginning, however, when the great common of the world first became populated, matters were quite otherwise. By cultivating the Earth, one gained dominion over a portion of it and acquired title to it. Originally, Locke maintains, nature set the limits on how much land an individual could appropriate, the limits having been the amount he could cultivate and enjoy; and since a portion as good and as large as that which was appropriated always remained, it was impossible for anyone to acquire property at the expense of his neighbour. The limits thus set on how much land one could work and enjoy confined everyone's possession to a moderate proportion.

Proceeding with his argument, Locke proposes that the same moderate rule of property could still be applied in his own day, notwithstanding the substantial increase in human population that had spread to all corners of the globe. Advancing a proposition that harks back to Aristotle and that profoundly influenced Thomas Jefferson and the other founders of the American Republic, Locke insists that the same principle of moderate property would hold in the world were it not for the intrusion of money, which has enabled some to aggrandize their property to the point of leaving none for others. It is the moneyed and commercial interests who have distorted the intrinsic value of things and who have denied to their fellow human beings the 'right to appropriate by their labour, each one to himself, as much of the things of nature as he could use' (#37, 279).

Of Paternal Power

Sir Robert Filmer's *Patriarcha*, published in 1680, was immediately embraced by the supporters of royal absolutism as a most cogent presentation of their views. It was Filmer's thesis that Adam, as the first man and father of mankind, was the rightful owner of the world and the king of all his descendants; that the powers of fathers and kings were identical and unlimited; and that kings should be regarded as Adam's surrogates and the fathers of their peoples. The first objection Locke raises to Filmer's thesis and to the concept of paternal power is that it places parental authority over children solely in the hands of the father, as if the mother is to have no share in it. This flies in the face of both revelation and reason, which bestow upon her equal title. Locke cites several biblical passages, beginning with the relevant one from the Decalogue: 'Honour thy father and mother' (Exod. 20:12); 'Whosoever curseth his father or his mother' (Lev. 20:9); 'Ye shall fear every man his mother and his father' (Lev. 19:3); 'Children, obey your parents' (Eph. 6:1). If Scripture had been well heeded, says Locke, and if the authority over children had been properly called 'parental,' the gross and egregious error of attributing absolute dominion and regal authority to the father might have been avoided. Moreover, once we see clearly that the power over children belongs to the mother too, it exposes the absurdity of the position of those who support the absolute and undivided power of kings; for it is evident that the fundamental authority on which they would base their government by one person was placed not in one, but rather in two persons jointly.

Locke's second objection to Filmer's thesis addresses the issue of how long parental authority over children should last. Although all human beings are by nature equal, it is evident that children are not born in the full state of equality. Parents therefore have a temporary jurisdiction over their children from the time they come into the world until they have grown up and developed the faculty of reason. Acquiring authority over their children by the law of nature, parents thereby take upon themselves the obligation to nourish, protect, and educate their offspring so that they may become mature, free, and intelligent agents aware of both their own proper interests and those of the society at large. When the son reaches the stage of maturity that had made his father a freeman, the son becomes a freeman too. Maturity, for Locke, means that the individual in question is supposed capable of knowing the laws, natural and civil, so that he can conduct himself in accordance with them. Only insofar as individuals so conduct themselves can they also be free, for where there is no law, there is no freedom. Liberty, that is, freedom from arbitrary restraint and violence, cannot exist where there is no law. (Locke, like Hobbes, posits the existence of laws of nature. However, whereas Locke seems to believe that such laws, in and of themselves, possess regulatory power in the state of nature, Hobbes maintains that as the state of nature is a state of war, only a Leviathan can ensure obedience to the laws.) Once a son has attained the stage of maturity, the father and the son are equally free, equally subject to the law, and the father's dominion over the son comes to an end. Therefore, Locke concludes, even the most adamant defenders of royal absolutism, by right of fatherhood, should now be able to see that the subjection of a child to his parents does not and should not preclude his attainment of full freedom and equality upon reaching adulthood.

For Locke, then, there is no sound reason to attribute an absolute, arbitrary dominion of the father over the child, since the power of the mother has a definite share with the father. It is equally unsound to deduce royal absolutism from a temporary parental authority, which lasts only so long as is required to bring children to the stage of free, equal, and responsible adulthood. The power of a father is that of a guardian of his children; it is a power that comes to an end once he ceases to care for them. As paternal authority is inseparable from the care, nourishment, and education of children, it is acquired as much by a foster father as by a natural one. And is it not true, Locke asks, that if the father dies while the children are still young, they naturally owe the same obedience to the mother as to the father, were he alive? That the authority of parents is far from being absolute and perpetual is further confirmed by the biblical injunction that a man shall 'leave his father and his mother, and shall cleave to his wife' (Gen. 2:24; cf. Matt. 19:5). So while children are required always to honour, respect, show gratitude, and give assistance to their parents, that is a far cry from the absolute obedience and submission that, according to Filmer, children owe their parents. In a word, Filmer and his admirers have confounded paternal and political power, two distinct and separate powers resting on different foundations and given for different ends. In a commonwealth parents, who are themselves subjects, retain no less authority over their children than do parents in a state of nature. Indeed, every subject who is a father possesses as much paternal authority over his children as does the prince over his; and every prince, until he has reached the age of majority, owes as much filial duty and obedience to his parents as the humblest of his subjects owe theirs. Hence, Locke concludes his all-too-patient rebuttal – paternal authority has nothing in common with the 'kind of dominion which a prince or magistrate has over his subject' (#71, 296).

Of Political or Civil Society

Human beings, like other creatures, are social by nature. The bonds between man and woman and parents and children arise out of the need for mutual aid, without which very young children could not survive. Such bonds last longer in the human than in other species because of the helplessness of the human infant and the prolonged dependency of the child. Moreover, a woman is capable of conceiving and giving birth to a new infant before the earlier one is out of dependence.

When husbands and wives disagree or their wills clash for whatever reason, Locke allows the final decision to rest with the husband. But this prerogative of the husband, which pertains only to matters of common interest, nevertheless leaves the wife in full possession of the rights she acquired through the marriage contract, and 'gives the husband no more power over her life than she has over his' (#82, 302). Families, however, even when they are large and complex – having acquired servants and slaves united under the master of the household – must not be confused with a commonwealth.

For Locke, a commonwealth or political society arises only when everyone concerned relinquishes his natural rights and powers and agrees to place them in the hands of the community, which now becomes the umpire that impartially settles disputes in accordance with the laws established by the community. A political society, then, is made up of all those who, united in one body and possessing a common established law and judicature to which to appeal, recognize the government's authority to arbitrate conflicts and punish offenders. Those who possess no such umpire to which to appeal are still in the state of nature, where each individual remains judge and executioner. In a commonwealth the government acquires the authority to protect the lives and property of its subjects and to punish outsiders (the powers of war and peace) for injuries perpetrated against them. The individual subject thus gives to the commonwealth the right to employ his force for the execution of the commonwealth's judgments. In such a political society the commonwealth's judgments are, in effect, the individual's own judgments, since they have been 'made by himself, or his representative' (#88, 305). It is the setting up of such a judge on Earth, with authority to resolve all controversies and redress injuries from within and without, that human beings leave the state of nature and enter a commonwealth.

The goal of civil society, Locke holds, is to avoid and remedy the dangers and defects of the state of nature in which everyone is judge and executioner in his own case. This is accomplished by establishing a common authority to which everyone may appeal when wronged. Without such a common and voluntarily constituted authority, human beings remain in the state of nature. It therefore followed, for Locke – and this is where he differed fundamentally from Hobbes – that all those who live under the dominion of an absolute prince are also in a state of nature. Locke reasoned that since an absolute monarch unites in himself alone both the executive and the legislative powers, no real umpire exists: there is no opportunity for appeal to anyone with authority who can fairly and impartially decide whether the inconveniences suffered by a subject due to the prince's orders are just. An absolute monarch, then, whether he be a czar or grand signor, 'is as much in a state of nature with all under his dominion as he is with the rest of mankind' (#91, 306).

Not only is the subject of an absolute prince in a state of nature, he is even worse off than in the original state of nature, where he retained the liberty to judge of his own right and, to the best of his power, to preserve it. Under royal absolutism, in contrast, whenever the subject's life or property is threatened by the monarch, he not only has no one else to whom to appeal, he is denied the freedom to defend himself. Supporters of absolutism had acknowledged that there must be laws and judges by which to mediate and arbitrate between subject and subject; but they denied that such laws and institutions were necessary for disputes between the ruler and his subjects. The ruler, such supporters insisted, ought to be absolute, and whatever he does is right. Moreover, it is considered faction and rebellion merely to ask how one might protect oneself from injury at the hands of the strongest power in the kingdom. It is as if men, when they left the state of nature and entered society, agreed that all of them except one should be under the restraint of laws, and that he should retain the power to injure with impunity. 'This is to think,' Locke remarks sardonically in a now famous passage, 'that men are so foolish that they take care to avoid what mischiefs may be done them by polecats or foxes, but are content, nay think it safety, to be devoured by lions' (#93, 308).

For Locke, then, no individual, no matter how lofty his position, is above the civil society of which everyone else is a member. The people can never be safe under the absolute power of even the most excellent and upright individual, if no other precaution is taken but the assurance of his uprightness and wisdom. The people should never consider themselves either safe or members of a genuine civil society unless the legislative power is placed in a separate collective body such as a parliament or senate. That is the only means by which every single person, whether lofty or mean, becomes subject equally to the laws that he himself has directly or indirectly established. The establishment of a separate and independent legislature ensures that no one can escape the rule of law or plead exemption on some pretext of superiority. Thus Locke argues, in effect, that absolute power is bound to become tyrannical, and that the only safeguard against tyranny is the separation of the executive and legislative powers so that the latter may check the former.

How do legislative decisions become binding, given that unanimity is seldom if ever achieved? Defending the majoritarian criterion, Locke affirms that whenever any number of individuals consent to form one community or government, the majority binds all the rest. The will of the majority must be taken as the will of the whole. Every individual who consents with others to form one united body politic assumes an obligation to all the other members of that society to submit to the decisions of the majority. Invoking Hobbes's biblical monster and applying it to a legislative body, Locke states that in the absence of majority rule, the variety of opinions and the diversity of interests 'would make the mighty Leviathan of a shorter duration than the feeblest creatures' (#98, 311).

Locke recognizes that at least two serious objections have been raised to the 'social-contract' theory of the origin of society: (1) no evidence exists of any such aggregate of equal and independent individuals who met together to set up a government; and (2) it is a theory that is morally wrong, because all humans are, in fact, born under government and therefore obliged to submit to it and, hence, not at liberty to begin a new one. To the first objection Locke responds that it is not surprising that history gives little or no account of how individuals lived in the state of nature, which was, after all, a primordial condition. However, it is altogether plausible, he insists, that political societies all began from a voluntary union, a mutual agreement of equal individuals freely acting in the choice and establishment of their government. The governments of the world that were begun in peace originated on the foundation of the consent of the people. Locke concedes that when we look back in history at the earliest commonwealths we generally find them under the rule of one man. Locke insists, however, that in such cases the individuals in question exercised their natural freedom, equality, and intelligence to select the one whom they judged the ablest to rule well over them. Besides, if monarchy seems early on to have been the dominant form of government, it is not difficult to understand why that should have been the case: people had too little experience with the insolence and encroachments of absolute power, and they had yet to learn the effective method of *balancing the power of government by placing several parts of it in different hands'* (#108, 315, italics added). Whatever one may think of Locke's general argument in this case, it is clear that the underscored passage represents his most important insight and contribution where the prevention of tyranny is concerned. In contrast to Hobbes, for whom tyranny was simply monarchy disliked, tyranny for Locke was a real political phenomenon that threatened the lives, liberties, and properties of those subject to it.

The second objection to social-contract theory, we recall, was that since all humans are born not in a state of nature, but under government, they have no liberty to form a new one. To this Locke replies with a rhetorical question: 'If this argument be good ... how came so many lawful monarchies into the world?' (#113, 319). History, he continues, is full of examples, sacred and profane, of individuals withdrawing themselves and their obedience from the government they were born under and setting up a new one either in its place or in other places. That is the origin of all those small and large commonwealths known to us from history.

Of the Ends of Political Society and Government

If every individual in the state of nature is free and equal, and master of his own person and possessions, why would he part with this condition and subject himself to the dominion and constraints of any other power? As Locke replies to this question we see again how close he comes to Hobbes's state of nature, which is at one and the same time a state of war. It is evident, says Locke, that notwithstanding the natural freedom and rights of an individual in the state of nature, those rights are very uncertain, since he is constantly exposed to the threats of others. Every other individual being his equal, with little or no concern for equity and justice, the enjoyment of his life and possessions is neither safe nor secure. However free the individual is in the state of nature, it is a condition 'full of fears and continual dangers' (#123, 325). It is such fears, dangers, and general insecurity that impel the individual to leave the natural condition and exchange it for life in society. He seeks out others whose experience has been the same, and together they unite to form a political society for the mutual preservation of their lives and possessions.

For Locke, there are lacking from the state of nature three conditions that prompt individuals to unite in commonwealths. First, there is no law, arrived at by common consent, that sets the standards of right and wrong for the adjudication of controversies and strife. (The laws of nature, or moral virtues, exist and are plain and comprehensible to all rational creatures; but humans are biased by their own interests and unlikely to abide by those laws when they conflict with their interests.) Second, there is no impartial judge with the authority to resolve conflicts in accordance with an established law. Third, there is no established power capable of enforcing just decisions. The absence of these conditions makes it virtually inevitable that individuals in a state of nature will seldom shy away from force in pursuing their own interests.

We see, then, that in Locke's state of nature individuals are mutually threatened, insecure, and unsafe. They are self-seeking and willingly employ force offensively against others. The primary reasons for the prevalence of distrust and strife are the absence of positive laws commonly consented to, an impartial judge to adjudicate conflicts, and finally, a common power who can ensure that the laws are enforced and just decisions carried out. All this, we need to observe, bears a striking resemblance to Hobbes's state of nature equalling a state of war. But we need to exercise care in deciding what this resemblance implies for the

respective theories of Hobbes and Locke. The resemblance does not necessarily mean that Locke's theory of the balance of powers is flawed.
Nor does it necessarily mean that Hobbes's theory of absolute and undivided sovereignty, as applied to monarchy, is sound. We have seen in
the epilogue to the previous chapter that Hobbes allowed for an original
democracy and for a democratically constituted common power whose
authority was limited, while the sovereignty of the people remained
absolute. In principle, then, there was nothing to prevent the original
democracy from establishing a constitutional form of government based
on law and a proto-Lockean division and balance of powers between the
executive and legislative branches of government. Hobbes, of course,
assumed that any such division inevitably brings factionalism, strife,
and ultimately civil war. He somehow found it impossible to imagine
peaceful conflict between the separate branches of government that
would preserve the commonwealth's unity.

As applied to monarchy, Hobbes's zealous advocacy of absolute and
undivided sovereignty caused him to sidestep the question of why royal
absolutism should not degenerate into tyranny. Indeed, he shrugged off
the problem, asserting that tyranny is simply monarchy disliked. Even if
Hobbes were right that a divided sovereignty brings with it conflict
between the distinct powers of government, that might be the price we
would willingly pay to prevent tyranny. History has shown that the conflicts in constitutional government between its branches have been
peaceful for long stretches of time; and this fact lends cogency to Locke's
position: a division and balance of powers are necessary for the 'peace,
safety, and public good of the people' (#131, 327).

Forms of Commonwealth

Locke allows for an original democracy in which the majority in the
state of nature had agreed to unite and form a community, employing
their united power to make laws and appoint officers for the execution
of those laws. He recognizes, however, that other non-democratic forms
of government, such as the rule of the few or the rule of the one, also
emerged from the state of nature. When Locke employs the word 'commonwealth,' he means neither a democracy nor any other specific form
of government. 'Commonwealth' means, simply, any independent society. What is paramount for Locke, as it was for Aristotle, is the rule of
law: a good commonwealth presupposes the supremacy of the legislature. In opposition to the supporters of royal absolutism Locke thus pro-

poses that the 'legislature is not only the supreme power of the commonwealth, but sacred and unalterable in the hands where the community have once placed it; nor can any edict of anybody else, in what form soever conceived, or by what power soever backed, have the force and obligation of a law which has not its sanction from that legislative which the public has chosen and appointed' (#134, 328)

Does the supremacy of the legislature carry with it the danger that its power will become absolute and arbitrary? Locke replies that no such danger exists. Although the legislative authority is supreme, its authority rests strictly on the body of laws enacted by the will of the majority. Whatever the form of the commonwealth, the ruling power ought to rule in accordance with the received laws. It is only in such a constitutional government, based on established laws, that the people can know their rights and duties; and it is only in constitutional government that the rulers can be kept in their due bounds. The legislative authority, being but a delegated power from the people, cannot be transferred to any other hands. 'The people alone,' Locke writes, 'can appoint the form of the commonwealth, which is by constituting the legislative, and appointing in whose hands that shall be' (#141, 334). And the laws must be administered impartially: there must not be one rule for the rich and another for the poor, one for the court favourites and another for the men at the plough.

In chapter 12 Locke explicitly introduces the doctrine of the separation of powers. The persons making the laws should not be the same as those having the power to execute them. Given the need for the laws always to remain in force, Locke stipulates that the executive should be the power always in being. Since each commonwealth is in a state of nature in relation to every other commonwealth, there has to be provision for what Locke calls the federative power – the power to manage the security and interests of one's commonwealth in relation to other independent states. Although the commonwealths of the world are in a state of nature with respect to one another, the federation of two or more commonwealths by means of diplomatic agreement takes them out of the state of nature for the duration of the agreement.

In all circumstances the delegated powers of the commonwealth remain subordinate to the people who retain in perpetuity the supreme power to remove or alter the legislative authority if and when it acts contrary to its mandate. The power of choosing representatives of the legislative and other branches of government is exercised by the people; and if, for whatever reason, the executive power should employ force or the threat of it to hinder the meeting or proceedings of the legislature, he thereby places himself in a state of war with the people. In all such circumstances the people's only remedy is to oppose force with force. The prince's only prerogative being to provide for the public good, he should have no distinct and separate interests from those of the community. For Locke, it is simply unthinkable in constitutional government that anyone should possess absolute, arbitrary power, for that is 'despotical power' (#172, 350).

Of Tyranny

Tyranny, like despotism, refers to the unjust and unlawful exercise of power. The tyrant employs his power not for the good of the people, but for his own personal advantage. He makes not the law, but his will the rule. The question that arises, then, is when a ruler who has exceeded or abused his authority may be opposed. If subjects resisted by force every time they felt themselves aggrieved, one would have anarchy, not government. Hence, Locke allows for forceful resistance to the ruler only when he or his men have themselves employed unlawful and unjust force. Armed resistance to the ruler is, however, not to be taken lightly. Only if his illegal acts have affected the majority of the people, or have affected only a few but the precedent and consequences appear to threaten the majority, does Locke allow subjects to resort to armed opposition. The assumption is that many are persuaded in their consciences that their laws, lives, liberties, and possessions are in danger.

Rebellion and revolution are, for Locke, virtually inevitable when the people are made miserable by arbitrary power. Not easily aroused, the people generally will rise up only after they have suffered a long train of abuses. Besides, it is not the people in such circumstances who are the rebels, but rather the tyrant who has destroyed the 'umpirage which everyone had consented to for a peaceable decision of all their controversies and a bar to the state of war amongst them' (#227, 377). For Locke, the question of who shall be the judge whether the prince has violated his trust can have only one reasonable answer: 'the people shall be judge.' And it is the people who, once they have removed the tyrant, have a right to establish a new form of government, 'or under the old form place it in new hands, as they think good' (#243, 387).

Chapter Six

Montesquieu

Montesquieu, a true son of his age, had thoroughly emancipated himself from the medieval heritage. Like other representatives of the eighteenth-century Enlightenment, he was well acquainted with the two philosophical movements of the previous century, rationalism and empiricism – movements that had remained relatively separate from each other and thus without any significant reciprocal influence. Descartes had played a key role in founding the first movement, while Galileo pioneered in the use of experimentation and Bacon explained its particular virtues. The Enlightenment thinkers made a sustained effort to bring together the two philosophical approaches and to integrate them into one unified method; and Montesquieu, a leading *philosophe*, believed he had succeeded in synthesizing the best elements of the rational and empirical movements. In his concern with regularities, he sought the laws of social and historical development. He studied facts not for their own sake, but for the laws that become manifest through them: 'I began to examine men and I believed that in the infinite variety of their laws and customs they were not guided solely by their whims. I formulated principles, and then I saw individual cases fitting these principles as if of themselves, the history of all nations being only the consequence of these principles and every special law bound to another law, or depending on another more general law.'

That was Montesquieu's mature theoretical standpoint as written in the preface to his chief work, *The Spirit of the Laws*, published in 1748. He did not, however, begin his intellectual career with this theoretical approach, which developed only gradually as the joint product of his vast reading knowledge and wide travels in Europe. His first published book, *The Persian Letters* (1721), preceded those travels and was a work of literary and sociological imagination that met with an enormous and immediate success. The workings of social laws and causes are, however, less clear here than they become in his next major work, *Considerations on the Causes of the Grandeur of the Romans and of Their Decline* (1734), published after his extensive travels in Hungary, Italy, Austria, Germany, and England. Let us briefly review the significance of the two earlier works, and then turn our attention to a full analysis of *The Spirit of the Laws*.

The Persian Letters

The Persian Letters is an epistolary novel about several Persians who leave their homeland in 1711, travel to Europe, and take up residence in France until 1720. During that entire stretch of time they comment critically and sardonically on French social institutions, mores, and customs, which differ so markedly from those of their native Persia. The novel unfolds in a series of letters presenting scenes from French social and cultural life and containing short essays on philosophical and political themes. There is, however, another element of the novel that probably accounts for its immense popularity. Usbek, the principal character, has left behind all his wives in his harem in Ispahan, where as a result of his nine-year absence the harem is torn by strife and, finally, open revolt against the master. The correspondence between Usbek and Rica and their fellow Persians back home thus satisfied the European craving for knowledge of the East by providing glimpses of polygamous life in the seraglios of Turkey.

The Enlightenment thinkers were not only rational and empirical, they were also critical of the old regime. Indeed, it was their primary aim to evaluate all social institutions before the judgment seat of Reason. Montesquieu accomplishes such an evaluation by centring his novel on the Persian visitors who view French society as diverging from what is right and proper in their homeland. This change in perspective enables Montesquieu to challenge the French standard as the one, purportedly, by which to measure the rest of humanity. From the Persians' perspective the follies of the French ways become evident when compared with their own practices in Persia. In this way Montesquieu's French readers are compelled to view their society through strangers' eyes and become aware of its flaws. The taken-for-granted status quo is scrutinized from a standpoint outside the prevailing consensus. So while French readers at first found the novel interesting and amusing, they soon came to recognize it as a serious questioning of the existing social and political arrangements.

It is for such reasons that *The Persian Letters* became a central philosophical text of the eighteenth century, especially among the *philosophes*, the liberal thinkers and writers who tore down the *ancien régime* intellectually and thus paved the way for the actual revolution of 1789. Early in the novel (*PL*, letters 11–14)[1] Usbek tells the story of a primitive, cave-dwelling people – Troglodytes – who were fierce and evil, lacking any principle of fairness or justice. Living in continual strife, they first depose a king who has conquered them, and then overthrow the magistrates they themselves have elected. Rejecting all forms of authority, they live in a state in which everyone pursues his own interest without concern for anyone else's. The Troglodytes have achieved absolute liberty, but at the price of an anarchy resembling a Hobbesian 'war of each against all.' From this lawless state where might is right, two families escape, inspired by the ideals of humanity, justice, and virtue, the last of which terms implies, for Montesquieu, both moral and civic virtue. The families begin a new society based on a shared concern for the common interest. In time they thrive because they have put into practice a civil ideal, teaching their children that self-interest should always be compatible with the common interest. Civic virtue is neither costly nor painful to the individual, since justice for others brings justice for oneself. Soon, however, outsiders, envious of the prosperity of the new society, threaten them with invasion. When the Troglodyte efforts at negotiating peace fail, they defend themselves vigorously, totally defeating their enemy because they fight not for special interests, but for the common good.

Despite their victory, feeling themselves insecure, they decide to choose a king to rule over them. They elect the most venerable, wise, and just man, but he is far from happy with their decision, seeing it as an abdication of their individual and common responsibility to maintain the high level of civic mindedness and mutual aid that has made their prosperity possible. He therefore admonishes them to the following effect: 'In your present situation, having no ruler, you must be virtuous; for without virtue you would fall back into the misfortunes of your first fathers. But virtue requires responsibility, a yoke that appears too heavy for you. You would rather submit to a prince and his laws, than to your own mores and customs.' Although the episode ends abruptly, and we are not told how the Troglodytes respond to the admonition, Montesquieu wants us to infer that such a change in government would have been contrary to the people's common interest.

Read as a parable, this story of the Troglodytes conveys a principle that remains fundamental to all of Montesquieu's later thinking: the imposition of laws from the outside cannot create a just and stable political society. Laws have to be internalized if they are to acquire their full effectiveness. Montesquieu's term *virtue* refers to this inner obligation on the part of citizens, a condition without which a state cannot thrive. Virtue is acquired through moral education and expresses itself in the society's customs and mores (*moeurs* in French) and in the citizens' obedience to them. In later letters Usbek attempts to define the most reasonable form of political society, proposing that the best government is one that leads individuals in the manner best suited to their needs and habits. Again the point is that the policies of a good government must resonate with the basic moral sentiments of the people, and not run counter to their time-honoured customs. The long-standing customs of the people, embodying the wisdom that comes from reflection on experience, should be respected and systematically imparted to the children. The people's traditions, as repositories of wisdom, should be carefully preserved, for 'customs and mores always produce better citizens than laws do' (*PL*, 129).

Montesquieu approaches the subject of religion with the same philosophical aim in view. Like the other *philosophes*, he was critical of Catholicism, the official organized religion of France, because he regarded many of its doctrines as irrational sources of superstition. For Montesquieu, the moral teachings of Christianity are its essential elements. He therefore has Usbek remark, concerning the religious disputes in France, that the parties to the controversies conduct themselves neither as good Christians nor as good citizens. What Usbek values most in religion is the respect for morally grounded laws, the love for one's fellow human beings, and the devotion to one's parents. In a word, dogmas and rituals are less important than trying to live in accordance with the Golden Rule.

The Enlightenment thinkers who held this deistic point of view believed in God, but interpreted God's teachings as intended to enhance human happiness in this world. Deism, therefore, also taught tolerance for diverse religious beliefs at a time when religions persecuted dissidents and rivals as heretics. It is in the tolerant, deistic spirit that Usbek closes a letter to Rhedi with this prayer: 'I cannot so much as move my head without being told that I am offending you; however, I wish to please you and employ to that end the life I have received from you. I do not know if I am mistaken; but I think that the best way to attain that end is to live as a good citizen of the society in which you have caused me to be born and as a good father of the family that you have given me' (*PL*, 46). The worldly essence of religion is to live one's life according to the highest ethical and moral standards. And insofar as members of a society abide by those standards, it enhances the goodness of the political state.

The Persian Letters is more in the nature of a literary work than a treatise on political philosophy. There are, of course, politically relevant insights to be found in this work; but by no stretch of the imagination do the letters anticipate the important ideas of Montesquieu's later works. Often one finds that a letter jumps from one topic to another, leaving issues unresolved. If one approaches *The Persian Letters* in the expectation that the disparate reflections will somehow be pulled together in a systematic fashion, one will surely be disappointed. So while this work may be regarded as a significant, eighteenth-century literary achievement, it is a weak source in which to search for the trans-historical insights of political philosophy. Montesquieu's chief work, *The Spirit of the Laws*, does deliver such insights; but before proceeding to that work, we need to say a word about his study of Roman history, a truly original and impressive achievement.

Considerations on the Causes of the Grandeur of the Romans and of Their Decline

The originality of this work lies precisely in Montesquieu's attempt to seek out the *causes* of historical processes, causes that operate beneath the surface and that, therefore, are not readily evident even to those who know the historical events quite well. While the *Considerations* did not enjoy anything like the popularity of *The Persian Letters*, it inspired Gibbon's great work on the Romans by uncovering some of the major factors that led first to Roman aggrandizement and political vitality in the period of the republic, and then to decline in the period of the empire.

Rome remained great, Montesquieu argued, so long as its territorial conquests had not undermined the unified spirit of devotion to the commonwealth that had characterized its civic life in the period of the early republic. Originally Rome had been a comparatively homogeneous and egalitarian entity supported by political virtue. With a large proportion of its population being young, vigorous, and well trained in military discipline and technique, Rome was able to achieve great victories in the wars against Carthage. The senate offered a model of stability and resoluteness for the Roman character, cleverly dividing Rome's enemies and maintaining its allies in a subordinate position. Enemies like Mithradates successfully resisted Rome for a long time because he possessed many of the same virtues and advantages that the early Romans themselves had possessed. Pompey's victory over him marks the high point of Rome's power and, ironically, the beginning of its decline. The vast expanses incorporated into the empire brought with them neither a real gain in power nor an enhancement of liberty for Rome's citizens.

To illuminate the causes of the decline, Montesquieu begins in chapter 8 to discuss the class divisions that had always existed in the city. From earliest times intense conflict prevailed between the patricians and the plebeians. For a long time the strife between them had the salutary effect of energizing the body politic. The tribunes and the other state organs mediated and moderated the conflict between the classes so that they remained in a dynamic equilibrium. However, the expansion of the empire interacted with other causes to create a new situation: each class now strove to dominate the other rather than to maintain the balance between them. Moreover, as Montesquieu suggests in chapter 9, two factors began to undermine the Roman national identity and character. First, the Roman soldiers began to feel a greater loyalty to their military commanders than to the senate or the state. No longer thinking of themselves as soldiers of the republic, they became, instead, the loyal followers of Sulla, Marius, Pompey, or Caesar. This attitude together with the growing number of foreign mercenaries radically weakened the army's spirit of unity on which the maintenance of the empire was ultimately based. The second factor tending to undermine Roman national unity was the granting of Roman citizenship to more and more foreigners who simply lacked the love of liberty and hatred of tyranny so characteristic of the Romans themselves. With the influx of foreign ethnic groups the concept of being a Roman lost its unifying power.

Another consequence of Rome's victories and the expansion of empire was moral corruption, as Montesquieu explains in chapter 10. Victories meant that the legions brought back to Rome enormous quantities of booty. The spoils of war introduced unprecedented wealth and luxury, so that many individuals came to look with contempt upon work, craftsmanship, and trade, abandoning those skills and delegating them to their slaves. At about the same time a hedonistic version of Epicurean philosophy was introduced in Rome, undermining the warrior ethic and the strict military discipline of earlier times.

The accumulating moral and structural changes are made more vivid

in chapters 14 through 16, where Montesquieu reviews the empire's disintegration under Tiberius, Caligula, Nero, and the weak emperors who
succeeded them, with only a brief interlude under Marcus Aurelius,
who attempted to restore the old values but failed. By the time the
empire was split in two, Asiatic pomp and ceremony had totally triumphed over the old Roman frugality. The root cause of Rome's fall,
Montesquieu proposes, is that the Romans 'established customs that
were entirely contrary to those that had made them masters of the world
[*maîtres de tout*]' (*Oeuvres complètes*, vol. 2, 173). Here, in chapter 18, Montesquieu lets us know more explicitly what he regards as the method
that has guided him in this study: 'It is not fate or fortune that rules the
world ... There are general causes, either moral or physical, that are at
work in each State, that raise it up, maintain it, or precipitate its fall; all
[so-called] accidents are subject to these causes; ... in a word, the principal cause drags along with it all the accidental particulars' (ibid.). This
statement describes succinctly a new approach to the study of history
and society, which Montesquieu will perfect in the work of his maturity
for which he is justly famous.

The Spirit of the Laws

Montesquieu opens his masterwork with a discussion of laws in general, by which he means not positive laws made by human beings, but
rather natural, physical, or invariable laws. A law in that sense refers to
'the necessary relations deriving from the nature of things.' Like the
other *philosophes*, Montesquieu was greatly impressed by the scientific
achievements of the seventeenth century, and in particular by the epoch-
making contribution of Newton. Galileo had discovered an invariable
law when he observed that falling bodies accelerate at a constant rate;
just as Kepler had discovered such a law in the fixed relationship
between the distance of a planet from the sun and the speed of its revolution. Newton modestly acknowledged that his own contribution was
made possible by standing on the shoulders of those two giants who
had preceded him. He meant that it was by employing the discoveries of
Galileo and Kepler that he arrived at the law that the sun attracted planets to itself at a rate directly proportional to their mass and inversely
proportional to the square of the distance between them. Eventually he
was able to demonstrate that all bodies of the universe took their positions and movements through the force of gravitation. Moreover, the
force that held the planets in orbit also made objects fall to the ground.

The law was operative throughout the universe. Here was a magnificent triumph of reason *and* observation, the new method that takes observed facts and advances an interpretation that accounts for what is observed so that if the interpretation is correct, it can guide observers in their quest for new facts. It is laws in this sense to which Montesquieu refers when he speaks of them as 'the necessary relations deriving from the nature of things.' And, Montesquieu reasoned, if the material world and the beasts have their laws, then surely the human condition must also have its laws.

However, Montesquieu posited a significant difference between laws in the physical world and laws in the intelligent world. For although the intelligent world is also governed by laws that are invariable, intelligent beings do not follow such laws consistently. Animals, for example, attracted as they are by members of the opposite sex, thereby preserve their species. That they are subject to physical laws is therefore evident in their being drawn together by feeling. Still, they do not invariably follow those laws, since they are creatures that possess a degree of autonomy. Plants, in contrast, which, we surmise, possess neither a cognitive capacity nor feeling, follow the physical laws more consistently. The human being as a physical being is also governed by invariable laws, just as all other physical bodies are. But the human being tends to violate both the laws of God and the laws of nature. The reason for this is that human beings, subject as they are to myriad passions, *are subject to ignorance and error.* Precisely because humans are driven by what are often destructive and self-destructive passions, they cannot live without moral and civil laws.

Montesquieu posits a state of nature quite the opposite of Hobbes's. If Hobbes insisted on the fundamental equality of humans in that state, Montesquieu holds that humans would hardly feel themselves as equal. Hence, they would refrain from attacking one another and seek peace as their first natural law. Like Rousseau after him, Montesquieu accuses Hobbes of having imported into his state of nature attributes that could only have emerged with or after the establishment of society. For Montesquieu, humans in their pre-social condition, feeling vulnerable and fearful, would rather flee from one another than fight. But humans in that condition would also feel the need for nourishment, and in the course of seeking it would, perforce, approach one another and form a society. Contra Hobbes, Montesquieu proposes that as humans enter society the state of war begins. It is in society that individuals begin to feel their strength; and in seeking to gain advantage over their fellows, they bring about a state of war. At the same time, since not one but many separate societies emerge from the state of nature, each society comes to feel its strength, and in seeking its own advantage produces a state of war among nations. These two states of war bring about the need for the enactment of laws to ensure the honouring of three distinct rights: (1) the right of peoples or nations (*le droit des gens*), laws governing the relations of separate and independent commonwealths; (2) political right, laws regulating the relations between those who govern and those who are governed; and (3) civil right, laws regulating the relations that all citizens have with one another.

Montesquieu now introduces his classification of governments: the republican, monarchical, and despotic. In a republic the people, or a portion of it, hold sovereign power; in a monarchy one alone governs, but according to established laws; in despotic government, one alone governs, but without law. A republic has two opposing tendencies, one democratic, the other aristocratic. When the people as a body hold sovereign power, it is a democracy; when only a portion of the people have sovereignty, it is an aristocracy. In a democracy the people are, so to speak, both monarch and subjects. The people may express their sovereign will either in assembly or by delegating authority to ministers. Although the people may be divided into classes, as was the case in Athens and Rome, great legislators have known how to mediate between the classes to preserve the stability and prosperity of a republic. In an aristocracy, democracy prevails only within the body of nobles, and the people are nothing. This is foreign to the essential nature of a republic. Therefore, the more a republic approaches a democracy, the more perfect it is. Monarchy refers to the rule of one who is bound by fundamental laws, and whose relation with the people is mediated by intermediate powers that serve to prevent the monarch's power from becoming absolute. Here Montesquieu somewhat anticipates the argument he will present in Book XI: where there exist neither laws that the monarch is obliged to observe, nor intermediate powers between the monarch and the people, the monarch becomes a despot and the people become abject subjects. Thinking primarily of the monarchies of his own time, Montesquieu proposes that the most natural intermediate power is the nobility. The contrast between Britain and France, in this regard, was quite enlightening. In seventeenth-century Britain the power of the landed and commercialized nobility was preserved and institutionalized in the parliament. In France, in the same period, the power of the nobles was so drastically reduced under Louis XIV that they became little more than an appendage to the Crown. Thus Montesquieu presciently remarks that if the prerogatives of the clergy, nobility, and towns are eliminated in a monarchy, it will eventually degenerate into either anarchy or despotism, or a vacillation between them.

When Montesquieu speaks of a republic, a monarchy, or a despotism, those terms refer to whole societies, not just political systems. As he advances in his exposition he shows that a definite relationship exists between a political system and other social and non-social conditions. Monarchy is suited to the conditions of the large nations of the Europe of his time. The peoples of antiquity also had 'kings' – the Greeks, the Latins, and the Germans, for example. But those kingdoms were quite different from the absolute and constitutional monarchies of eighteenth-century Europe. Forms of despotism have also been known to have existed in various places and periods, often resulting from the corruption of other political forms. Still, despotism had its 'natural' or 'perfect' existence only in Asia.

The republican form has been found primarily in towns and is best suited to a small population. When numbers grow beyond a certain point, the republican form tends to break down. The despotic state, in contrast, is found in highly populous societies, spread over vast areas, as in Asia. The monarchical state stands in between: it is of medium size, having a population larger than that of a republic, but smaller than that of a despotic state. All citizens are equal and even alike in a democratic republic. A kind of homogeneity and, hence, order are evident. There exist definite restrictions on the excessive accumulation of wealth and power that might undermine the solidarity and the very existence of a democratic republic. Democracy can become debased by transforming itself into an aristocracy.

In a monarchy, social-class divisions have become more pronounced than in a republic. Farming, trade, and manufacturing, and an increasingly complex division of labour, produce class conflict. Yet, it is in a monarchy that Montesquieu envisions maximal political freedom. Classes, such as the nobility and the bourgeoisie, check and limit not only the power of the monarch, but one another as well. Each class, in preventing the other from becoming too powerful, remains free to pursue its special interests, but in moderation. Individual interest, envy, and rivalry emerge as strong forces in a monarchy, and individuals and groups tend to disregard the general welfare of society in favour of personal and class interests. However, anticipating the utilitarian doctrine, Montesquieu argues that individual and class interests prompt the citizens of a monarchy to perform their respective functions as well as possible, which conduces, ultimately, to the common good. Under despotism, in contrast, all intermediate orders of society have become so weakened that they can offer no organized resistance to the despot. All subjects are equal in their condition of servitude. If *virtue* is the basis for participation in a democratic republic, and *honour* is such a basis in a monarchy, then *fear* is the ground for submission to a despot.

As observed earlier, Montesquieu conceives of a 'law' as the 'necessary relations arising from the nature of things.' Laws, in this sense, are no less operative in human societies than they are in nature. Laws depend on the form of political society. Hence, the laws of a republic differ from those of a monarchy. The latter, being structurally more complex, requires the recognition of laws most appropriate for the regulation of its component elements. Laws would remain hidden and implicit, however, if some great legislator had not discerned and formulated them explicitly. Furthermore, laws may be at variance with the requirements of a certain type of society because what the nature of a society requires is, after all, a matter of judgment, and judgment is subject to ignorance and error. An element of contingency is thus introduced. A society would be what its nature prescribes, were it not for the erroneous judgments of those who decide what the prescriptions are.

Montesquieu's conception of law as expressing the necessary relations among things thus retains ambiguous elements. He proposed that by studying the conditions of a particular society, one can discover its laws (what its nature requires) and create legal forms and other institutions that best suit that nature. But the creation of such institutions inevitably involves an interpretation of what a society's true nature is, and is therefore subject to error. Were it not for ignorance and error, human beings would devise positive laws in perfect accord with a society's nature. The elements of society would then be perfectly articulated and integrated. However, the element of contingency that Montesquieu has introduced implies that humans can never achieve such perfect articulation. Moreover, Montesquieu's element of contingency leads to no small deviations. For example, though the institution of slavery was present in the ancient Greek and Roman republics, Montesquieu insists in Book XV that the institution is repugnant to the nature of republics and monarchies alike. In an ideal republic slavery is unnatural and, therefore, unnecessary. In a real republic of history, slavery was the result of certain social conditions, but one of those conditions was the misinterpretation of the true nature and requirements of a republic. The true nature, expressing not what is but what ought to be, remained hidden from those directly concerned.

Montesquieu's social laws, therefore, sometimes are and sometimes are not like other laws of nature, inherent in phenomena. Laws in the social realm may remain unrecognized and therefore inoperative. The ambiguity in Montesquieu's conception of a social law flows from his recognition of certain degrees of freedom in human conduct. The degrees of freedom that enabled individuals to institute slavery – contrary to the true nature of a republic – also enable them, once having recognized their mistake, to eliminate it.

On the Laws That Form Political Liberty

In Book XI, one of the best-known and most influential parts of *The Spirit of the Laws*, Montesquieu takes up the question of the relation of liberty to power. What is liberty? Does liberty consist in doing what one wants to do? No, says Montesquieu emphatically. Liberty 'can consist only in having the power to do what one *should* want to do and in no way being compelled to do what one should not want to do' (XI, 3, italics added). The ethical-moral element of true liberty is thus underscored. 'Liberty is the right to do all that the laws permit.' The term 'laws' in this context refers to positive laws formulated and enacted by legislators. So a fundamental question emerges: What is the relation of such laws to ethical and moral principles? Are positive laws arbitrary prescriptions and proscriptions imposed by government? Or is it Montesquieu's meaning that positive laws should embody fundamental moral principles?

Some commentators have employed the term 'relativism' to describe Montesquieu's philosophical attitude towards the bewildering variety of human laws, customs, and traditions. But that term does Montesquieu an injustice. It is true, as we have seen, that the whole of *The Persian Letters* seems designed to convey what anthropologists call 'cultural relativism.' The Turkish visitors to France are dismayed at customs the French take for granted. Some customs have no definite moral implications. Montesquieu remarks, for example, that a European shakes with his right hand, a Turk with his left. There are many such morally neutral examples in *The Persian Letters*, but there are also many with a definite moral significance. So, was Montesquieu a 'relativist'? This question can be answered with certainty: he was a cultural relativist with respect to the vast array of morally neutral cultural patterns. But he was certainly no relativist where morality was concerned.

In his *Notes on England*, Montesquieu makes a statement that some commentators have taken as evidence of his relativistic outlook: 'When I travel to a country, I do not investigate whether there are good laws, but whether those that exist are executed, for there are good laws everywhere.'[2] But this passage is followed by another that speaks directly to the issue at hand: 'It seems to me that no nation's customs and practices, *when not contrary to morality*, can be judged superior to those of others. For by what rule would one judge? They do not have a common measure except that each nation makes an example of its own and by them judges all the others.'[3] It is clear, then, that for Montesquieu one nation's customs and practices, insofar as they are contrary to morality, can be judged inferior to those of other nations, and that Montesquieu's so-called 'relativism' applies only to morally-neutral practices. He accepted the absolute validity of certain moral principles, which led him to prefer liberty over subjection to a despot.

In Book XI it is presupposed that positive laws have to embody fundamental moral principles if liberty and justice are to prevail. Political liberty is found only in republics and monarchies where power is not abused. But how does one prevent the abuse of power? Montesquieu responds by laying down an axiom: only power can check power. It is therefore necessary to constitute government so as to create a balance of powers that guarantees freedom under the laws. This theory of an equilibrium of powers as the precondition of freedom leads to the famous chapter on the British Constitution, which profoundly influenced the framers of the American Constitution. In every state there are three governmental powers: a legislative power, an executive power over foreign affairs, and what Montesquieu calls an executive power over the civil rights of the members of the commonwealth. The first power makes laws, the second engages in diplomacy and decides on peace and war, and the third adjudicates disputes between citizens and determines policy with regard to crime and punishment. Montesquieu calls the second 'executive' power, the power of judging. And although this power is not an explicitly independent judiciary, as it is in the American Constitution, it nevertheless has some of the features of such a judiciary, as further discussion of it makes clear.

Liberty implies a tranquillity of spirit, which comes from the opinion of the citizenry that they have nothing to fear from one another. And there can be neither tranquillity nor liberty where the legislative and executive powers are united in the same person. 'Nor,' Montesquieu continues, 'is there liberty if the power of judging is not separate from legislative power and from executive power. If it were joined to legislative power, the power over the life and liberty of the citizens would be arbitrary, for the judge would be the legislator. If it were joined to executive power, the judge would have the force of an oppressor' (XI, 6). In a word, when all three powers are concentrated in the same hands, a terrible despotism reigns.

The three powers are so organized as to provide counterweights to one another. Each of the powers has the capacity both to enact and to veto. The executive power should be in the hands of a monarch, because executive responsibilities almost always demand immediate action and are better administered by one than by many. The responsibilities of the legislative power require deliberation and are therefore better accomplished by an assembly. Liberty is always endangered if the executive power is entrusted to the legislative body, just as liberty is threatened if the legislative body fails to convene for a long stretch of time; for then either the legislative power would become defunct and the state would fall into anarchy, or legislative resolutions would be made by the executive power, which would then become absolute. The legislative body should not convene itself; for if it had the right to prorogue itself, it might never do so. Therefore, it should be the executive who decides the suitable times for convening the legislative assembly.

It is noteworthy that Montesquieu somehow views the executive as inherently weaker than the legislative. He allows the executive to check the resolutions of the legislative body, but he denies to the legislative body the reciprocal right to check the executive power: 'For as the executive has the limits of its own nature, it is useless to restrict it' (XI, 6). The person of the executive should be sacred and inviolable, since his role is essential to the state in preventing the legislature from becoming tyrannical. In this respect Montesquieu is very much the product of the French monarchical system. If wrong is done in the king's name, it is not the king himself, but his ministers and wicked counsellors who are to blame. The impeachment provision of the American Constitution would seem to be too democratic for Montesquieu; just as putting the king on trial, as was done in the French Revolution, would have been unthinkable to him. And yet it is curious that Montesquieu, writing after the English civil war and the Glorious Revolution, and inspired as he was by the British Constitution, should have viewed the king as inherently weak – unless, of course, he drew this conclusion from the aftermath of the Glorious Revolution when the power of the parliament was substantially increased. Although Montesquieu denies to the legislature the right to check the executive power, he nevertheless gives it the right to examine the manner in which the laws it has made have been executed.

The executive, legislative, and judicial powers are distinct, but not necessarily separate, since Montesquieu provides for their interpenetration by means of the veto – but not with perfect reciprocity. So though he stipulates that the executive power should take part in legislation by means of the veto, he does not extend the same right of veto to the legislature. Moreover, the judicial power, in contrast to provisions of the American Constitution, plays no significant role as a counterweight similar to that of the other two powers. Neither the executive nor the legislature may raise public funds without the consent of the other, but there is no provision for assessing the 'constitutionality' of either executive actions or legislation.

While Montesquieu speaks of the executive monarch as inherently weak in Book XI, chapter 6, he acknowledges in chapter 7 that a monarchy can degenerate into despotism since a monarchy tends to concentrate power in the prince, thus threatening the equilibrium of powers. Moreover, based as it is on the ruling passion of honour, a monarchy primarily pursues glory, not liberty. And yet, glory can lead to a 'spirit of liberty.' To illustrate this, Montesquieu briefly considers the history of the Germanic peoples. After their conquest of Rome, the Germanic tribes evolved from a form of direct democracy in which 'the whole people could assemble' (XI, 8) to government by representatives. As the intermediate powers gradually emerged, checking each other and working cooperatively, the boundaries of freedom were actually widened: 'Soon the civil liberty of the people, the prerogatives of the nobility and clergy, and the power of the kings found themselves in such harmony that I do not think there has been in any part of Europe a government ... so well tempered as this one' (XI, 8). As for Rome, one can learn much from its history about the preconditions of liberty. After his work on the causes of the grandeur and decline of the Romans, Montesquieu was well equipped to explore the relationship of liberty to power.

He begins with an analysis of the conditions that led to the overthrow of the tyrant Tarquin in early Rome. By acquiring too much power and abusing it, Tarquin led to his own downfall. He had himself placed in the seat of power without the consent of either the senate or the people. He murdered most of the senators and ignored those who remained. 'His power increased, but what was odious about his rule became still more odious: he usurped the power of the people; he made laws without them; he even made some in opposition to them. He would have united the three powers in his person, but the people remembered at a certain moment that they were the legislator, and Tarquin was no longer' (XI, 12).

By thus employing his concept of constitutional balance, Montesquieu illustrates how the likelihood of tyranny increases when powers are not divided, and how political stability and liberty are restored with the division and balancing of governmental powers. Montesquieu proceeds to show how the distribution of the three powers began to change after the expulsion of the kings. Four main obstacles to liberty remained in effect: the patricians monopolized power in the religious, political, civil, and military realms; the consul held excessive power; the state subjected the people to outrages with impunity; and, finally, the people had almost no political influence. The people corrected these abuses in the following ways: (1) they demanded that the plebeians be made eligible to serve in the magistracies, and gradually succeeded in acquiring posts in almost all of them; (2) the original consulate was dismantled and transformed into several magistracies, and the prerogatives of a consul were drastically reduced; (3) laws were enacted to create the institution of the tribunes, who could check the power of the patricians; and (4) the plebeians, in gaining the right to judge patricians, expanded considerably their influence in public matters.

But the people's liberty was soon threatened from another quarter. In the heat of the conflict between the patricians and the plebeians, the latter demanded the enactment of definite laws to ensure that judgments would no longer be made arbitrarily. Though the senate long resisted this demand, it eventually acquiesced, and the Decemvirs, ten men, were appointed to formulate the laws. On the premise that their task would be exceedingly difficult – making laws for parties that were incompatible – the ten were granted extraordinary powers. The appointment of magistrates was suspended during the tenure of the ten, who now became the sole administrators of the republic. They were invested with both the power of the consuls and the power of the tribunes. Although the former gave the ten the right to convene the senate, and the latter the right to call the people to assembly, the Decemvirs did neither. Thus ten men alone in the republic held in their hands the executive, legislative, and judicial powers. Rome now saw itself subjected to a tyranny as cruel as that of the Tarquins, though Tarquin had acquired his power by usurpation while the ten had obtained theirs due to the naïvete of the people, who were stunned by the power they had given away. Like Machiavelli, Montesquieu was impressed with the historical fact that it required an outrageous offence against the sentiments of the people to topple the ten from power. One of the Decemvirs had arrogantly supposed that he could have a young woman, Virginia, against her will. Her father, however, chose to prevent this by means of the most extreme measure: 'The spectacle of the death of Virginia, sacrificed by her father to modesty and liberty, made the powers of the Decemvirs evaporate. Each man was free because each was offended; everyone became a [concerned] citizen because everyone was a father. The senate and the people returned to a liberty that had been entrusted to ridiculous tyrants' (XI, 15).

In Book XII, on laws that form political liberty in relation to the citizen, Montesquieu reminds us that just laws stipulate punishments that are not arbitrary, but rather adapted to the nature of the crime. The rule of law is so fundamental to liberty that, paradoxically, a citizen who has been justly convicted in accordance with the law, and who, therefore, is to be executed the next morning, 'would be freer than a pasha in Turkey' (XII, 2). Offences against religion such as sacrilege, when they entail no injuries to citizens or to the state, are not to be regarded as criminal. Montesquieu recognized the danger that political leaders, on the pretext of defending the divinity, might create an inquisition. He defends freedom of thought, insisting that only external actions injurious to citizens should be punished, and freedom of speech unless it leads directly to criminal action: 'Thus a man who goes into the public square to exhort the subjects to revolt becomes guilty of high treason, because the speech is joined to the act and participates in it. It is not speech that is punished, but an act committed in which speech is used. Speech becomes criminal only when it prepares, accompanies or follows a criminal act' (XII, 12). To appreciate the boldness of Montesquieu's liberal position in this regard, we need to remind ourselves that he is writing in an era of French absolutism when arbitrary imprisonment, censorship of all written materials, and spying on the mails were common, everyday occurrences. In advocating freedom of expression, Montesquieu was actively supporting the ideological struggle of his fellow *philosophes*.

Liberty may also be threatened by the way in which taxes are levied. The revenues of the state derive from the portion each citizen gives of his goods in order to have the security and comfort shared by his fellow citizens. In fixing the amount of these revenues both the real needs of the state and the real needs of the citizens should be considered: 'One must not take from the real needs of the people for the imaginary needs of the State.' There 'is nothing that wisdom and prudence should regulate more than the portion taken away from the subjects and the portion left to them' (XIII, 1).

Climate

Books XIV through XIX are devoted to the question of how climate and other geographical conditions influence human conduct. There can be little doubt that Montesquieu overstated the impact of diverse climates on the constitution of societies. Indeed, in some cases his propositions are plainly silly. He asserts, for example, that 'people in warm climates are as timid as old men while those in cold countries are as brave as young ones' (XIX, 2). In northern climates individuals tend to be vigorous and libertarian while in southern climes they tend to be servile: 'There was in cold climates a certain strength of mind and body which made men capable of actions that were prolonged, difficult, great and audacious ... We should not be surprised, then, that the cowardice of people from warm climates has almost always made them slaves and the courage of those from cold climates has kept them free' (XXII, 2). Maintaining that Asia, unlike Europe, has no temperate zone, Montesquieu tries to correlate climate with liberty: 'That is the main reason for the weakness of Asia and the strength of Europe, the liberty of Europe and the servitude of Asia, a cause that to my knowledge has never before been noticed' (XVII, 3).

On the other hand, one finds among his aphorisms on climate – Montesquieu's style of exposition throughout *The Spirit of the Laws* is aphoristic – qualifications of what often seems to be a form of climatic determinism. He writes, for example:

Many things govern men: climate, religion, laws, maxims of government, examples of past things, mores, and manners; a general spirit is formed as a result.

To the extent that, in each nation, one of these causes acts more forcefully, the others yield to it. (XIX, 4)

The last sentence may help us to grasp the complexity of the theoretical approach being proposed. For Montesquieu, all the causal factors are interactively connected. As the causal weight of one increases, the weight of the others diminishes correspondingly. The recognition of multiple and interdependent causes in the above-quoted aphorism may be taken as a corrective to the apparently rigid theory of climate expressed in many of the other passages in Books XIV through XIX.

Religion

As a *philosophe*, Montesquieu was bound to find himself in opposition to the Catholic Church, the chief disseminator of irrational doctrines and the ideological mainstay of the old regime in France. He knew, of course, that approaching the subject of religion from a rational perspective was dangerous. And although he formulated his ideas with due caution, hoping the church would find them inoffensive, *The Spirit of the Laws* was placed on the Papal Index in 1751. In Book XXIV, Montesquieu's primary concern is with the political and social effects of religious doctrines and institutions. He is careful to say that the Christian religion, commanding human beings to love one another, desires the best political institutions and the best civil laws for each people. He is also prudent enough to call the other faiths he touches upon 'false religions,' as he describes his primary aim to be a search 'among the false religions those that are the most compatible with the good of society' (XXIV, 1). But the fact that he proposed religion in general as an essential element of social order – which meant that even the so-called 'false religions' had positive political and social functions – was enough to antagonize the church.

Montesquieu begins by opposing the view of Pierre Bayle, who had claimed it is better to be an atheist than an idol-worshipper and less dangerous politically to have no religion at all than to have a false one. But Montesquieu recognized – as did so many of the great political thinkers who had preceded him – that for both subjects and princes religion is the only 'bridle that can hold those who have no fear of human laws' (XXIV, 2). Even if religion had no direct utility for subjects (which Montesquieu does not grant), it would have great indirect utility for them if the prince were religious. For 'a prince who loves and fears religion is a lion who yields to the hand that caresses him or the voice that pacifies him; the prince who hates religion is like the wild beasts who gnaw the chain that keeps them from throwing themselves on passers-by; he who has no religion at all is that terrible animal that feels its liberty only when it claws and devours' (XXIV, 2). Since even so-called false religions are most often in agreement with morality, religion 'is the best warrant we can have of men's integrity.'

As for Christianity, it is remote from pure despotism owing to the teachings of the Gospels. If we reflect on the cruelty and massacres perpetrated by the ancient Greek and Roman rulers, and on the massive destruction of peoples by Tamerlane and Genghis Khan, 'we shall see that we owe to Christianity both a certain political right in government and a certain right of nations in war, for which human nature can never be sufficiently grateful' (XXIV, 3). Montesquieu also offers us a generalization about the social and political effects of the Reformation: Catholicism is better suited to a monarchy, and Protestantism to a republic. As Protestantism struck deep roots in northern Europe and Catholicism did so in the south, the geographical distribution that either encouraged or discouraged political freedom coincided with his climatic theory. The 'northern peoples,' he writes, 'have and always will have a spirit of independence and liberty that the peoples of the south lack ... A religion that has no visible leader is better suited to the independence fostered by the climate than is the religion that has one' (XXIX, 5).

In Book XXV, where Montesquieu continues his discussion of the relation of religion to civil matters, he follows Locke in advocating religious toleration. Montesquieu makes the important distinction between tolerating a religion and approving of it, a distinction that neither the ecclesiastical nor the civilian authorities of the old regime wished to recognize. If several different religions or denominations are present in a state, then the laws of the state 'must oblige them to tolerate one another. It is a principle that every religion that is repressed becomes repressive itself. For as soon as it throws off oppression, by some chance, it attacks the religion that repressed it, not as a religion, but as a tyranny' (XXV, 9).

Montesquieu also takes up the question whether the Jewish religion ought to be tolerated, and what status Jews should have in an enlightened civil state. Entitled 'Très humble remontrance aux inquisiteurs d'Espagne et de Portugal' (Very Humble Remonstrance to the Inquisitors of Spain and Portugal), chapter 13 of Book XXV is in the tradition of the French *conte philosophique*, a philosophical tale designed to convey an ideal as effectively as possible. Montesquieu places bitingly ironic words into the mouth of the imaginary Jewish author of a long soliloquy, only a portion of which is reproduced here:

You want us to be Christians and yet you do not want to be Christians yourselves ...

You live in a century when natural enlightenment is more alive than it has ever been, when philosophy has enlightened minds, when the morality of your gospel has been better known, when the respective rights of men over one another and the empire that one conscience has over another conscience, are better established. If, therefore, you do not give up your old ideas which, if you do not take care, are but [blind] emotional prejudices, it will be generally acknowledged that you are incorrigible, incapable of any enlightenment or instruction, and that a nation that gives authority to men like you is very unfortunate ... You will be cited to prove that these times were barbaric, and the idea one will have about you will be such that it will stain your century and bring hatred on all your contemporaries. (XXV, 13)

Montesquieu joins his liberal predecessors in separating the civil realm from the religious in matters of law: 'one should not enact by divine laws that which should be enacted by human laws, or regulate by human laws that which should be regulated by divine laws' (XXVI, 2). The separation of church from state means that matters such as suicide and divorce should not be the concerns of the civil authority; and it means, too, that the infamous Inquisition is to be condemned because it violated the principles of good government by treating religious beliefs and practices as concerns of the state. 'This tribunal,' Montesquieu writes, 'is unbearable in all governments. In monarchy it can make only informers and traitors; in republics, it can make only dishonest people; in the despotic state, it is as destructive as the state' (XXVI, 11). Returning to the relation of law to liberty, Montesquieu underscores again that one is free only because one lives under civil laws. It follows that princes of independent commonwealths, in relation to one another, cannot be free because they do not live under common civil laws.

Princes of independent states are governed by force. They live in a Hobbesian state of nature and war, though Montesquieu makes no direct reference to Hobbes in this context. Montesquieu's primary aim here (chapter 20) is to distinguish the principles for the 'right of nations' from the principles of civil law. He proposes that treaties between states imposed by force are as obligatory as those made voluntarily. 'When we who live under civil laws,' Montesquieu writes,

> are constrained to make some contract not required by law, we can with the favour of the law, recover from the violence; but a prince, who is always in the condition of forcing or being forced, cannot complain of a treaty that violence has had him make. It is as if he complained of his natural condition; it is as if he wanted to be a prince in regard to other princes and wanted other princes to be citizens in regard to him; that is, as if he wanted to run counter to the nature of things. (XXVI, 20)

Montesquieu is unconvincing in this regard. If independent states are in a state of nature and war, and their relations are ultimately regulated by force, then it is not at all evident why treaties imposed by force should be regarded as no less obligatory than those made willingly. Is it not inevitable in a state of nature and war that a nation will submit to a forcibly imposed treaty only so long as it lacks the force to nullify it? Indeed, from a Hobbesian standpoint the very term 'right of nations' would appear to be a contradiction in terms, since rights of nations do not and cannot exist so long as the international arena lacks a single, common, absolute and sovereign power.

As Montesquieu approaches the end of Book XXVI, he strikes a loud Lockean chord on the right of revolution:

> When the political law, which has established in the state a certain order of succession, becomes destructive of the political body for which it was made, there must be no doubt that another political law can change that order; and far from that law being in opposition to the first, it will be at bottom entirely in conformity with it, because both will depend on this principle: THE WELL-BEING OF THE PEOPLE IS THE SUPREME LAW (LE SALUT DU PEUPLE EST LA SUPREME LOI). (XXVI, 23)

There is a sixth part of *The Spirit of the Laws*, comprising books twenty-eight to thirty-one. Scholars are in general agreement, however, that this disproportionately long part, comprising about one-third of the whole, is so poorly integrated with the rest of the work that it is more in the nature of an oversized appendix. There Montesquieu addresses issues of Roman and feudal law relevant to the origin of the French monarchy. One school, represented by Abbé Dubos, maintained that the French king traced his authority back to Roman law. The opposing school, led by Boulainvilliers, insisted that French royal authority was rooted in the constitution of the Germanic peoples, where the king was only the first among equals, depending for his power on the nobles who surrounded him. Not surprisingly, Montesquieu favoured Boulainvilliers's view that the Franks had already possessed the concepts of limited monarchy and a responsible aristocratic class that mediated between the monarch and the people; and it is on that note that *The Spirit of the Laws* ends.

As we reflect on the many timeless insights of this monumental work, we come to understand why it exercised so profound an influence on the founders of the American Republic. But before we take up the question of how the founders applied not only Montesquieu's but other classical principles, the political theory of another *philosophe*, Jean-Jacques Rousseau, needs to be considered.

Chapter Seven

Rousseau

Like Hobbes and Locke, Rousseau recognized the need to posit a pre-social human condition. The perfectibility, freedom, and happiness of humanity, and the increasing control of its destiny, all depended on a clear understanding of the laws of nature. In common with the other *philosophes*, Rousseau assumed that both the physical universe and society worked in accordance with such laws. Like Montesquieu, however, Rousseau believed that society could deviate from the requirements of its natural laws because humans often fail to interpret the laws properly. Owing to limited perspectives and inadequate knowledge, humans err; they act contrary to the laws of nature and thus establish societies that not only preclude perfectibility, but actually oppress and violate their members. It was Rousseau's ultimate aim, therefore, to propose an alternative to the prevailing social order.

For Rousseau, then, there were two conditions, the natural and the social; and he understood that in order to allege that a social order is at variance with human nature, one must truly know that nature. But how can one know human nature when humans nowhere live outside society? For it is no light task, Rousseau recognized, 'to separate that which is original from that which is artificial in man's present nature, and attain a solid knowledge of a state which no longer exists, which perhaps never existed, and which will probably never exist, yet of which it is necessary to have sound ideas if we are to judge our present state satisfactorily.'[1] Thus Rousseau, in his *Discourse on Inequality*, posits a 'state of nature,' a hypothetical condition in which the human species is divested of all its social and cultural attributes.

Rousseau begins his thought-experiment by proposing two principles that govern human conduct in the natural state. The first provides us with an ardent interest in our own preservation and well-being, while the second evokes in us a natural aversion to witnessing the destruction or suffering of another sentient creature, especially if it is one of our own kind. For Rousseau, these two principles form the foundation of all the rules of natural law and do not require the assumption of a third principle, namely, that of *sociability* – a problematic view to which we shall return. Natural law is antecedent to reason and expresses the natural human attitude towards other sentient beings. So long as a human being responds and does not resist his inner promptings of sympathy, he will never do injury to another creature; only when his own preservation is at stake will he prefer his own survival over that of another. In these terms, though animals presumably lack the capacity to recognize this natural law, they ought nevertheless to have a share in it. Because animals are sentient creatures, human beings are bound by a definite duty towards them. For Rousseau, our obligation to refrain from harming a fellow human being derives less from the fact that he is a reasoning being than from the fact that he is a sentient one. Since man and beast share this sentient quality, it follows that the latter ought not to be ill-treated by the former.

After proposing this natural law, Rousseau proceeds to present his conception of human beings in a state of nature who are, in all physical respects, very much like ourselves: they are bipedal and employ their hands and senses as we do ours. Though they are less strong and agile than other species of the animal kingdom, these pre-social humans possess greater potential advantages than other species. Rousseau's state of nature is infinitely more benign than that of his predecessors. It is a virtual springtime on Earth in which a bountiful nature provides for all creatures' needs: food, water, and shelter. The vast and naturally fertile Earth, covered with nutritious vegetation and immense virgin forests, affords abundant nourishment to every species of animal. In these conditions the naked human being grows accustomed from infancy to the seasonal changes in weather, and learns to defend himself against or to escape from wild predators. Children, coming into the world with the excellent constitutions of their parents, strengthen themselves with rigorous physical exercises, acquiring all the vigour of which the human race is capable. Nature, says Rousseau, treats these children just as the Spartan regime treated the children of citizens: the well-constituted were preserved and made strong and robust, while the others were left to perish.

If these human individuals in a state of nature are to be distinguished from the animals, it is only in the *human capacity for self-improvement*. The source of this capacity is the passions, for it is by the activity of the passions that human understanding and reason advance. We strive to know because we desire to enjoy. The passions, in turn, owe their origin to human needs. In societies, progress in the power of the mind is exactly proportionate to the circumstances imposed upon humans, and therefore proportionate to the passions impelling them to satisfy their needs. But since humans in a state of nature satisfy their needs with ease, they have no need to employ their faculty for self-improvement, which therefore remains latent and dormant.

Rousseau refuses to attribute to these natural humans social qualities of any kind. They roam the Earth as lone individuals possessing neither language nor even the need for communication. Rousseau summons support for this view by citing the research of Abbé de Condillac, who had established that there can be no language without society; and since Rousseau denies to these humans sociability and association of any kind, he must also deny them language. Indeed, Rousseau considers it an egregious error to suppose that humans in a state of nature had formed families. To suppose that families would exist in that state is the error of attributing to the state of nature associations derived from civil society. In the primitive but bountiful conditions of nature, people possessed neither houses nor huts nor any kind of property, for they slept wherever they happened to find themselves. Males and females united only in brief and temporary encounters in response to desire and opportunity. They had no need for speech to express what they felt for each other, and immediately after the encounter they each went their own way. Rousseau is willing to grant mother and child a somewhat longer relationship for the duration of nursing; but as soon as the child has gained the strength to obtain his own food, he leaves the mother to herself. Once the child has left and become a youth, mother and child would not even recognize each other. Somewhat inconsistently, however, Rousseau appears to open the door to association even in this primordial state when he allows for cries of nature – cries uttered in times of emergency, to beg for help in great danger or for relief of intense suffering. This suggests more than a mere aversion to witnessing the death or suffering of a sentient creature; it suggests enough sociability to prompt individuals to come to the aid of a suffering or endangered creature. Yet Rousseau is adamant in denying sociability to these individuals in a state of nature.

Rousseau's view in this regard is problematic in the extreme. He claims that nature would not have provided humans in a state of nature with the quality of sociability because they have no real mutual needs. 'Indeed,' he writes,

> it is impossible to imagine why in the primitive state one man should have more need for another man than a monkey or a wolf has need for another of its own kind, or, if such a need were assumed, to imagine what motive could induce the second man to supply it, and if so, how the two would agree between them on the terms of the transaction ... In instinct alone man had all he needed for living in a state of nature; in cultivated reason he has what is necessary only for living in society. (*Oeuvres complètes*, III, *Discourse*, 151–2)

There are at least two errors in this conception of the state of nature in which every human being is an island unto himself. First, it is an error to suppose that monkeys and wolves in their natural habitat have no mutual needs. Think of wolf-packs and bands of monkeys. It is simply a fact that most if not all animals in their intra-species' behaviour reveal mutual need that is satisfied by mutual aid. Throughout the animal kingdom we find indisputable evidence of gregariousness, cooperation, and social organization. Even where there is rivalry and conflict, as between males for females, the victory of one over the other redounds to the benefit of the group by providing the best leadership. Second, it is an error to suppose that animals in nature possess some kind of 'instinct,' or built-in biopsychic mechanism that tells them how to behave in a specific situation. Since animals possess brains, nervous systems, and sensory equipment, they naturally possess a cognitive capacity, or a 'reasoning' ability; and it is this cognitive capacity that enables them to acquire the experiential knowledge and skills essential for their survival. A wolf comes into the world with the *capacity* for hunting, but that capacity will remain unrealized if it never *learns* to hunt from its elders. And if mutual need gives rise to mutual aid within animal species, there is no good ground for denying such qualities to human beings in a state of nature. What makes the denial of such qualities appear to be logical to Rousseau is his unrealistic and implausible construction of the state of nature.

It is clear that this construction was intended as a repudiation of Hobbes's state of nature. However, Hobbes's position is summarized by Rousseau with less precision and care than it might have been. Hobbes never asserted what Rousseau attributes to him, namely, 'that man is naturally evil just because he has no idea of goodness, that he is vicious for want of any knowledge of virtue, that he always refuses to do his fellow-men services which he does not believe he owes them, or that on the strength of the right he reasonably claims to things he needs, he foolishly imagines himself to be the sole proprietor of the whole universe' (*Oeuvres complètes*, III, *Discourse*, 153). What Hobbes did assert, as we have seen, is quite different. Human beings naturally desire power, defined as an individual's present means to some future apparent good; and when two or more individuals desire the same good that they nevertheless cannot have, they tend to fight over it. There is nothing in this conception of things that suggests humans are either good or evil. Hobbes could not imagine a state of nature – whether based on animals in that state or on the relations of sovereign nations in the international arena – in which peace would reign because no goods were scarce and there was, therefore, nothing to fight about. Rousseau's state of nature, in contrast, is one in which peace prevails because an individual's care for his own preservation cannot be prejudicial to that of others. Rousseau can entertain this view because all goods are infinitely abundant in his state of nature. He accuses Hobbes of having failed to notice that the ferocity of human pride is moderated: man's 'desire for self-preservation serves to moderate the ardor he has for his own well-being by giving him an innate repugnance against seeing a fellow creature suffer' (154). For Rousseau, then, it is not only the absence of scarcity, but the additional factor of this 'innate repugnance' that accounts for the peaceful condition of his state of nature.

This additional factor of compassion or pity assumes considerable importance in Rousseau's argument. He cites Mandeville favourably for realizing that for all their morality, humans would be no better than monsters if nature had not given them the capacity for *pity*. But Rousseau criticizes Mandeville for failing to realize that all the social virtues flow from this capacity alone. 'In fact,' Rousseau writes, 'what are generosity, mercy, and humanity but compassion applied to the weak, to the guilty or to the human race in general ... Pity is a natural sentiment which, by moderating in each individual the activity of self-love, contributes to the mutual preservation of the whole species. It is pity which carries us without reflection *to the aid of those we see suffering*' (*Oeuvres complètes*, III, *Discourse*, 155–6). This last phrase has been underscored here to call attention to a contradiction. Up to this point in his depiction of the state of nature Rousseau has insisted on the absence of mutual need resulting in mutual aid. Although he had posited the capacity for pity, it had not led to any real association. Now, however, in the above-quoted passage, there is an explicit acknowledgment of mutual need, or at least the need of the weak and the suffering. Pity, says Rousseau, 'will always dissuade a robust savage from robbing a weak child or a sick old man of his hard-won sustenance *if he has the hope of finding his own elsewhere*' (156, italics added). Here again we see how Rousseau's entire argument rests on the premise of a nature so bountiful that scarcity is unknown, for the italicized passage clearly implies that if the savage had no hope of finding his sustenance elsewhere, he might in fact be inclined to take it by force from the child or the old man.

There are inconsistencies in Rousseau's conception of the state of nature. Notwithstanding the interaction and association implied in giving aid to those we see suffering, Rousseau continues to insist that humans in nature 'had no kind of intercourse with one another' (*Oeuvres complètes*, III, *Discourse*, 157). At the same time, employing the example of 'savages,' he allows for a measure of conflict. Savages, he says, are more intent on protecting themselves from the harm that might be done to them than tempted to do harm to others. Hence, humans in a state of nature, he infers, were not prone to especially dangerous quarrels. It is noteworthy that Voltaire, finding this proposition naïve and unconvincing, countered by calling attention to the prevalence of tribal wars among the native peoples of North America.

Equally problematic is Rousseau's conception of man–woman relations in a state of nature. Rousseau distinguishes between the physical and moral elements of love, refusing to allow for the moral element in his state of nature. The moral part of love, he believes, was invented and cultivated by women in society to gain dominance over men. Rousseau again invokes the example of 'savages' and alleges that the moral element in love, based on the notions of merit and beauty, is something of which a savage is incapable. Not only is the savage incapable of discerning merit and forming stable relations, he has no aesthetic faculty. Taste and distaste never enter into the savage male's selection of a mate: 'for him every woman is good' (*Oeuvres complètes*, III, *Discourse*, 158). In this way Rousseau expunges from his condition of nature all forms of sexual rivalry while at the same time he eliminates the possibility of lasting ties between men and women. The proportions of males to females are perfectly balanced; and since they are denied an aesthetic faculty where the selection of a sexual partner is concerned, and scarcity of sexual mates is non-existent, the state of nature is free of conflict. In sum, Rousseau's state of nature is a condition in which humans live as self-sufficient and equal individuals without any need for their fellow human beings and without any desire to hurt them. They wander about alone, without work, without language, without love, without taste for beauty, without conflict, and without relationships.

The Perfect Balance Is Upset

Humanity in Rousseau's state of nature never would have voluntarily surrendered its springtime on Earth, a paradise of plenty and sunshine. But, alas, the perfectly harmonious balance between humanity and the physical environment was upset. Difficulties presented themselves, which human beings had to learn to overcome. The fruits of nature became less plentiful as the competition of humans and animals for the same fruits became keener. Fierce beasts threatened the lives of humans who were therefore obliged to develop their physical prowess. They learned to use the natural weapons of sticks and stones to defend themselves against animal predators and to fight other humans for subsistence. Conditions worsened: 'Barren years, long hard winters, scorching summers consuming everything, demanded new industry from men' (part 2, 163).

Humans now learned to fish, hunt, and fight. They killed beasts not only for food, but for their skins to protect them from the cold. They discovered how to use fire to cook the meats they had previously eaten raw. In time humans gained superiority over other creatures, outwitting them in a thousand ways. Consciously reflecting on their new challenges and experiences, humans now recognized the love of one's own well-being as the sole motive of their conduct. They sensed, for the first time, when common interest justified a reliance on the aid of their fellows, and when rivalry justified a distrust of them. In the latter case each pursued his own advantage, either by force if he felt himself stronger, or by cunning if he believed himself weaker. For Rousseau, these emergent social beings have acquired a crude idea of mutual commitment, though their communication is hardly more sophisticated than that of crows and monkeys. No longer able to rely on nature's bounty, humans now discovered how to use hard, sharp stones as tools with which to dig the soil and cut branches with which to build huts.

This was the epoch of the first revolution, which gave rise to families and property and, indeed, conflict over property. It is only in this epoch that conjugal love and paternal love appear together with stable families and a sexual division of labour. Now that people are learning to live together in distinct groups, each society develops a common tongue and common customs. At the same time differences in property together with sexual rivalry give rise to envy, jealousy, discord, and bloody violence. Humans have become bloodthirsty and cruel. This is a stage, for Rousseau, far removed from the original state of nature, a stage reached by most of the savage societies of his time. It is therefore wrong, Rousseau insists, to attribute violence and cruelty to the original state.

In this first stage following the upset of the original balance, families formed and banded together to create larger societies. As humans learned to cooperate, they learned to speak to facilitate cooperation. With speech they acquired the ability to accumulate knowledge and pass it on to their children. At this stage great social inequalities had yet to emerge. Such inequalities as did exist were primarily within families, as children were dependent for their survival upon parents. That was not a harmful dependence, since it was natural and temporary. Rousseau regards this stage as a happy one for humanity, for though people were capable of vanity and envy, they were also capable of love, loyalty, and the desire to please. Rousseau therefore prefers this epoch to the original, natural state in which humans were lonely, never having experienced love or companionship.

This epoch is, however, left behind as the cultivation of plants, the domestication of animals and a division of labour opened the way to all kinds of social inequalities that appeared for the first time. Some families, prospering more than others, accumulated wealth and passed it on to their children. Once inequalities came into being, they created greater opportunities for the rich than for the poor. The rich increasingly dominated the poor, who became correspondingly resentful. Classes emerged, and society was now for the first time divided against itself. Some of the poor acquiesced in their condition of servitude, while others lived by plundering the rich. Insecurity and violence – from which everyone stood to lose, but the rich more than the poor – were now felt and feared. In these circumstances the rich invented a device from which all could benefit, but the rich more than the poor. Laws were instituted, and political society came into being.

Like Locke, Rousseau proposed that government originated to protect property – ultimately to protect the rich. Rights, obligations, and property laws – the products of society – emerged as humans learned to act against one another. War, for Rousseau, is not a conflict of individuals; it is a socially organized phenomenon. Hobbes, Rousseau argues, is therefore wrong to assume that humans entered society and submitted to a common power to escape the war in nature. On the contrary, humans make war as members of organized communities – one community against another. A human being becomes a warrior only after he becomes a citizen. However, aggression and war also emerge within societies as a consequence of social inequality. The social condition in which the rich dominate and the poor serve gives rise to class warfare. It is for the purpose of controlling class conflict that the civil state is established. This is quite the reverse of Hobbes's view, in which war in the natural state prompted the multitude to establish a civil state for their mutual protection. For Rousseau, tranquillity reigned in the original natural state owing to the perfect equilibrium between humanity and the physical environment; and it was only after the equilibrium was disturbed and upset that human beings created society. The emergence of society led to inequality, inequality to war, and war to the civil state.

In the society of unequals that has now arisen, 'mutual need' is highly asymmetrical, even spurious. Rousseau writes: 'You need me, for I am rich and you are poor. Let us therefore make a contract with one another. I will do you the honour to permit you to serve me under the condition that you give me what little you still have left for the trouble I shall take in commanding you.'[2] Since such a relationship clearly involves coercion, Rousseau replies to Hobbes that this contract is absurd and unreasonable. It is unreasonable to suppose that individuals would throw themselves into the arms of an absolute master unconditionally and irrevocably, for that would be like trying to ensure their common security by rushing headlong into slavery. For Hobbes, one had to choose either to be governed or to be free; one could not have both, because security required civil obedience. Rousseau, as will be seen, agreed with Hobbes that sovereignty must be absolute; but he could not accept Hobbes's proposition that we must choose between being ruled or being free. If, in forming society, Rousseau argued, people give themselves to a sovereign, it is not merely for the purpose of bringing the internal war to an end and defending the commonwealth against external aggression. Their aim is also to protect their liberties. The worst thing that can befall an individual is to find himself at the mercy of another. It is therefore contrary to common sense that individuals would surrender into the hands of a chief the very thing they wish to preserve with his help.

Liberty, for Rousseau, is a fundamental natural right that must be preserved in society. He asks what equivalent a chief can offer individuals in return for giving up that fundamental right. We know how Hobbes would answer that question: the equivalent is security – the protection of their lives and possessions. But this is not enough for Rousseau, who sees no reason why life, property, *and* liberty cannot be secured under an absolute and undivided sovereignty – *provided that that sovereignty resides in the people.* Here in the *Discourse* Rousseau thus anticipates the proposition he will develop systematically in the *Social Contract*. In contrast to Hobbes's contract in the *Leviathan*, which is made only among the individual members of the original multitude, Rousseau's contract, like Locke's, would establish the body politic through a covenant between the people and the leaders chosen by them. In such a contract both parties commit themselves to observe the laws that are written down and that form the bonds of their union. The people have thus combined all their individual wills into a single united will, based on the fundamental laws that are obligatory on every member of the state without exception. One of these laws regulates the election and defines the limited authority of the chief magistrate.

As we have seen in Chapter 4 of this book, Hobbes, in his *The Elements of Law*, anticipates Rousseau by allowing for an original democracy and for the preservation of that democracy through a democratically constituted common power to whom authority is delegated *conditionally.* Rousseau, however, like most of his contemporaries, had most probably read only the *Leviathan*, not *The Elements of Law*. His polemic is therefore directed against Hobbes of the *Leviathan*, where the members of the multitude agree to form a commonwealth by giving up their liberty and accepting the absolute sovereignty of a chief whose only obligation is to protect them from one another and from foreign aggression. In contrast, Rousseau's social contract is made between the people and their magistrates, so that the latter explicitly bind themselves to use the powers entrusted to them only in accordance with the laws and intentions of their constituents. Moreover, insofar as in the particular case of Britain Hobbes defended royal absolutism, it was not only the multitude, but also the laws that were subject to the monarch's will. For Rousseau, however, since the power of all magistrates is established solely on the basis of the fundamental laws, magistrates cease to be legitimate as soon as they ignore or act contrary to the laws. In such an eventuality the people no longer owe them obedience.

Rousseau recognizes that in thus imparting to the people the right to renounce their dependence, he is opening the door to dissension and infinite disorders. The danger of such disorders, Rousseau avers, demonstrates that stable government requires a foundation more solid than reason alone. The divine will should therefore intervene, as it were, and give to the sovereign authority a sacred and inviolable character that would restrain the people from exercising their right to rebel. 'If religion had done men only this service,' Rousseau writes, 'it would be enough to impose upon them the duty of adopting and cherishing religion' (*Oeuvres complètes*, III, *Discourse*, 186). The need for 'civil religion' is a subject to which Rousseau will devote an entire chapter in *The Social Contract*.

In concluding the *Discourse on Inequality*, Rousseau restates his thesis that social inequality, emerging in response to the challenge posed by the decline in nature's bounty, establishes itself through the institution of private property. Though legitimized by positive law, social inequality is contrary to natural law whenever it fails to coincide with 'physical' inequality, as it does throughout civilization. In Rousseau's words: 'It is manifestly contrary to the law of nature, however defined, that a child should govern an old man, that an imbecile should lead a wise man, and that a handful of people should gorge themselves with superfluities while the hungry multitude goes in want of necessities' (*Oeuvres complètes*, III, *Discourse*, 194). In *The Social Contract* Rousseau proposes to remake society in order to eliminate such injustices.

The Social Contract

Rousseau opens this 'little treatise' by considering political relations based on force. If by force or the threat of it a people is coerced into obedience, it does well to obey in order to avoid worse consequences. History demonstrates, however, that as soon as a people gains the opportunity to shake off an oppressive yoke, it does so. Moreover, in a political system based on the forceful repression of the people, they have the right to regain their freedom by force. However, in a political system founded not on force but on a covenant, order is a sacred right, which serves as the basis of all other rights. To substantiate his thesis that a social order founded on covenants is a sacred right, Rousseau turns to a critical consideration of the views of Hugo Grotius and Thomas Hobbes.

Rousseau agrees with Hobbes that the need for liberty and the pursuit of it is inherent in human nature. The first law of nature is self-preservation, and as soon as an individual attains the age of reason, he becomes the sole judge of the best means by which to preserve himself. He becomes, in a word, his own master. It followed, for Rousseau, that in exiting the state of nature human beings retain the natural right to preserve their lives and liberty. In forming political society they also remain the sole judges of whether the society in question will aid or hinder them in preserving life and liberty. In a word, government should be established for the good of the governed. Grotius, however, had rejected this principle, citing the example of slavery. His characteristic method was to point to historical instances of political relations based on coercion as if such facts were a proof of right. What Grotius failed to recognize was that he was merely recounting the history of ancient abuses. By citing slavery to deny that all human government should exist for the benefit of the governed, Grotius was thereby also denying to humanity the natural right to preserve both life and liberty.

As for Hobbes, though he posits equality and liberty in the state of nature, he deprives humans of those rights once they enter the state of society. The reasoning of Grotius and Hobbes, Rousseau remarks sardonically, coincides with that of the Emperor Caligula, who conducted himself according to the prejudice that just as shepherds are superior to their flock, rulers are naturally superior to their subjects. For Caligula, kings were gods or alternatively the people were beasts. Rousseau also takes Aristotle to task for asserting that humans are unequal by nature, some born to be slaves and others to be masters. Aristotle, thus mistaking the effect for the cause, had failed to recognize that slavery, far from being natural, is social in origin. When human beings are born in slavery, they often behave as if they were born for slavery. In their bondage they become wantless, losing even the desire to be free, and making peace with their servitude. But, Rousseau emphasizes, if they appear to be slaves by nature, it is only because force made them slaves and fear perpetuated their submission.

Rousseau, of course, rejects the 'might is right' doctrine and the moral nihilism it implies. When humans yield to force, it is an act of self-preservation and prudence, but certainly no moral duty. Force is the physical means by which the strong dominate the weak. How, then, could it ever produce morality? Once humans enter society no individual should be regarded as ruler unless he transforms power into right and obedience into duty. Without such a legitimation of power and its transformation into lawful authority, the so-called 'right of the strongest' resolves itself into a tissue of amoral nonsense. Once might alone claims to be right, every force that overcomes another force acquires the 'right' previously held by the now vanquished. So the word 'right' adds nothing to our understanding of relations based on force.

An armed robber, says Rousseau, may compel me to hand over my purse; but if I successfully resist him, am I still obliged to surrender it? It is clear, then, that if one says 'might is right,' it is merely an ironic comment on much of history. Might cannot make right, and the duty of obedience is owed only to legitimate powers. *If there is no such thing as a natural right to dominate, and if force bestows no such right, then it is evident that all legitimate power must be based on covenants.* But Grotius had argued that if an individual can alienate his freedom and become a slave, so may a whole people alienate its freedom and become the subject of a prince. To this Rousseau responds that an individual becomes a slave not by giving himself to another, but either by yielding to superior force or by selling himself for subsistence. But in return for what could a whole people be supposed to sell itself? Here, following Machiavelli, Rousseau dramatically inverts Grotius's view of the relationship of a prince to the people: a prince, far from nourishing his people, derives his nourishment from them. And in response to the Hobbesian proposition that an absolute monarch gives his subjects the assurance of civil peace, Rousseau replies with this question: What if the monarch's greed and ambitions lead to wars against other states, wars requiring the oppression of the people and resulting in a devastation of the country far worse than that caused by civil strife? In such cases the people lose rather than gain from the condition of civil order. There is peace in dungeons, Rousseau adds, but that does not make dungeons desirable; and there was peace in Cyclops's cave where Odysseus's men awaited their turn to be devoured.

Returning to Grotius's view of the alienation of freedom, Rousseau insists it is erroneous on another account. Even if, for the sake of argument, one were to grant that an individual can alienate his own freedom, he cannot alienate that of his children who are born free. Their liberty is strictly their own, and no one but they themselves have the right to dispose of it. Before they reach adulthood, it is true, their parents may make rules for their protection and welfare. But parents have no right to give away their children's liberty irrevocably and unconditionally, for that would be contrary to natural law. Hence, even on Grotius's terms, an arbitrary government would be legitimate only if each new generation were able to accept or reject it, and in that case the government would no longer be arbitrary. For Rousseau, the renunciation of one's freedom is tantamount to the renunciation of one's humanity. Indeed, renouncing one's freedom is contrary to human nature. In renouncing one's liberty, moreover, one loses one's freedom of will, thus stripping one's actions of any moral significance. It follows, for Rousseau, that the Hobbesian covenant, which stipulates absolute dominion for the king and absolute obedience for the subjects, is unreasonable and

nugatory. It is nullified by the absence of reciprocity and mutual obligation. Although there is a degree of reciprocity in Hobbes's covenant –
the protection offered by the monarch in return for the subjects' absolute
obedience – this is, for Rousseau, so little as to amount to nothing.

Rousseau again returns to Grotius's claim that war gives the victor the
right to enslave, the argument being that the victor's right to kill the
vanquished implies that the latter has the right to purchase his life at the
expense of his liberty. For Grotius, the legitimacy of such a contract is
borne out by the fact that it thus becomes advantageous to both parties.
In his rebuttal Rousseau argues that the so-called right to kill the vanquished cannot be derived from the state of war: 'It is the conflicts over
things that constitute war. War arises not from conflicts in personal relations, but only from property relations. Private wars between one individual and another can exist neither in a state of nature, where there is
no fixed property, nor in society, where everything is under the authority of law' (*Oeuvres complètes*, III, 357). Here we see Rousseau basing his
rebuttal on his original state of nature as a bountiful springtime on
Earth, a condition diametrically opposed to Hobbes's state of nature as a
state of war.

War, for Rousseau, is a conflict between states, not between individuals. Furthermore, a prince who kills, robs, or captures the subjects of
another prince without first declaring war is a despicable brigand. In a
declared war, on the other hand, a just prince, though he will seize what
he can of the enemy's territory, will nevertheless respect the principles
on which his own rights are based. The aim of war being to subdue the
hostile state, a soldier has the right to kill the defenders of that state
while they are armed; but as soon as they lay down their weapons and
surrender, they cease to be enemies, and no one any longer has the right
to take their lives. History has shown that it is sometimes possible to
conquer a state without killing a single one of its members, and war
imparts no right to kill or destroy more than is necessary for victory. For
Rousseau, these principles are derived from the nature of things and
founded on reason. Since war gives the victor no right to massacre a
vanquished people, it follows that no right exists to justify their enslavement. The so-called right of enslavement cannot be derived from the
right to kill, since one has the right to kill an enemy only when he
refuses to accept defeat and fights on. 'It is therefore an iniquitous
exchange,' Rousseau avers, 'to make the conquered enemy purchase, at
the expense of their liberty, their lives over which the conqueror has no
right' (*Oeuvres complètes*, III, 358).

The option of massacring a defeated enemy is not a right, as Grotius claims, but an arbitrary and unreasonable use of force, and as such places a conquered people under no obligation to obey. Furthermore, by sparing the lives of the vanquished and exploiting instead of destroying them, the victor gains no genuine authority over them. Indeed, the domination and exploitation of the defeated enemy, far from giving the victor authority over the vanquished, means that the state of war between them continues, and that the defeated will employ force whenever possible to resist their enslavement and to oppose their temporary masters as deadly enemies. In sum, there is no 'right' of slavery. Whether it is between individuals or between a prince and a people, it is always absurd to say: 'I make with you a covenant entirely at your expense and wholly to my advantage, a covenant I shall respect so long as I please and you will respect so long as it pleases me' (*Oeuvres complètes*, III, 358).

For Rousseau, then, there is a fundamental difference between dominating a multitude and ruling a society. Although he does not expressly refer to Hobbes in this context it is apparent that Rousseau is continuing his rebuttal of Hobbes's notion that the social contract was made by the individual members of the original multitude, each of whom agreed with every other member to transfer his rights and liberties to an absolute sovereign power. Such a 'contract,' Rousseau insists, is an aggregate of slaves dominated by one master, not an association between a people and its ruler created for the common good. Hobbes had posited an original multitude of warring individuals to counter the view that an organized *people* had emerged from the state of nature, and that it was the people, therefore, with whom the social contract was made. Grotius, however, had said that 'a people may give itself to a king,' thereby acknowledging that a people had existed before the gift to the king was made. The gift, says Rousseau, was a civil act that presupposed public deliberation. Rousseau thus takes advantage of this opening to set the stage for his own conception of the social covenant, which differs so radically from that of Grotius and Hobbes – though we need to recall again that in his *The Elements of Law* Hobbes anticipated Rousseau by allowing for a democratic constitution of the common power.

Rousseau's Social Pact

With the loss of the original springtime on Earth and the onset of scorching summers and harsh winters, individuals faced a condition in which the obstacles to their preservation in a state of nature proved greater than the ability each had to preserve himself in that state. Rousseau now makes an assumption Hobbes had refused to make in the *Leviathan*. Hobbes's state of nature, which was at one and the same time a state of war, meant that the members of the original multitude were incapable of uniting their separate powers, for that would have required first bringing the war of each against all to an end. Rousseau's state of nature, being no state of war, allows him to posit a combination of individual powers strong enough to overcome any resistance to the creation of a single, unified will. Such a combination of powers could be created only by a union of separate individuals. However, the strength and liberty of each individual being the chief means of his self-preservation, how can he merge with others without imperilling the care he owes to himself? Rousseau formulates the problem in these words: 'How to find a form of association which defends and protects the person and goods of each member with the collective force of all, and in which each individual, in uniting himself with the others, obeys no one but himself, and remains as free as before' (*Oeuvres complètes*, III, 360).

That is the fundamental problem, Rousseau believes, to which his conception of the social contract provides a solution. Each individual associates himself with others by alienating from himself all his rights and transferring them to the community as a whole. Because each individual gives himself absolutely, the conditions of the association are the same for all; and being the same for all, it is in no one's interest to make the conditions onerous for others. Since the alienation of one's rights is absolute and unconditional, the individual associate no longer has any special rights to claim. Rousseau believes he has eliminated the conflict between the individual and the common interest, because each individual 'in giving himself to all, gives himself to nobody; and as there is no associate over which he does not acquire the same right as he yields to others over himself, he gains an equivalent for everything he loses, and an increment of force for the preservation of what he has' (*Oeuvres complètes*, III, 361). Each individual, by giving his person and powers to the community and placing them under the supreme direction of the general will – *volonté générale* – becomes an indivisible part of the whole. The association creates an artificial body politic composed of as many members as there are voters in the assembly.

The sovereignty of this association resides in the assembly of which it is constituted. The sovereign assembly is now like a single person who can neither alienate a part of himself nor submit to another sovereign. Though the sovereignty of the assembly is absolute, it cannot become tyrannical: formed entirely of the individuals composing it, it cannot have any interest contrary to theirs. But if in the relation of the sovereign to a subject there is no conflict of interest, that is not true of the relation of a subject to the sovereign. For an individual may have a private interest different from or contrary to the interest he has as a citizen in the general will. In a word, private interest may clash with the public interest, so that an individual might seek to enjoy the rights of a citizen without fulfilling the duties of a subject. Whoever, therefore, refuses to obey the general will may be forced to do so by the whole body politic. That is the way Rousseau leaves himself open, in chapter 7 of *The Social Contract*, to the charge of having overlooked the danger of a 'tyranny of the majority.'

Sovereignty, for Rousseau, is absolute, inalienable, and indivisible. The sovereign assembly of the people may delegate some of its powers, but not its will. Rousseau expressly states: 'Just as nature gives each individual an absolute power over all his own limbs, the social pact gives the body-politic an absolute power over all its members' (*Oeuvres complètes*, III, 372). If we recall from our discussion of Hobbes that he prescribed absolute and undivided sovereignty for all forms of government, including democracy, we have the ironic circumstance that for all his disagreement with Hobbes, Rousseau converges with him on this salient principle. We have to remember, however, that Rousseau evidently had read only the *Leviathan* and even that with less care than it deserved. He therefore believed that Hobbes was defending royal absolutism, pure and simple. Converging with Hobbes in another respect, Rousseau employs virtually identical terms to describe an individual's condition as he exits the post-springtime state of nature and enters society. Arguing that individuals make no real renunciation by becoming parties to the social pact, and that their very lives which they have pledged to the state are protected by it, Rousseau writes: 'And even when they risk their lives to defend the state, what more are they doing than returning what they have received from the state? What are they doing that they would not do more frequently, and with greater danger, *in the state of nature, where every man is inevitably at war and defends at the risk of his life whatever serves him to preserve life?*' (375, italics added).

The sovereign body politic that emerged with the social pact requires positive legislation. The reason for this, Rousseau explains, is that considered realistically the laws of divine and natural justice, lacking as they do any natural sanction, are ineffectual. Indeed, since just individuals obey them and others do not, divine and natural laws injure the innocent and benefit the wicked. Positive laws are therefore indispensable, and they are the acts of the general will. Such laws being but the enactments of what the people themselves desire, the people are both free and subject to the laws. Government, or the prince, is but one integral element of the state and, as such, can never be above the law. Rousseau thus reaffirms the principles of classical political theory in this regard, asserting that any state ruled by law is a 'republic'; for it is only under law that the public interest governs and the 'public thing' – *res publica* – becomes a reality. All legitimate government is 'republican.' As Rousseau clarifies in a footnote, however, the term can refer to either an aristocracy or a democracy, and even to a monarchy. The term therefore implies a condition – the delegation of authority by the general will in accordance with the laws. However, the people cannot by themselves undertake the formidable and complex project of creating a just system of legislation. The people always will what is good, but cannot always discern it. That is why a lawgiver is necessary.

Rousseau views the lawgiver as an extraordinary individual whose genius enables him to formulate laws that would bring about the highest degree of cooperation among the citizens. By means of good laws and institutions the power acquired by the whole republic becomes greater than the sum of the natural powers of each citizen. The lawgiver's office is neither that of the government nor that of the sovereign. The lawmaker has nothing to do with the execution of the laws. The Greek lawgiver Lycurgus had set a good example by abdicating his monarchical functions before assuming his duties as legislator. Many Greek cities turned to foreigners to frame their laws, as did the modern republics of Italy and Geneva. Already in antiquity it was understood that when the legislative and executive powers are placed in the same hands, tyranny is the likely outcome. Sovereignty must remain with the people who give the lawgiver authority to frame the constitution of the republic, but no authority to command.

Rousseau's extraordinary lawgiver is wise enough to recognize that in order to persuade without convincing, he must attribute his wisdom to the gods. By putting his own ordinances into the mouths of the deities, he compels by divine authority those who cannot be moved by human prudence. Then the people, identifying the laws of the state with the divine laws of nature, bear the yoke of the public welfare more easily. Quoting Machiavelli in this regard, Rousseau writes: 'The truth is that there has never been in any country an extraordinary legislator who has not invoked the deity; for otherwise his laws would not have been accepted. A wise man knows many useful truths which cannot be demonstrated in such a way as to convince others' (quoted by Rousseau in Italian, *Oeuvres complètes*, III, 384). Rousseau's lawgiver, like Machiavelli's, is not merely shrewd; for it is not every individual who can gain credence when he claims to be the interpreter of the divine word. The lawgiver must be a great-souled individual like a Moses or Lycurgus.

Following Montesquieu, Rousseau underscores that even the wisest of legislators is doomed to failure in the absence of certain preconditions. The state for which the laws are made must be neither too large to be well governed, nor too small to maintain itself. Accepting Montesquieu's view, Rousseau proposes that the larger the territory over which the social bond is stretched, the slacker it becomes. A small state is therefore stronger proportionately than a large one. In his discussion of the administrative difficulties of a large state, Rousseau was influenced by what Montesquieu had said about oriental despotism, the highly centralized agrarian bureaucracies of Asia. But Rousseau overlooked the fact that Montesquieu had allowed for the federation of many small republics so as to form a unified large state under a republican form of government (*The Spirit of the Laws*, Book IX). This principle, as we shall see, did not go unnoticed by the framers of the American Constitution. Rousseau further stipulates that a people best fit to receive new laws is bound together by common origin and interest, strong enough to repel invasion, and neither rich nor poor, but possessing enough to maintain itself. As for the moral-political aims of good laws, they may be summed up in two words: *freedom* and *equality*. By equality Rousseau does not mean that the amount of wealth should be the same for all, but rather that no citizen should be rich enough to buy another and none so poor as to be compelled to sell himself.

Government

Sovereignty, for Rousseau, is absolute and undivided, and in this respect he follows Hobbes. The powers of government, on the other hand, must be divided, and in this respect he follows Locke and Montesquieu. The will of the sovereign people – the democratic state – is represented, respectively, by the legislative and executive powers, and nothing should be done in the body politic without the concurrence of both. Sovereignty must not be confused with government, a body established between the sovereign and the subjects, a body responsible for the execution of the laws and the maintenance of the civil and political freedom of the citizens. Government derives its authority from the sovereign.

In Rousseau's republican political theory there are, therefore, three components: the sovereign assembly of the people, the prince or government, and the people, again, who as subjects obey the government in power and as citizens may exercise their sovereignty by changing the government if and when it tends to abuse its authority. Rousseau recognized that it was impossible outside a very small community to have democracy without representatives, without the delegation of authority. He understood that government, though it called itself a public force and though it professed to represent the general will, could usurp power and act against the common good. Government is a constant threat to freedom and yet indispensable; government is a potentially corrupting element in society, capable of undermining the sovereignty of the people. A republic should, therefore, always be ready 'to sacrifice the government to the people and not the people to the government' (*Oeuvres complètes*, III, 399).

In his classification of governments in Book III, chapter 3, again relying on Montesquieu, Rousseau asserts that 'democratic government suits small states' (*Oeuvres complètes*, III, 403), though he recognizes there may be exceptions to this rule owing to the particular circumstances of the state in question. In chapter 4 Rousseau then makes this statement: 'In the strict sense of the term, there has never been a true democracy, and there never will be. It is contrary to the natural order that the greater number should govern and the smaller number be governed. One can hardly imagine that all the people would sit permanently in an assembly to deal with public affairs; and one can easily see that they could not appoint commissions for that purpose without the form of the administration changing' (404). This statement has been cited by certain theorists to support their claim that the emergence of a ruling political élite, or ruling class, is inevitable in all forms of government, including republics. Read in its context, however, it is clear that Rousseau's real point was quite different: *government* by all would be against 'the natural order' because it would result in anarchy, just as sovereignty, which is inalienable, would be against the natural order if possessed by less than all the people. Rousseau did, however, say, 'If there were a nation of gods, it would govern itself democratically. A government so perfect is not suited to men' (406). It seems, then, on balance, that the best and most realizable option, in Rousseau's view, was an aristocracy, but elective rather than hereditary. It is of the utmost importance, he says, that the election of magistrates be regulated by law, for if this is left to the will of the prince there will be an unavoidable decline into a hereditary aristocracy. And yet Rousseau has reservations even about an elected aristocracy. It is best and most natural for the wisest individuals to govern the multitude, 'if one is sure that they will govern for its advantage and not for their own.' For it must be noted, he adds, 'that the corporate interest begins at this point to direct the forces of the state less strictly in accordance with the general will, and that a further inevitable tendency is for a part of the executive power to escape the control of law' (407).

Rousseau thus recognizes both the necessity of government and its dangers. There can be no doubt, however, that like Machiavelli before him Rousseau is morally and politically committed to popular sovereignty and to a republican form of government. He recognizes that Machiavelli's *Prince* is actually a handbook for republicans (*Oeuvres complètes*, III, 409), and he would agree with Montesquieu that the more democratic the republic, the more perfect it is. An essential and inevitable defect, he writes, 'which will always make monarchical government inferior to republican government, is that in republics the popular choice almost always elevates to the highest places only enlightened and capable men, who fill their office with honour; those who rise under monarchy are nearly always muddled little minds, petty knaves and intriguers ... The people is much less often mistaken in such choices than is a prince' (410). And, Rousseau adds, it is clear that 'if there is more cunning in a royal court, there is more wisdom in a republican senate, and that republics have a more stable and effective guidance' (412).

Although Rousseau thus prefers a republic to other forms, the more democratic the better, he understands that 'democracy,' 'aristocracy,' and 'monarchy' are pure types, and that strictly speaking, no pure type of government exists in reality. After all, even a government of the people must have a head. Admiring, therefore, the government of England in which the component parts are interdependent and balanced, Rousseau advocates *mixed government*. Following Locke and Montesquieu, Rousseau adds: if the power of the prince in relation to the sovereign is greater than the power of the people in relation to the prince, this has to be remedied by dividing the government so that the separation of the executive from the legislative will make them less powerful in relation to the sovereign.

Rousseau understood, as we have seen, that government can act against the sovereign. When government ceases to administer the state according to the law and usurps the sovereign power, democracy may degenerate into *mob rule*, aristocracy into *oligarchy*, and monarchy into *tyranny.* How, then, can such degeneration be prevented? For Rousseau, the most effective way in which the sovereign people can defend itself against the prince's abuse or usurpation of power is by instituting fixed and periodic assemblies. When the people are lawfully assembled as the sovereign body, the executive power is immediately suspended. Frequent assemblies of the people are the strongest shield of the body politic and a check upon the degenerative tendencies of government. In these terms Rousseau is profoundly distrustful and even opposed to the political institution of representation. For a variety of reasons, the expedient of deputies and representatives has been adopted to replace the assemblies of the people. For Rousseau, however, sovereignty cannot be represented for the same reason that it cannot be alienated. It is clear that Rousseau's rejection of representation presupposed a demographically and geographically small state. His proposal of fixed and periodic assemblies, he recognized, might be practicable in one small town, but hardly practicable in a state consisting of several towns. Moreover, adding an admonition, Rousseau observes that 'it is always an evil to unite several towns in one nation, and whoever wishes to form such a union should not flatter himself that the natural disadvantages can be avoided' (*Oeuvres complètes,* III, 427). There is, therefore, only one right means by which to prevent a government's usurpation of sovereignty, and that is periodic assemblies of the people as stipulated by the law. At such assemblies two motions should be placed before the people: (1) Does it please the sovereign to retain the present form of government? (2) Does it please the people to leave the administration to those currently charged with it? Rousseau subscribes to the rule that the votes of the greatest number always bind the rest.

Civil Religion

Centring attention on Christian commonwealths, Rousseau observes that from the time of Jesus of Nazareth, who had come to establish a spiritual kingdom on Earth, Christian doctrine has tended to separate the theological order from the political. As a consequence the state ceased to be a unity, and the strife between the two orders has incessantly disrupted Christian societies. The two coexisting centres of power and the endless conflict over jurisdiction has made any kind of good polity impossible in Christian states. People have never known whether to obey the civil ruler or the church. Rousseau acknowledges that Hobbes understood the problem: 'Of all Christian authors the philosopher

Hobbes is the only one who saw clearly both the evil and the remedy, and who dared to propose reuniting the two heads of the eagle and fully restoring the political unity without which neither the state nor the government will ever be well constituted' (*Oeuvres complètes*, III, 463). For Rousseau, however, Hobbes's solution was defective for two reasons: (1) he failed to recognize that the dominant spirit of Christianity was incompatible with his proposed system; and (2) he failed to recognize that the interests of the prince will always be stronger than those of the commonwealth.

In his chapter on 'Civil Religion' Rousseau therefore addresses two fundamental questions: Is religion useful to the body politic? Does Christianity provide the best ideological support of a commonwealth? Responding to the first question in the affirmative, Rousseau points to the fact that no state has ever been founded without religion as its base; and responding to the second question in the negative, he asserts that Christian doctrine is at bottom more injurious than serviceable for the strong constitution of a state. To defend his response to the second question Rousseau begins by dividing religion into two categories, religion of the individual and religion of the citizen. The first, devoid of temples, altars, and ritual, is expressed in the inward devotion to God and the eternal moral obligations. This is the pure and simple religion of the Gospel that enjoins obedience to the divine natural law. The religion of the citizen, in contrast, is the official, organized religion established in a single country. This category consists of tutelary deities, dogmas, and rituals that are laid down by law in a given state. To a nation practising such religion, its own ways are sacred while all outside ways are infidel and barbarous. It is this category to which Rousseau gives the name civil religion.

Civil religion is good, says Rousseau, in that it unites divine worship with a love of the civil laws and homeland, teaching citizens that service to the state is at the same time service to the tutelary deity. But this kind of religion is also bad, based as it is on error and lies. It makes people superstitious, replacing the true worship of the divine with empty ceremonials. It is bad, too, insofar as it becomes tyrannical, making the people intolerant and bloodthirsty. In sharp contrast there is the Christianity of the Gospel, in which individuals look upon themselves and all others as children of the same God and, therefore, as brothers. From a political standpoint, however, the Christianity of the Gospel is defective in that it contributes nothing to the strengthening of the civil laws, the chief social bonds of a good society. Far from attaching the citizens to the state, the

Gospel detaches them from it and, indeed, from all worldly matters, since the Christian's homeland is not of this world. In order for a true Christian society to prevail in peace, every citizen without exception would have to be an equally good Christian, since all it would take is one ambitious hypocrite to establish a tyranny over his pious compatriots. A Christian republic is a contradiction in terms, for in preaching submission and servitude, Christianity is too favourable to tyranny for tyranny not to take advantage of it. True Christians are servile because this short life has so little value in their eyes.

Given, then, the shortcomings of the two types of religion he has reviewed, Rousseau proposes a form of civil religion wholly positive in its effects. In Rousseau's social contract, subjects have no obligation to account to the sovereign for their beliefs, except when those beliefs are important to the community. Since the civil sovereign has no competence in the other world with which religion is concerned, he has no business even taking notice of individuals' religious opinions, so long as they are good citizens in this life. For Rousseau, there is a purely civil profession of faith, and it is the sovereign's responsibility to determine the articles of that faith, not as religious dogmas, but as moral principles of civic duty without which it is impossible to be either a good citizen or a loyal subject. The positive dogmas of this civil religion are simple and few in number: 'the existence of an omnipotent, intelligent, benevolent divinity who foresees and provides; the life to come; the happiness of the just; the punishment of the sinners; the sanctity of the social contract and the laws ... As for the negative dogmas, I would limit them to a single one; it is intolerance. Intolerance belongs to the cults we have rejected' (*Oeuvres complètes*, III, 468–69).

Theological intolerance, Rousseau argues, inevitably threatens the sovereignty of the sovereign even in the temporal sphere. For in conditions of religious intolerance the priests become the real masters. Under the laws of good civil religion there can be no exclusive national religion. In a good polity 'all religions which themselves tolerate others must be tolerated,' so long as their dogmas prompt no actions contrary to the laws of the state and the duties of the citizen. That is the note on which Rousseau ends his 'little treatise' on political theory.

Chapter Eight

The Federalist Papers

The thirteen American colonies had declared and won their independence by joining together under the Articles of Confederation. But the Articles had proved to be woefully inadequate to ensure the union of the separate states, each of which regarded itself as sovereign and independent.[1] Under the Articles there was no central government in the United States with the authority to tax, regulate commerce, or enforce laws. The Confederation was considered a temporary expedient required by the war against Britain, an organization that would dissolve as soon as victory and peace were achieved. Even during the war the separate states of the Confederation had been so independent that some honoured their financial obligations to the Continental Congress and others did not. With the end of hostilities in 1783, the Continental Congress, the wartime centre of power, became defunct and all effective power was returned to the states. The result was that the precarious wartime union was now threatened with complete disintegration.

This was the context in which a few perspicacious political leaders, including Alexander Hamilton and James Madison, called for a meeting of the states at Annapolis, Maryland, to plan for amendments to the Articles of Confederation. Only five states, however, sent delegates to Annapolis. Recognizing that they were too few to presume they had the authority to draft amendments, they called for a convention of all the states to meet at Philadelphia the following May. It was this convention that drafted the Constitution of the United States. Most of the framers of the Constitution thought it good even when it had not fully incorporated their own personal proposals. But the Constitution still had to face public opinion. It had to be ratified by the popularly elected state conventions, and not until nine states had done so could the new union it was designed to create come into being.

In state after state opposition to the Constitution was bitter and deep-seated. It was attacked on several related grounds: it created too strong a central government; it threatened individual liberty; it granted too much power to the executive; it created a dangerous federal judiciary; it failed to provide a bill of rights; and it opened the door to oppressive taxation. Two camps soon emerged: the Federalists who supported ratification of the Constitution, and the anti-Federalists who opposed it. A great debate ensued wherever politics was discussed – in the press, in the public arena, and most importantly in the popularly elected state conventions. Five small states promptly ratified the Constitution: Delaware, Maryland, New Jersey, Connecticut, and South Carolina. The fiercest battles were waged in Pennsylvania, Massachusetts, Virginia, and New York. In those states the majority of the populace appeared no less than hostile to ratification, though due to the eloquence and political skills of the Federalists, Pennsylvania, Massachusetts, and Virginia were won over, albeit by narrow majorities. New York being a key state politically and geographically, it was essential to gain ratification there; and it was with the aim of persuading the inhabitants of New York that Alexander Hamilton, the brilliant young leader of the Federalists, conceived the idea of a series of newspaper articles highlighting the political virtues of the new Constitution and refuting objections to it. To collaborate with him in this task, he enlisted two friends, James Madison of Virginia and John Jay of New York. Together these three highly learned and skilful men planned the series of articles that came to be known as *The Federalist Papers*.

The first paper appeared in the *Independent Journal* on 27 October 1787 and was signed *Publius*, a signature that all subsequent articles bore, for authorship was secret. 'Publius,' the collective pseudonym employed by Hamilton, Madison, and Jay, ultimately produced some 175,000 words in defence of the new federal Constitution. Hamilton chose the pseudonym for what it represented in the history of Rome. Publius Valerius was a Roman hero celebrated for establishing a stable republican government in Rome after Lucius Brutus overthrew Tarquin, the last king of Rome. Plutarch describes Publius as a great lawgiver whose achievements for Rome were equivalent to those of Solon for Greece. The later articles appeared in the *New York Journal*, the *New York Packet*, and the *Daily Advertiser*, and eventually were reprinted in other newspapers.

The series continued until April 1788, the six final numbers appearing first in book form. In spite of the persuasiveness of these articles, the New York ratifying convention was at first strongly opposed to ratification, and it was Hamilton's presence there that finally won the convention over to ratification. While the New York convention was still in session, steeped in debate, nine states ratified the Constitution and the new United States came into being.

It is important to note, however, that an essential element of the Constitution as we know it was the contribution of the anti-Federalists. Like Thomas Jefferson, they objected to the absence of a bill of rights. A major concern of theirs in the ratification debates was the threat to personal liberty represented by the Constitution's centralization of power; and it was out of the Virginia debates between Patrick Henry and James Madison that there emerged the outline for the Bill of Rights, the first ten amendments to the Constitution guaranteeing individual rights against government interference.

Jefferson, who was no Federalist and certainly no Hamiltonian Federalist, favoured the adoption of the Constitution and described *The Federalist Papers* as 'the best commentary on the principles of government which ever was written.' There can be no doubt that he was right in this judgment. *The Federalist Papers* is one of the greatest political treatises of all time because it is so much more than the best exposition of the virtues of the Constitution by three extraordinarily wise and able statesmen. *The Federalist Papers* is a truly great work because it is a profound treatise on political theory and practice, which bases its analysis on the classical principles of political philosophy, on logic, and on the experience of history. It is a rigorous and realistic analysis of political power that addresses such questions as these: How may the social forces of a society and the branches of government be properly balanced? How may thirteen separate states be brought together in a large, federated republic? Both questions presupposed that the new republic's central mission was to achieve liberty *and* order, and to avoid the extremes so well known in history of tyranny and anarchy.[2] To take just one example of the Federalists' originality in applying classical political philosophy, there was the troublesome question of whether a republic necessarily implies government over a small population and area. At the centre of the debate between the Federalists and the anti-Federalists was the latter's dedication to a Rousseauian form of participatory democracy and the Federalists' commitment to republican government. Madison defined a republic as a government by representatives in contrast to democracy where the people govern directly in popular assemblies. Madison argued effectively that whereas democracy necessarily implies a small state, a republic can govern a great number of citizens and a large territory. The view of Madison and his colleagues, which became so crucial if republican principles were to be realized in a large territory, was definitely prompted by a careful reading of Montesquieu. In Book IX of *The Spirit of the Laws*, Montesquieu states that if a republic is too small it is liable to be destroyed by a foreign enemy, and if it is too large it is liable to be undermined by internal vice. These drawbacks need not forever plague republics, since there exists a kind of constitution that has all the internal advantages of republican government and the external force of monarchy. 'I speak,' Montesquieu wrote, 'of the federal republic. This form of government is an agreement by which many political bodies consent to become citizens of the larger state which they want to form. It is a society of societies which makes a new one, which can be enlarged by new associates which unite with it' (Book IX, ch. 1).

The three authors of *The Federalist Papers*, though they were immensely learned in the classics of political philosophy, successfully combined an active public life with study and thought. Hamilton was the initiator and most important figure in the venture. He wrote about two-thirds of the papers, Madison about one-third, and Jay only five papers. A few were jointly authored by Hamilton and Madison. With these few introductory remarks as background, we can turn to the actual collection of papers, which originally appeared under the title of *The Federalist*.

The Federalist

Hamilton opens the series of articles by underscoring that the Confederation has proved its inefficacy as a unifying force. Large sections of the citizenry have recognized the need for a new Constitution for the United States, which can only overcome the crisis they face by demonstrating their ability to establish good government based on common interests and aiming for the general good. The most formidable obstacle to the new Constitution, Hamilton avers, is the obvious interest of a certain class of men in every state to resist all changes that are likely to diminish the power of the offices they hold. In a sharp polemical tone Hamilton asserts that it is personal ambition that most often lies behind the proclaimed zeal for the rights of the people. To demonstrate that strong, vigorous, and efficient government is essential for the security of American liberty, Hamilton announces to his readers that the series of papers will discuss the following subjects: the inadequacy of the existing Confederation to preserve the desired union; the utility of the proposed union for the prosperity of all concerned; the necessity of a federal government at least as strong as the one proposed; the proposed Constitution's true republican principles; its parallels with the state constitutions; and, finally, the additional security to liberty and property that the proposed form of federal government will provide.

The first task of a free people is to provide for its common safety. This entails defence against the threat of foreign aggression; and it should be clear that an efficient national government offers the best security against hostilities from abroad. Publius (Jay) points specifically to the many potential sources of conflict between the United States and other nations: rivalry with France and Britain in the fisheries, especially with America's ability to supply the markets more cheaply than they can; rivalry with them and most other European countries in navigation and the carrying trade; rivalry with all those nations in trading with China and India. Moreover, the expansion of American commerce is bound to antagonize the nations possessing territories on or near the American continent. Spain strives to control the Mississippi just as Britain excludes Americans from the Saint Lawrence. One could bring many more examples, says Jay (IV), to show that the exercise and advancement of American power by land and by sea are not likely to be regarded with indifference by other nations. It is only wise and prudent, therefore, that there be created a national government strong enough to discourage aggression instead of inviting it. A central national government would unify and harmonize the member states so as to produce an effective collective security.

What would be the state of Britain's security if the military forces of England, Scotland, and Wales obeyed only their respective governments and not the central government of Great Britain? Or what would be the state of the celebrated naval prowess of Britain if, instead of one national government having created and regulated its fleets, England, Scotland, Wales, and Ireland had each maintained separate navies? With these and additional rhetorical questions Jay makes his point: If America is left divided into thirteen independent and sovereign governments, what armies and naval fleets could they hope to raise in an emergency? If one is attacked could it ever be sure that the others would risk blood and money and fly to its defence? Would not the danger exist that some would maintain neutrality rather than hazard their tranquillity for the sake of a neighbour? Jay cites the experience of ancient Greece where the city-states remained at odds with one another. But even if one assumes for the moment, Jay continues, that if one of the American states were invaded the others would come to its aid, who would command the allied armies? Who would negotiate the terms of the peace, and how would conflicts between states be settled in the absence of an umpire who could decide between them and compel obedience? Looking at Britain again, Jay observes that although common sense dictates that the people inhabiting such an island should be united in one state, they were for ages divided into three or four nations. Why, then, should Americans suppose that we would not also be embroiled in quarrels and wars just as the English, Scots, and Welsh were before they were brought together in one sovereign state? Given the historical experience of other nations, it stands to reason that even if three or four confederacies were to start out on an equal footing, they would not long remain so. Whenever one would rise in power over the others, its neighbours would regard it with jealousy and fear. Those persons, Jay concludes, who oppose the uniting of the thirteen states in one sovereign nation, proposing instead that the states should form several defensive alliances, are therefore greatly mistaken.

Continuing in the same vein, Hamilton (VI) calls it utopian to doubt that thirteen states, either wholly disunited or partially united in confederations, would have frequent violent confrontations with one another. Such doubt ignores the fact that human beings are 'ambitious, vindictive and rapacious,' and ignores, too, the experience of history. The anti-Federalists maintained that it is the genius of republics, especially commercial republics, to pursue peace and to eschew mutually ruinous contention with one another. The thirteen separate republics, they believed, would be governed by a mutual interest in peace, cultivating amity and concord. In response Hamilton also poses several rhetorical questions: If mutual amity is, purportedly, the true interest of republics, have they in fact pursued it? Have republics in practice been less inclined to war than monarchies? Are not republics also governed by men, and thus inclined to strive for power? Are not popular assemblies also subject to resentment, envy, avarice, and violence? Has commerce hitherto lessened the inclination to war? Is not the love of wealth as enduring and domineering a passion as the love of power and glory? Let history be our guide: Athens, Sparta, Rome, and Carthage were all republics. Were the predominantly commercial republics of Athens and Carthage any less often engaged in offensive and defensive warfare than the others? Carthage was the aggressor in the very war that ended in its destruction. Venice, in later times, was far from pacific in its relation to its neighbours; and Holland, a pre-eminently commercial republic, was an implacable foe of Louis XIV and engaged in a fierce struggle with Britain for control of the sea. In a word, commercial interests and rivalry – the desire to supplant and the fear of being supplanted – have been a salient cause of war.

Apart from commercial interests, what about territorial disputes, which from earliest times have been a chief source of hostility among nations? Given the vast tracts of unsettled territory within the boundaries of the United States, would not the dissolution of the union open the door to competing claims on the part of the states? Hamilton reminds his readers that in the absence of an umpire to mediate between the contending parties, the western territory affords ample opportunity for hostile encounters between the states. He cites the dispute between Connecticut and Pennsylvania over the lands of Wyoming, and admonishes his readers not to expect easy, mutual accommodations of such differences. States, like individuals, says Hamilton, seek their own advantage. New York, for instance, out of the need for revenue, imposes duties on imports from Connecticut and New Jersey. Would the latter states submit indefinitely to this condition? And since it is as true as it is trite that issues over money are a major cause of strife, it is beyond doubt that the public debt of the union, incurred during the revolution, would be an additional cause of clashes between the separate states or confederacies.

Hamilton warns, moreover, that war between the separate states would be not only likely, but also more destructive than in Europe where regular military establishments and fortifications render sudden conquest difficult. In America, where military establishments are non-existent, the open frontiers between states would make inroads easy. The more populous states could overrun their less populous neighbours with little difficulty. Although, however, the initial conquest would be easy, maintaining it would be difficult. War would therefore be protracted and predatory. To forestall such consequences, neighbouring states would resort to standing armies, an institution inimical to liberty. The weaker states or confederacies would first have recourse to standing armies to compensate for the deficiency in population and resources; and then the more powerful neighbours would respond by increasing their armed forces. At the same time the power of the executive in all the states concerned would grow at the expense of the legislative authority, for it is in the nature of war and the preparation for war to produce that result.

For Hamilton, a valuable lesson is to be learned from Britain in this regard. Being an island, but possessing a large and powerful naval fleet, Britain was able to secure itself against invasion without the threat to liberty that a standing army and an inordinately strong executive entail. It is not unlikely, Hamilton convincingly suggests, that if Britain had been situated on the European continent it would have been compelled to create a military establishment at home very much like that of the other great powers of Europe and would have fallen under the rule of a single man. America, Hamilton observed, has an advantage similar to the insular situation of Britain, an advantage, however, contingent upon the forging of a real union of the states. Since Europe is at a great distance and separated by an ocean, a true union of the states would make military establishments unnecessary for American security. If, on the other hand, the states were to remain separated or thrown together in a few confederacies, it is certain that they would soon find themselves in the unenviable position of the continental powers of Europe.

A true union would not only safeguard America against foreign aggression, it would more firmly secure it against civil strife and insurrection. Some individuals, however, have questioned the validity of this proposition, citing the history of the small republics of ancient Greece and Italy, which oscillated perpetually between the extremes of tyranny and anarchy. From the history of those republics some individuals have drawn arguments against republican government. In response, Hamilton suggests that the political science of his time has discovered principles unknown or imperfectly known to the ancients: the distribution of power into distinct departments so that the three branches of government may check and balance one another; and the representation of the people in the legislature by deputies of their own election. Another new principle recognizes that the republican form of government may be adapted to a vast geographical area like that of America.

Hamilton here responds to opponents of the Constitution who, relying on Montesquieu, maintained that republican government is only suited to a relatively small territory. He begins his rebuttal by reminding his readers that the geographical area Montesquieu had in mind as appropriate for a republic was much smaller than the area of almost every one of the states. Virginia, Massachusetts, Pennsylvania, New York, North Carolina, or Georgia would all be far too large for Montesquieu's model of a republic. If, therefore, we were to stop there in our careless reading of Montesquieu, Hamilton cogently argues, America would be driven to the alternative of either opting for a monarchy or splitting itself into an infinity of petty, jealous states clashing constantly with one another. Hamilton proceeds to quote the passage from Book IX, chapter 1, of *The Spirit of the Laws*, where Montesquieu explicitly posits a federal republic as an effective means of extending the sphere of popular government and gaining the advantages of both a monarchy and a republic. Montesquieu explained how a republic can withstand both external invasions and internal corruption. He reasoned that if a single member state attempted to usurp supreme authority, it is unlikely that all the other member states would acquiesce. Short of attempting to seize supreme power, if a member state were merely to acquire too great an influence over another, that, too, would surely alarm the rest. Finally, if one state were to subdue another, or a part of the large, federated republic, the states remaining free could oppose the aggressor and overpower it before it succeeded in its aggression. 'Should a popular insurrection happen in one of the federated states,' Montesquieu continues,

> the others are able to quell it. Should abuses creep into one part, they are reformed by those that remain sound. The state may be destroyed on one side, and not on the other; the federation may be dissolved, and the federated states preserve their sovereignty.
>
> As this government is composed of small republics, it enjoys the internal happiness of each; and with respect to its external situation, it is possessed, by means of the association, of all the advantages of large monarchies. (*The Federalist Papers*, Number IX, 120–21, Hamilton's translation of the relevant passages from Book IX, chapter 1, of *The Spirit of the Laws*)

Madison, continuing the argument along the same lines, proposed that one of the chief advantages of a well-constructed union is its ability to control and end violent factional strife. The Federalists employed the classical concept of 'faction' to refer to a number of citizens who, prompted by common passions or interests, combine to act contrary to the rights of other citizens or the collective interests of the community. The Federalists recognized, of course, that the diversity in human faculties and interests, and the pursuit of honour, pre-eminence, and power, made it inevitable that society would be divided by classes and parties. They recognized that 'the most common and durable source of factions has been the various and unequal distribution of property. Those who hold and those who are without property have ever formed distinct interests in society. ... The regulation of these various and interfering interests forms the principal task of modern legislation and involves the spirit of party and faction in the necessary and ordinary operations of government' (X, 124).

The Federalists were disinclined to rely on enlightened statesmen to mediate the clashing interests and subordinate them to the common good. Enlightened statesmen will not always be at the helm. Since one cannot remove the causes of faction without destroying liberty, one must seek relief from factional strife by controlling its effects. When a faction consists of a minority, the republican principle enables the majority to defeat it by regular vote. When, however, a faction is the majority, popular government carries with it the danger that the majority will subordinate to its own interests both the rights of other citizens and the public good. The great challenge of popular government, therefore, is to preserve liberty, while securing individual rights and the public good against such faction. A pure democracy in the Rousseauian sense – a small number of citizens who assemble and administer the government in person – has no way to prevent either the consequences of faction or the tyranny of the majority. No check exists on the ability of the majority to exercise its will against the minority. Political theorists, Madison remarks in a possible reference to Rousseau, have failed to recognize that a republic is more effective than a democracy in mitigating the effects of faction.

The two basic differences between a democracy and a republic, Madison explains, are the delegation of government in the latter to a small number of citizens elected by the rest and the larger population and geographic area over which the government may be extended. Furthermore, Madison suggests, a national legislature based on large representational units would

> refine and enlarge the public views by passing them through the medium of a chosen body of citizens, whose wisdom may best discern the true interest of their country and whose patriotism and love of justice will be least likely to sacrifice it to temporary or partial considerations. Under such a regulation it may well happen that the public voice, pronounced by the representatives of the people, will be more consonant to the public good than if pronounced by the people themselves, convened for the purpose. (X, 126)

Madison realizes, however, that the 'medium of a chosen body of citizens' may open the way to the opposite effect: ambitious and corrupt individuals obtaining political office and betraying the interests of the people. So Madison raises the question whether small or large republics are most capable of electing true guardians of the common weal; and he proceeds to explain why an extensive republic is best able to deal with corruption and the abuse of power. Inasmuch as the pool of prospective representatives is larger in an extensive than in a small republic, it would be more difficult for unworthy candidates to be chosen; and the people would be more likely to choose individuals of the greatest merit and the best character. In determining the number of electors, Madison stresses, one must seek the mean: the number must not be so large as to render the electors too little acquainted with their local circumstances, and not so small that it makes them unduly attached to local interests and less comprehending and caring of important national objects. For Madison, the proposed Constitution provides the most reasonable solution in this regard, 'the great and aggregate interests being referred to the national, the local and particular to the State legislatures' (X, 127).

Elaborating on Montesquieu's insight, Madison observes that the smaller the society, the fewer will be the distinct parties and interests composing it; and the fewer the parties, the more likely that the majority will constitute the dominant party. In a small republic such a majority realizes its will more easily and succeeds in accomplishing its aims of oppression. In a large republic, in contrast, the greater number and variety of parties makes it less likely that a majority of citizens would have a common interest in encroaching on the rights of the other citizens. And even if such a common interest were to exist, it would be more difficult in a large, complex republic for all who share it to act in unison. In a large, federated republic factious leaders may kindle a flame within their own states, but they would surely fail to spread a general conflagration throughout the nation.

The new and extensive federated republic proposed by the Constitution stood in sharp contrast to the existing Confederation and its inadequacy for the preservation of the union. To the Federalists, the defects of the Confederation could hardly be more obvious: the debts incurred to foreigners and citizens during the revolution remained without any proper arrangement for their discharge; valuable territories on the American continent remained in the hands of foreign powers in spite of their express agreement to surrender them. The retention of those territories by foreign powers, widely regarded as a gross violation of America's interests and rights, gave the Federalists the opportunity to press their point: the nation lacked the power to expel the aggressor, having neither the army nor the money nor, of course, the strong central government with which to accomplish the task. Hamilton therefore underscores that the chief defect of the existing Confederation resided in the principle that the government of the United States had no authority either to raise money or requisition men as *individual* citizens of America. The result was that though in theory the resolutions of the Confederation were binding on the members of the union, in practice they were mere recommendations that the states could either accept or reject at their option. The union was more in the nature of a league than a federal government. The only way to lead America out of this perilous situation, Hamilton insisted, was to extend the authority of the union to individuals as citizens of one nation – 'the only proper objects of government' (XV, 149). If America fails to create such a union, Hamilton argued, it will remain in its current state of paralysis, in which the concurrence of thirteen distinct sovereign wills are required, under the Confederation, for the execution of every measure deemed essential for the union. Legislating for states that regard themselves as sovereign is impossible. In the confederations of antiquity, such as the Delian League in Greece, the aim of legislating for sovereign states, even when supported by military coercion, had never proved effectual. For the Federalists, then, it could not have been clearer that a federal government capable of regulating the common concerns and preserving the common good had to carry its authority to the *persons* of the citizens.

Although this seemed logical enough to the Federalists, the anti-Federalists were concerned that the federal government would undermine state and local autonomy. Legislating for the individual citizens of America would render the government of the union too powerful, enabling it to absorb authorities more properly left to the states and local communities. To this objection Hamilton replied that he could not imagine why those entrusted with the administration of the general government would ever be tempted to divest the states of their authority. Granted that the love of power is a strong and prevalent passion, it would surely be satisfied by authority over commerce, finance, and negotiations with foreign states where war and peace are concerned. Those are the powers that ought to rest with the national government. As for the administration of justice between the citizens of a state, the supervision of agriculture, and other state and local concerns, those can never be the primary responsibilities of the national jurisdiction. It is therefore improbable, Hamilton assures his readers, that the federal councils would ever wish to usurp powers which would contribute nothing to the dignity, importance, and splendour of the national government. But let us admit for argument's sake, says Hamilton, that in their lust for domination the national representatives would attempt to extend their power. Given such a tendency, Hamilton argues, the constituents of the national representatives, that is, the people of the respective states, would effectively counter it; for the state governments are inherently more powerful than the national authorities. 'The proof of this proposition,' writes Hamilton, 'turns upon the greater degree of influence which the State governments, if they administer their affairs with uprightness and prudence, will generally possess over the people; a circumstance which at the same time teaches us that there is an inherent and intrinsic weakness in all federal constitutions; and that too much pains cannot be taken in their organization to give them all the force which is compatible with the principles of liberty' (XVII, 157).

To support his argument further, Hamilton cites the experience of the feudal system, which though it was no confederation strictly speaking, was an organization consisting of a chieftain or sovereign and a number of vassals over which he extended his authority. Each principal vassal, however, was sovereign in his own domain. As a result, there was a continual struggle between the sovereign head and the great barons in which the power of the head was typically too weak to preserve the peace and in which the powers of the barons triumphed over the prince. For Hamilton, the state governments in the proposed Constitution are analogous with the feudal baronies: insofar as the states will earn the goodwill and confidence of the people, they will generally be able to oppose all encroachments by the national government. Of course, Hamilton knew recent European history well enough to realize that the French Crown, for example, by overwhelming the nobility and rendering it an appendage of the central government, became absolutist and despotic. Where monarchy was concerned, therefore, it was the British model after the Glorious Revolution that he admired; for it was a constitutional government based on checks and balances and the principles of liberty. In defending the federated republic of the proposed American Constitution, Hamilton and his colleagues were confident that the new American commonwealth would embody the advantages of both the republican and monarchical forms of government: composed of small republics, it would enjoy the liberties of the internal government of each one, and by the force of the unified association of those republics, it would acquire the power of a large, constitutional monarchy.

In the judgment of the Federalists, the anti-Federalists understood well enough how essential it was to preserve popular government and liberty in their respective states. But they understood poorly or not at all that America can have no secure future if its association of states fails to acquire the force of a large, unified monarchy. The existing Confederation, in the Federalists' view, could be likened to the amphictyony of ancient Greece, where each city-state retained its independence and sovereignty and had an equal vote in the central, amphictyonic council. In theory, all the city-states were equal. In practice, however, the more powerful members tyrannized over all the rest. Even in the face of invasions by powerful enemies such as Persia and Macedon, the members of the amphictyony never acted in concert against the common enemy. Indeed, some members even sided with the enemy. Although Athens and Sparta and their respective allies had successfully repulsed the Persians, Athens and Sparta soon became rivals and enemies inflicting on each other in the Peloponnesian War more destruction than they had suffered from Xerxes. For the Federalists, the lesson was clear: the historical experience of previous confederations, whether Greek, German, or Polish, demonstrated 'the tendency of federal bodies rather to anarchy among the members than to tyranny in the head' (XVIII, 164).

The historical experience of previous confederations assisted the Federalists in exposing the defects of the existing American Confederation. No means existed by which the United States could exact obedience or punish disobedience to their resolutions. Nor was there any provision in the Articles of Confederation guaranteeing the mutual assistance of the state governments in dealing with domestic dangers such as the Shays rebellion. Another defect was the attempt to regulate state contributions to the common treasury by means of quotas. Neither the value of the lands of the respective states nor the numbers of their inhabitants were regarded as a just criterion by which to impose quotas; and the Federalists believed that there was no general rule by which the ability of a state to pay taxes could be determined. Moreover, any attempt by a central government to enforce quotas based upon that government's perception of a state's ability to pay would inevitably produce glaring inequalities and extreme oppression, leading to the eventual destruction of the union. For the Federalists, the just solution was to authorize the national government to raise its own revenues by imposing excises on articles of consumption. The built-in advantage of this method is that it determines its own limit, which cannot be exceeded without defeating its purpose. If duties are excessive, they reduce consumption and with it the revenues of the national treasury. This alone would dictate that taxes of this kind be confined within moderate bounds.

Another shortcoming of the existing Confederation was the absence of authority on the part of the national government to regulate commerce. This shortcoming had already produced tariff barriers between the states; and if such mutual protectionism were to continue, the Federalists warned, the citizens of each state were liable one day to be regarded by the citizens of others as no better than foreigners and aliens. Just as the method of raising taxes by quotas had proved inadequate during the revolution, so had the method of recruiting men for the revolutionary armies. To furnish the quotas the states competed with one another in offering bounties to recruits, until bounties grew to an insupportable size. Often men who were ready and willing to serve deliberately procrastinated in their enlistment, hoping for a still further increase in the bounties offered. Moreover, this method brought with it an unequal distribution of the burden. States near the seat of war made efforts to furnish their quotas even at great cost to themselves, while those far from the danger were often remiss.

Suffrage and Other Issues

The demand for equal suffrage among the states produced another inequality and injustice among them. The Federalists argued that to give, say, Rhode Island equal weight with New York contradicted the central principle of republican government, requiring that the will of the majority should prevail over that of the minority. Hamilton labelled it sophistry to argue that sovereigns are equal and that a majority of the sovereign states is a proper majority of a confederated America. Hamilton pointed out in reply that a majority of the states could be but a small minority of the American people: 'New Hampshire, Rhode Island, New Jersey, Delaware, Georgia, South Carolina and Maryland are a majority of the whole number of states, but they do not contain one third of the people' (XXII, 179, fn. 31). The anti-Federalists sought to strengthen their case by proposing that not seven but nine states – or two-thirds of the total number – must consent to the national government's resolutions. Hamilton replied, however, that he could also enumerate nine states that contained less than a majority of the people: 'Add New York and Connecticut to the foregoing seven, and they will be less than a majority' (XXII, 179, fn. 32). So if Americans were in earnest about giving the union the concentrated energy it needed, they would have to recognize the basic error of legislating for the states in their collective capacities. The union had to rest on a truly solid foundation, the consent of the people. Hence, the laws of the federal government had to apply to the individual citizens of America. In place of the old system of quotas and requisitions, the union had to acquire full power to raise an army, build and equip naval fleets, and raise revenues for those purposes.

The anti-Federalists raised the objection that 'standing armies,' as provided for in the proposed Constitution, are a threat to liberty, a potential instrument of an aspiring tyrant. To this Hamilton replied that the power of raising armies was lodged in the *legislature*, not in the executive, and that the legislature was to be a popular body consisting of representatives of the people periodically elected. The provision in question, far from favouring standing armies unconditionally, contains an important qualification even of the legislative authority: it forbids the appropriation of money for the support of the army for any period longer than two years. Moreover, although a wide ocean separates the United States from Europe, the presence of settlements on the American continent subject to Britain on the one side and to Spain on the other demonstrates the real need not merely for occasionally organized detachments from the militia, but 'a standing army in times of peace; a small one, indeed, but not the less real for being small. Here is a simple view of the subject that shows us at once the impropriety of a constitutional interdiction of such establishments, and the necessity of leaving the matter to the discretion and prudence of the legislature' (XXIV, 191). Hamilton and his colleagues understood that judging from the history of the human race the passions for war were much more powerful than the sentiments for peace among sovereign states. In light of the fact that foreign nations maintained on the American continent disciplined armies ready for action, the new American Republic was obliged to create a force adequate for its defence. A standing army was a necessary institution; and the best precaution against the potential danger of that institution was the constitutional limitation of the term for which revenue was appropriated for the support of standing armies.

The Structure of Government

The anti-Federalists also raised the objection that the proposed Constitution violated the political maxim that the executive, legislative, and judicial departments of government must be distinct and separate. The Federalists not only agreed with this maxim, but emphasized that the concentration of all executive, legislative, and judicial powers in the same hands was the very definition of tyranny. They disagreed, however, that the Constitution, did in fact violate the 'separation of powers' principle. What required clarification in this regard was whether Locke and Montesquieu had intended this principle to mean that the three departments of government were to be totally separate from one another. Judging from the British Constitution which was for Montesquieu the model of political liberty the three departments were by no means totally separate. The executive magistrate participated in the legislative authority in that it was his prerogative to make treaties with foreign sovereigns which, when approved by parliament, acquired the force of law. He also appointed all members of the judiciary, some of whom often participated in legislative deliberations. Hence, the Federalists argued, Montesquieu could not have meant that there was to be no interpenetration of the three departments, and that they were to have no *partial agency* in, or no *control* over, the acts of each other' (XLVII, 304).

The Federalists averred that unless these departments were connected and blended so as to give each a constitutional control over the others, the degree of separation that Montesquieu's maxim requires as essential for liberty, could never be put into practice properly. A good example of the blending the Federalists had in mind was the presidential veto: the power to return all bills with his objections, thus preventing their becoming law unless they are afterwards ratified by two-thirds of each house of the Congress. Opponents of this 'negative' prerogative of the president feared that it would inordinately strengthen the powers of the executive; but their fears were assuaged when they understood that it was not an absolute but a qualified veto power. The anti-Federalists, most often speaking for the popular state legislatures, feared the ambitions of their executive magistrates, seeing in them the source of the danger of tyranny. The Federalists therefore had to assure their readers that in a representative republic, where the executive power is carefully limited, there is no such danger. Indeed, the Federalists argued, insofar as the danger of tyranny exists, the source of the danger lies in the existing Confederation where the popular legislative assemblies rule without any constitutional limits of their powers. Citing the example of Virginia, which had declared in its constitution that the three departments of government ought not to be intermixed, Madison invoked the authority of Thomas Jefferson, who in his *Notes on the State of Virginia* wrote the following:

All the powers of government, legislative, executive, and judiciary, result to the legislative body. The concentrating these in the same hands is precisely the definition of despotic government. It will be no alleviation that these powers will be exercised by a plurality of hands, and not by a single one. One hundred and seventy three despots would surely be as oppressive as one. Let those who doubt it turn their eyes on the republic of Venice. As little will it avail us that they are chosen by ourselves. An *elective despotism* was not the government we fought for; but one which should not only be founded on free principles, but in which the powers of government should be so divided and balanced among several bodies of magistracy as that no one could transcend their legal limits without being effectually checked and restrained by the others. For this reason that convention which passed the ordinance of government laid its foundation on this basis, that the legislative, executive, and judiciary departments should be separate and distinct, so that no person should exercise the powers of more than one of them at the same time. *But no barrier was provided between these several powers.* The judiciary and the executive members were left dependent on the legislative for their subsistence in office, and some of them for their continuance in it. If, therefore, the legislative assumes executive and judiciary powers, no opposition is likely to be made; nor, if made, can be effectual; ... They have accordingly, in *many* instances, *decided rights* which should have been left to *judiciary controversy,* and *the* direction of the executive during the whole time of their session, is becoming habitual and familiar. (XLVIII, 310–11, italics in original)

Jefferson, then, agreed that the 'tyranny of the legislature' was more to be feared than the executive's lust for power. The anti-Federalists may have had a valid point in maintaining that the proposed Constitution was much more a mixed government of shared powers than a strict separation of powers; but Madison also had a valid point in insisting that some intermixing was necessary, but that this, paradoxically, precluded neither the division of powers nor a system of checks and balances. In his words:

The great security against a gradual concentration of the several powers in the same department consists in giving to those who administer each department the necessary constitutional means and personal motives to resist encroachments of the others. The provision for defence must in this, as in all other cases, be made commensurate to the danger of attack. Ambition must be made to counteract ambition. The interests of the man must be connected with the constitutional rights of the place. It may be a reflection on human nature that such devices should be necessary to control the abuses of government. But what is government itself but the greatest of all reflections on human nature? If men were angels, no government would be necessary. If angels were to govern men, neither external nor internal controls on government would be necessary. (LI, 319–20)

From the standpoint of the Federalists and the framers of the Constitution, the people had to be protected from themselves, from their temporary errors and delusions. Misled by men with special interests, the people may at any given moment call for measures that they themselves will afterwards regret and condemn. It was in the popular legislative assemblies of the states where the people were most vulnerable to demagoguery; and it was in those same assemblies that the abuse of both power and liberty was most likely, owing to the absence of checks and balances. The potential for such abuses by large, popular legislative assemblies meant for the framers of the Constitution that in order to prevent legislative tyranny, the legislative function had to be divided and delegated to two houses. The new republic required, in addition to a House of Representatives, a well-constructed Senate. 'The people,' Madison explained, 'can never wilfully betray their own interests; but they may possibly be betrayed by the representatives of the people; and the danger will be evidently greater where the whole legislative trust is lodged in the hands of one body of men than where the concurrence of separate and dissimilar bodies is required in every public act' (LXIII, 372). However, adversaries of the Constitution feared that the Senate would gradually acquire a dangerous pre-eminence in the government and finally transform itself into a tyrannical aristocracy. To this objection Madison replied that history informs us of no long-lived republic that had no senate; and that the British example ought to quiet such fears, since the 'senate' there, instead of being elected for six years and open to all candidates regardless of their family backgrounds and fortunes, is a 'hereditary assembly of opulent nobles' (LXIV, 374).

The Constitution provided that the president is to be elected for four years and is to be re-eligible as often as the people of the United States shall consider him worthy of their confidence. Although Jefferson favoured adoption of the Constitution, this indefinite re-eligibility worried him, especially as the president was to be 'the commander-in-chief of the army and navy of the United States, and of the militia of the several states, when called into the actual service of the United States.' But Hamilton argued in favour of re-eligibility on several grounds: given that energy in the executive is a leading quality in the definition of good government, duration in office is a prerequisite for energy in the executive authority. Excluding an individual from the office after he has served one term would diminish his incentive to discharge his duties well. Most individuals fulfil their responsibilities better when they have the hope of showing they deserve to remain in office. Another ill effect of exclusion would be the temptation it would afford to an avaricious man to abuse his power; while the same man, with the prospect of being re-elected, would, most likely, content himself with the regular perquisites of office. 'His avarice,' Hamilton astutely observed, 'might be a guard upon his avarice' (LXXII, 414). Exclusion would also deny the community the experience and wisdom gained by the individual in the exercise of his duties, just as exclusion would prevent outstanding individuals from serving the community in national emergencies. Finally, exclusion would work against stability in the administration of the chief magistrate.

In concluding this exposition of the Federalists' views a word needs to be said about the absence of a bill of rights in the Constitution as it was originally formulated. Jefferson objected to the absence, as did Patrick Henry and other anti-Federalists. Hamilton, however, maintained that such a bill was not only unnecessary, but positively dangerous. A bill of rights, he argued,

> would contain various exceptions to powers which are not granted; and, on this very account, would afford a colorable pretext to claim more than were granted. For why declare that things shall not be done which there is no power to do? Why for instance, should it be said that the liberty of the press shall not be restrained, when no power is given by which restrictions may be imposed? I will not contend that such a provision would confer a regulatory power; but it is evident that it would furnish, to men disposed to usurp, a plausible pretense for claiming that power. (LXXXIV, 476)

At the Virginia convention held to decide whether to ratify the proposed Constitution, Madison debated Patrick Henry, who spoke for the anti-Federalist cause. When the votes were counted, the result was close, with Madison winning by a vote of eighty-nine to seventy-nine. And yet it was out of this Virginia debate that there emerged the outline for the Bill of Rights, the first ten amendments to the Constitution, which guaranteed personal rights against government interference and which were passed by the first Congress convened under the new Constitution.

Notes

CHAPTER ONE **Plato**

1 Thucydides, *History of the Peloponnesian War*, trans. Rex Warner (London: Penguin Books, 1988)
2 All references in parentheses to Plato's *Republic* are abbreviated as *Rep.*

CHAPTER TWO **Aristotle**

1 Herodotus, *The Histories*, trans. Aubrey de Sélincourt (London: Penguin Books, 1972)

CHAPTER THREE **Machiavelli**

1 Niccolo Machiavelli, *The Discourses*, ed. with an Introduction by Bernard Crick, using the translation of Leslie J. Walker, S.J., with revisions by Brian Richardson (London: Penguin Books, 1970), I, 39. Hereafter all references to this work will be indicated in parentheses immediately following the cited or quoted passage. Book and chapter numbers are indicated by roman and arabic numerals, respectively.
2 Niccolo Machiavelli, *The Prince*, trans. with an Introduction by George Bull (Harmondsworth: Penguin Books, 1975), IV, 47. Hereafter the book and page numbers of references to this work will be cited in parentheses immediately following the quoted passage.

CHAPTER FOUR **Thomas Hobbes**

1 Thomas Hobbes, *Leviathan*, ed. by Richard Tuck (Cambridge: Cambridge University Press, 1992). All chapter and page references to this work will appear in parentheses immediately following the cited passage.

2 Thomas Hobbes, *The Elements of Law*, ed. F. Tönnies, 2nd ed., with a new Introduction by M.M. Goldsmith (London: Frank Cass and Company, 1969)

CHAPTER FIVE John Locke

1 See Wootton's illuminating Introduction to John Locke, *Political Writings* (London: Penguin Books, 1993). This particular observation of Wootton's appears on page 61. Hereafter all references to this volume will be cited in parentheses immediately following the quoted passage.

CHAPTER SIX Montesquieu

1 Montesquieu, *Oeuvres complètes*, texte présenté et annoté par Roger Caillois, 2 vols. Bibliothèque de la Pléiade (Paris, 1949), vol. 1, *Lettres persanes*; vol. 2, *Grandeur et décadence des Romains: De l'esprit des lois*. Hereafter all references to *The Persian Letters* will be indicated by the letter number immediately following the cited passage. References to Montesquieu's other works will also be indicated immediately following the cited passage.
2 Cited in David Wallace Carrithers's Introduction to *The Spirit of the Laws* (Berkeley: University of California Press, 1977), 35.
3 Ibid., 35

CHAPTER SEVEN Rousseau

1 Jean-Jacques Rousseau, *Oeuvres complètes*, III, Bibliothèque de la Pléiade, sous la direction de Bernard Gagnebin et Marcel Raymond (Paris, 1964), preface, 123. Hereafter all references to Rousseau's writings will be cited in parentheses immediately following the quoted passage.
2 From Jean-Jacques Rousseau's article, 'Économie politique,' in *Encyclopédie*, quoted in Ernst Cassirer, *The Philosophy of the Enlightenment* (Princeton, NJ: Princeton University Press, 1951), 260.

CHAPTER EIGHT The Federalist Papers

1 See Gordon S. Wood, *The Creation of the American Republic, 1776–1787* (Chapel Hill: University of North Carolina Press, 1969), chaps. 12 and 13.
2 For a fuller account of the historical and political context of the papers, including the nature of the debate between the Federalists and their opponents, see Isaac Kramnick's splendid Introduction to *The Federalist Papers* (New York: Penguin Books, 1987). All references to the papers will be indicated in parentheses immediately following the cited or quoted passage.

Bibliography

Aristotle. *Nichomachean Ethics*, Loeb Classical Library, vol. 19. Translated by H. Rackham. Cambridge: Harvard University Press, 1982
– *Politics*. Loeb Classical Library, vol. 21. Translated by H. Rackham. Cambridge: Harvard University Press, 1977
Herodotus. *The Histories*. Translated by Aubrey de Sélincourt, revised with an Introduction and Notes by A.R. Burn. London: Penguin Books, 1972
Hobbes, Thomas. *The Elements of Law*. Edited by F. Tönnies. 2nd ed., with a new Introduction by M.M. Goldsmith. London: Frank Cass and Company, 1969
– *Leviathan*. Edited by Richard Tuck. Cambridge: Cambridge University Press, 1992
Locke, John. *Political Writings*. Edited with an Introduction by David Wootton. London: Penguin Books, 1993
Machiavelli, Niccolo. *The Prince*. Translated with an Introduction by George Bull. Harmondsworth: Penguin Books, 1975
– *The Discourses*. Edited with an Introduction by Bernard Crick, using the translation of Leslie J. Walker, S.J., with revisions by Brian Richardson. London: Penguin Books, 1970
Madison, James, Alexander Hamilton, and John Jay. *The Federalist Papers*. Edited with an Introduction by Isaac Kramnick. New York: Penguin Books, 1987
Montesquieu. *Oeuvres complètes*. Texte présenté et annoté par Roger Caillois, 2 volumes, Bibliothèque de la Pléiade, Paris, 1949. Vol. 1, *Lettres persanes*; Vol. 2, *Grandeur et décadence des Romains: De l'esprit des lois*
Plato. *Gorgias, Republic, Statesman, Laws*. In *Platonis Opera*. Edited by John Burnet. 5 vols. Oxford: Oxford University Press, 1987
Rousseau, Jean-Jacques. *Oeuvres complètes*. III. Bibliothèque de la Pléiade, sous la direction de Bernard Gagnebin et Marcel Raymond. Paris, 1964

– 'Économie politique.' In *Encyclopédie*. Quoted by Ernst Cassirer, *The Philosophy of the Enlightenment*. Princeton, NJ: Princeton University Press, 1951

Thucydides. *History of the Peloponnesian War*. Translated by Rex Warner, with an Introduction and Notes by M.I. Finley. London: Penguin Books, 1988

Wood, Gordon S. *The Creation of the American Republic, 1776–1787*. Chapel Hill: University of North Carolina Press, 1969

Index